It's All About the Style

Blake Matthews

It's All About the Style

A Survey of Martial Arts Styles Depicted in Chinese Cinema

Blake Matthews

*For my brother Anthony, who changed my life forever when he decided one Saturday evening that he just had to tape the movie **Kickboxer** off HBO.*

For Jacob, who spent hundreds of hours watching kung fu movies with me, even after I moved up to São Paulo.

For all my friends and family who have ever been coerced into watching a kung fu movie, or even just a single fight scene (especially my brother-in-law, Xande, and his wife, Eliza, bless their hearts)—sorry about the flying ninja, Mom.

Special Thanks to David McRobie for introducing to such greats like Avenging Eagle; Five Shaolin Masters; Book of Heroes; Invincible Shaolin; and Avenging Warriors of Shaolin; not to mention his believing in this project from the outset AND supplying this book with its wonderfully-written Foreword.

Blake Matthews

Table of Contents

Foreword

Ever watch a kung fu movie and wonder if the style being used is a true martial art or not? Or perhaps, is that a real weapon? Is there a difference between a three sectional staff, a two sectional staff and nun-chaku? Is there such a thing as *blind white leopard* fist? These are questions I've asked myself and friends many times (well, not about the *leopard* fist, I just made that up) and never got an answer. My next question was usually "why isn't there a book about these things?"

Now there is one.

There have been a lot of books about martial arts, and there have been a lot of books about martial arts movies. Blake has written a great book about different authentic styles of martial arts and talks about specific movies one can view them in. Of course, you won't be reading about the completely made up styles that exist in nearly every kung fu movie (i.e. sadly, there is no real "Venoms" clan style) but the real styles more than make up for it. It's not just the Chinese martial arts he covers, he goes to Japan, Korea, Thailand and even India as well. Didn't think *yoga* was a martial art? Think again! Even hula has a history of being a hidden fighting form, but sadly, it doesn't appear that anyone has ever made a Hawaiin martial arts movie.

He also covers weapons as well. That's a daunting task, as there are as many weapons as there are martial arts in the world. There's nearly as many different kind of swords- broadswords, straight swords, Japanese katana... and I've already mentioned jointed weapons. We also get the more esoteric and exotic weapons, though sadly the awesome flying guillotine is nowhere to be seen.

There is history here as well, and it's fascinating. Did I mention the book is well written? It's also really well researched. Blake has a sense of fun about the whole subject, even though he treats the entire thing seriously.

The best part is he picks out the movies with the finest examples of weapons and styles to watch. These may not be the greatest martial arts movies, but if you want to see a certain form or if a dragon trident is actually used, that's the film you want to see. These run the gamut from the classics like *HEROES TWO* to Taiwan based movies like *GOOSE BOXER*. If this book doesn't make you want to watch a bunch of these movies in a row, check your pulse, because I'm sure it's not beating properly. It's a wonderful resource that deserves to be in the library of anyone who loves martial arts and the movies about them.

I am kind of bummed the flying guillotine isn't a real weapon.

-David McRobie

Introduction

A History of Chinese Martial Arts

In any discussion about Chinese martial arts films, there are some things that need to be explained about Chinese martial arts and their history, much of which can be inaccessible to Western audiences unfamiliar with the Chinese language, customs or history. For starters, there are three words in Chinese generally used to speak of martial arts: *wushu*, *kuoshu*, and *kung fu*. *Wushu* literally means "military skills", and has generally referred to martial arts in general, regardless of their origin. *Guoshu* means "skills of the kingdom[1]", and refers specifically to Chinese martial arts. *Kung Fu* means "individual accomplishment" and is often used colloquially in other contexts. Throughout the book, we will use *kung fu* to describe Chinese martial arts in general and *wushu* to describe the modern, exhibitionist martial arts practiced on the Chinese mainland, which we will get into more detail later on in this section.

Before we get into the history of Chinese martial arts, we feel it necessary to advise the reader that discussing the history of martial arts can often be an exercise in futility. Martial arts have often been passed down through generations from one father to son, and thus when one style has several different lineages stemming from a single master, oral tradition often distorts the history of the style and the story differs from one family to another. Moreover, practitioners of a number of styles have often liked to link their style with different historical figures, even though the style may have been founded after that person's lifetime. For example, in the case of *tai chi chuan*, the man generally considered to be the founder, *Chang Sanfeng*, is doubted by many to actually have existed. It's not common to have several variations of the same legend in circulation, followed by some historian claiming to have found records that prove all of the legends false.

The first Chinese martial arts are said to have been created as early as the Xia Dynasty[2]. Soldiers practiced hand-to-hand combat and weapons techniques in preparation for battle and to help them in hunting as well. During the Shang Dynasty[3], records indicate that a fighting style called Shoubo was practiced. By the following dynasty, the Zhou Dynasty[4], a martial art similar to modern kickboxing, known as *Xiangbo*, had been

---

[1] - The Chinese word for "China" is *Zhongguo*, which means "Middle Kingdom."

[2] - The Xia Dynasty (2205- 1766 B.C.) is the first dynasty to be recorded in Chinese history texts. Some modern historians, however, doubt that the dynasty ever actually existed. There is something of a mythical air about the Xia Dynasty, and the legends surrounding it have parallels in the legends surrounding many styles of *kung fu*.

[3] - The Shang Dynasty (1766 – 1066 B.C.) is generally considered to be the first dynasty of which there is no doubt actually existed. Centered on the Yellow River (Huang He) in Nothern China, it is the dynasty in which China went through its bronze age. Records from the Shang Dynasty have been found written the bones of animals, including turtle shells, and are known as "oracle bones". It has been confirmed that the Chinese writing system by this time had been fully developed. Culturally, it was during this period that the doctrine of ancestor worship, which has been a long been a part of Chinese culture, developed.

[4] - The Zhou Dyntasy (1045 – 256 B.C.) was one of the longest-lasting dynasties in the history of China. During this period, the idea of the "Mandate of Heaven", in that a ruling dynasty justified itself by claiming to have been backed by heaven itself, was created. The government practiced an early variation of the feudal system in its economy. The Zhou Dynasty is most well-known for the many different philosophies

developed. During the same dynasty, a combat system called *jiao di*, similar to wrestling, was common. *Jiao Di* consisted of techniques including throws, pressure point attacks, and joint locks. It would eventually become a sport during the following dynasty, the Qin[5] Dynasty. By the Tang Dynasty[6], swordplay had advanced to the point that many of the elegant, dance-like movements we see in sword demonstrations today had been developed. *Xiangpu*, a predecessor to modern *sumo* wrestling, was practiced by the beginning of the 10th century A.D.

The greatest influence to *kung fu* was the influence of the Shaolin Temple. The Shaolin Temple was a Buddhist temple erected around 495 A.D. in the northeastern province of Henan, located on the Shaoshi Mountain. The name *Shaolin* means "Little Forest" and refers to the location of the original temple. According to most legends, around 527 B.C., a Buddhist monk from India, named Bodhidharma (Tamo in Chinese) came to China. According to one source, he was introduced to the emperor, who had ordered the copying of Buddhist texts from Sanskrit to Chinese[7], thinking that such a deed was enough for him to attain Enlightenment. Bodhidharma was opposed to such course of action, and eventually left the court for his own safety. He arrived at the Shaolin Temple, who denied him access for thinking that he was come to make trouble.

Bodhidharma spent the next nine years meditating in a cave near the temple, which eventually gained him the respect of the Shaolin monks and entrance into the temple. According to legend, it was from there that he taught a number of exercises, meditation techniques, and even techniques taken from Indian fighting styles (Bodhidharma had been a warrior prince in India before converting to Buddhism) to the monks. The reasons for him doing such are debated: some say that the Shaolin monks had spent so much time in meditation that they had become physically weak and thus Bodhidharma's teachings were to help the monks strengthen their bodies; others say that monks had already long practiced martial arts for self-defense against wild animals and bandits and Bodhidharma's teachings helped to systemize and methodize the practice of *kung fu*.

---

which came into being during this period, namely Confucianism, under Kong Fuzi; Taoism, under Laozi; Mohism, under Mo Zi; and Legalism, under Shang Yang and Han Feizi.

[5] - Qin Dynasty (221 – 206 B.C.) – The Qin Dynasty is the dynasty in which the numerous kingdoms in China were unified by emperor Shi Huangdi. It is from the Qin dynasty that "China" got its western name. Although the dynasty is credited with unifying the nation, Emperor Shi was known as a butcher and heavily persecuted intellectuals and burned Confucian books. It was also during this time that the Great Wall of China was built. By the time Shi Huangdi's son, Huhai, took the throne, there were numerous revolts by peasants, soldiers, and other oppressed peoples, leading to the end of the short-lived dynasty. Chinese films like *The Emperor and the Assassin* (1998), *Hero* (2002), and *The Myth* (2005) tell the story of Emperor Shi Huangdi.

[6] - Tang Dynasty (618 – 907 A.D.) – One of the more prosperous dynasties, the empire during the dynasty took up most of modern-day China, with the exception of the Tibetan plateau. It was during this dynasty that the government maintained a strong civil service system, using public standarized examinations to select public servants. Hydraulic fans, woodblock printing, and substantial improvements in cartography also mark this time period. Buddhism also enjoyed a surge in popularity in China during this period. It was through the Silk Road that a lot of Western and Middle Eastern influences, including musical instruments, chairs, ceramics, and silver-smithing, reached China; who in turn directed these influences to Korea and Japan. The film *House of the Flying Daggers* (2004) deals with the fall of the Tang Dynasty.

[7] - Some legends say that the Bodhidharma had come to purge Buddhism in China of a lot of its external rites and ordinances, which had been added to the religion. The main idea is that Bodhidharma's intent was to reform Buddhism in China.

As Shaolin kung fu developed, there were times in which it would be tested in battle and ultimately prove victorious. At the beginning of the Tang Dynasty, a man named Wang Shichong, who had been a general of the previous dynasty, declared himself to be emperor. The Tang emperor Li Yuan sent his son, Prince Li Shimin, to combat Wang. Thirteen armed monks from Shaolin joined Prince Li's army in consequence of Wang's invasion of their sacred temple grounds. The monks helped the army to win subsequent battles and the monks gained great fame for their deeds. During the Ming Dynasty[8], China suffered numerous attacks from Japanese pirates. The government employed a massive army to repel such attacks, among which were a group of armed monks, including a monk named Yuekong. They were able to win some victories against the pirates, although eventually were killed in a subsequent ambush by their enemies.

The Ming Dynasty fell to foreign invaders in 1644, which marked the beginning of the Qing Dynasty, China's final dynasty. The Qings, or Manchus, hailed from Manchuria, a region in Northeastern China bordering on what is now North Korea. The Qings carried out a number of reforms in order to consolidate their power, including the institution of the queue, or pigtail, as a mandatory rule for all Han (native Chinese) men. Censorship and literary inquisitions were also instituted, not to mention the massacre of both peasants and educated men on a number of occasions. Most Han Chinese opposed the rule of the Qings, a number of people started forming secret societies that aimed to depose the Qing government and restore the previous Ming Dynasty.

It was in this context that the Shaolin Temple started accepting laymen as disciples[9]. This had happened on occasion over the centuries, but by this time most of the laymen disciples were those who were involved in anti-Qing activities. The Qing government, who up to this point had left Shaolin alone out of respect for religious customs, started getting suspicious of Shaolin and eventually accused it of harboring rebels and fostering an insurrection. The temple[10] was eventually attacked and burned down by the Qing army, with the help of a traitor[11]. Five monks and a number of laymen were able to escape, going all over China in order to spread their cause as well as knowledge of Shaolin kung fu. Among these disciples were Hong Xiguan, Fong Sai-Yuk (Fang Shiyu), Luk Ah-Choy, Hu Huichen (Wu Wai-Kin), and others, all of whom have become folk heroes because of their exploits (some real, some legendary) in fighting against the Qings and trying to restore the empire to the Han people. Despite the persecution by the Qing government, quite a few styles were founded during that

---

[8] - The Ming Dynasty (1368 – 1644) – The final dynasty where China was ruled by the Han (native Chinese) people. It was during this period that China began to establish maritime trade with European peoples, notably the Portuguese and the Dutch. The dynasty saw a flourishing period for the arts, as well as one of the greatest periods of political, economic, and social stability in world civilization.

[9] - The credit of expanding the teaching of Shaolin kung fu to regular people is generally given to a monk named San Te, whose story is told in films like *The 36th Chamber of Shaolin* (1978) and *Young Hero of Shaolin* (1986).

[10] - A lot of films and stories portray the Shaolin Temple at Fukien as being the one that was destroyed. Most historians, however, agree that it was the original temple at Henan that was attacked.

[11] - There are a lot of stories about who the traitor was. Most films and accounts point to one of two people: a layman disciple named Ma Ling-Yee or Pai Mei, who was one of the Five Elders of the temple. The story of the latter is told in films like *Executioners of Shaolin* and *Shaolin Rescuers*, and the character appears in Quentin Tarantino's *Kill Bill Vol. 2* (2004). The former shows up in films like *New Legend of Shaolin*, *Five Shaolin Masters*, and *Shaolin Temple* (1976).

dynasty, including *hung gar*, *wing chun*, *choy li fut*, *pa kua*, Yang style *Tai chi chuan*, and others.

Following the fall of the Qing Dynasty and China's entrance into its Republic Era, *kung fu*'s popularity grew and was taught all over the country as a way of bringing to the Chinese people together in the face of growing foreign occupation and exploitation, principally by the Japanese. However, following the fall of the republic to Communist forces led by Mao Zedong in 1949, *kung fu* in its then current form was discouraged by the government. Martial arts in Mainland China eventually became regulated and standardized by government committees, becoming more of a sport than a system of self-defense techniques. As a result, Chinese martial arts, referred to as *wushu*, became somewhat watered-down, exhibitionist affairs, full of flashy and acrobatic moves with much of the actual fighting techniques removed[12]. In competitions, performers are judged on their forms, although there is a branch of *wushu*, known as *sanda*, which is dedicated to sparring. There has been some de-regulation of *wushu* that has permitted people to choose between studying the more aesthetically-pleasing *wushu* and traditional *kung fu*, whose practice had been controlled and regulated by the government. Actors like Donnie Yen, Jet Li, Wu Jing, and Vincent Zhao Wen-Zhuo are among those who are *wushu*-trained, and the word *wushu* in this book will generally be used to describe this homogenized form of martial arts promoted by Communist China.

I.   Classification of Chinese Martial Arts

There are three main ways in which Chinese martial arts can be classified: region, external/internal, or religious foundation. The way that they are organized in this book is a combination of the first two: external styles being divided into region and internal styles with a section of their own.

When we speak of region, what we mean is that styles are often divided into the Northern and Southern. The admittedly overgeneralized difference between the two styles is that Northern styles are characterized by high stances; wide, sweeping hand techniques; and a greater emphasis on kicking. On the other hand, Southern styles tend to feature a greater emphasis on the hand strikes; short, snappy movements; and lower, wider stances. Northern styles include *changquan* (Long Fist), Tanglangquan (Northern Praying Mantis Fist), Ying Jow Pai (Eagle Claw), and the Black Tiger style. Southern styles include *wing chun*, *hung gar*, white crane, Southern tiger, Southern dragon, Panther/Leopard, *choy li fut*, and *chow gar* (Southern Praying Mantis). In a lot of older kung fu films, principally those produced in Hong Kong and Taiwan, there was a certain bias for Southern styles, and thus the villain was often a master of a Northern style, generally the Northern Praying Mantis or Eagle Claw styles. When the Chinese Mainland started producing kung fu films in the early 1980s featuring entire troupes of *wushu* students in their casts, this practice became a little less prevalent, as the action directors often wanted to show off as many styles as possible, and thus less attention was paid to the whole North vs. South conceit.

---

[12] - The general exception to this rule was people in the military, who were trained in actual *kung fu* with the emphasis on the practical applications of the art, rather than the demonstrative aspects of it.

External and Internal styles may be another way to classify different fighting styles. Internal styles focus on the development of one's *qi*, or inner energy. This is often done by practicing the style performing slow, flowing movements and controlling one's breathing. Examples of Internal styles are *tai chi chuan (taijiquan), baguazhang (pa kua chang)*, and *xingyiquan (hsing-i chuan)*. External styles often focus on the strengthening of the practitioner's muscles, tendons, and overall physical strength. Movements in the style are often performed in a quick and explosive manner. Most Chinese martial arts are external[13].

Some styles could be classified according to their religious foundation. A lot of Chinese martial arts can trace their origins back to the Shaolin Temple, and thus could be classified as Buddhist kung fu styles. Other styles, like *taijiquan, baguazhang*, and *wudanquan*, have their roots in Taoist philosophies. Finally, there are some styles that were founded by the Hui people, the Islamic Chinese living in western China, including *tan tui*, a kicking style, among others.

If one desires, he/she can further divide individual styles into groups based on the family/lineage. It is common for a single style to have different lineages sprouting from a single master, each lineage adding some unique touch the style. Imagine a style that father passes to son, who then passes it to his own son, and so forth during a number of generations. Then, in one generation, the master takes on a disciple who had previously studied one or more different styles. The disciple learns his master's style, and then incorporates elements from the other styles into what he learned, creating a variation on the master's style. Thus, you now have two lineages of the same style, each one performed and practiced a little different than the other. An interesting example is *taijiquan*, which has a number of different variations such as Yang style, Chen style, and Wu style, all named after those who founded said systems, each with its own additions to the technique. Another example is *jeet kune do*, the style founded by Bruce Lee. There are currently two main schools of the style, one led by Lee's students Taky Kimura and Jerry Poteet, in which the curriculum adheres solely to what Bruce Lee himself taught; the second, championed by Dan Inosanto and others, seeks to follow Bruce's philosophy, constantly evolving the style by including elements of other styles.

II.   A History of Modern *Wuxia Pian* (1966 – Present)

The term *wuxia pian* refers to a genre of period piece film that deals with the exploits of noble swordsmen, often referred to as cavaliers or knights errant. *Wuxia pian* usually tells the story of rival clans who vie for superiority in the "Martial World", or the world of martial arts. Oftentimes these films are based on well-known legends or on Chinese

---

[13] - There is a difference between "External" and "Internal" styles and "hard" and "soft" styles of fighting. "Hard" and "Soft" generally refer to the style when applied in an actual fight. "Hard" techniques focus on the destroying the opponent's "structure" through hard blows and kicks, powerful blocks, and devastating locking and breaking techniques. "Soft" techniques include parries, evasive techniques, some throws and other movements meant to stop a fight without crippling or killing one's opponent. *Xingyiquan*, despite being an internal style, is a very hard style in application, as opposed to the other two internal styles. Some external styles, like the Northern Praying Mantis and the Southern Dragon (at its highest level), are soft in their application.

literature. *Wuxia pian* have had the reputation for being ridiculously convoluted plots, with a simple conflict being intensified by an ungodly number of characters, different clans, and more plot twists than can be healthy for a single film. *Wuxia pian* have existed on Jade Screen for quite some time, although we're more interested in the "modern" examples of the genre.

The first modern *wuxia* film is generally considered to be *Come Drink with Me*, a 1966 film directed by a man named King Hu. The film stars Cheng Pei Pei, a young, pretty actress who would become one of the staples of the genre for the rest of the decade. The film is considered to be one of the all-time genre classics, and heavily influenced other films of that era, from the strong swordswoman lead to the style of swordplay on screen. The style of fighting in the mid-late sixties can be described as having been influenced by Western swashbucklers and Japanese *chambara*, or samurai, films. The intricate, drawn-out choreography that would characterize Chinese cinema in the 1970s had not yet existed, and thus a single sword fight would consist of a few simple strokes, instead of more than a hundred.

If King Hu and his team created the first modern *wuxia pian*, it was director Chang Cheh and his team that upped the testosterone on the genre, which had often cast women as the stoic heroine and men as the effeminate foil. Chang's first major foray into the genre was *One-Armed Swordsman* (1967), which cast swimming champion Jimmy Wang Yu in the title role. In this film, all women were pushed back into supporting roles as the "weaker vessel" while the men did the dirty work of hacking each other to pieces with swords. Jimmy Wang Yu would become the first modern male hero in Chinese action cinema. The film was a resounding success and Chang Cheh would continue to make a number of the genre's most beloved films, including *Have Sword, Will Travel* (1968) and *Trail of the Broken Blade*.

By the beginning of the 1970s, the *wuxia* genre experienced a bit of decline with the rise of the modern kung fu film, which we'll talk about in the next part. Nonetheless, a number of independent studios based in Hong Kong and Taiwan continued to churn out films in the same style as those from the late 1960s. The Shaw Bros studio, which has produced all of the aforementioned films, was by this time the biggest movie studio in Hong Kong and was able to supply a bigger budget to most of the films they produced. They continued to produce some *wuxia pian* in the early 1970s, notably films like *The Water Margin* (1972), which is based on the classic Chinese novel *Heroes of the Marsh*, and *Heroes of the Sung Dynasty*, which features some early action direction from the Yuen Clan, who would go on to be the most famous action directors worldwide. Nevertheless, the Shaw Bros would take advantage of the competition brought by the rise of another big studio, Golden Harvest, to dabble in other genres, including adult films, kung fu films, and horror films (and sometimes a combination of them all).

It was the Shaw Bros studio who brought new life to the *wuxia pian* in the mid-1970s, when director Chor Yuan started making a series of *wuxia pian* based on the novels of Gu Long, a famed author. Chor cast actor Ti Lung, who had appeared in most of Chang Cheh's films from the late 1960s through the mid 1970s, in most of his films as the heroic, yet stoic swordsman. Chor's films were characterized by convoluted plots, bizarre weapons, some female exploitation, and other weird elements. Some of his more famous films include *Legend of the Bat*, *Killer Clans*, and *The Magic Blade*. The action direction was generally provided by a man named Tong Gaai, who had been one of

Chang Cheh's principal action directors since the mid-1960s, and he must've had a field day choreographing the action scenes with so many strange weapons and fighting techniques.

By the early 1980s, the Shaw Bros began to enter into decline, especially with the growing popularity of Jackie Chan and Sammo Hung, who were working primarily with the Shaws' rival, Golden Harvest. They continued to churn out *wuxia pian*. Chang Cheh turned to the novels of then-contemporary author Louis Cha for inspiration, making films like *Ode to Gallantry* (1981) and *Sword Stained with Royal Blood* (1981). Tong Gaai finally took up directing and gave us the marvelously weird *Shaolin Prince* (1983). Nevertheless, these films were not enough to keep the genre from basically withering away and the Shaw Bros studio from moving out the film business.

Although *wuxia* films lost a great deal of their popularity on the big screen during the 1980s, there were several important films made that would end up playing a big role in the genre's revival in the following decade. The first is *The Sword* (1980), in which action director Ching Siu-Tung would use wires and quick cuts to create a new, kinetic style of filming a swordfight. Ching Siu-Tung's directorial debut, *Duel to the Death* (1983), was a big success for Golden Harvest and featured great advances in the use of wire tricks to enhance and exaggerate fight action. The film featured flying swordsman, giant ninja who split up into several regular-sized ninja, ninja flying on kites and burrowing underground, and much, much more. Ching Siu-Tung would then keep the period piece alive with the cult classic *A Chinese Ghost Story* (1987), a love story about a mortal man and a female ghost peppered with supernatural action and wire-enhanced fight scenes. The success of that movie would inspire dozens of imitators well into the early 1990s.

At the same time, Tsui Hark produced a large-budget fantasy *wuxia* film that would raise the bar for optical effects for years to come. That film was *Zu: Warriors from Magic Mountain* (1983). Featuring special effects from some one of the men who worked on *Star Wars* and fight choreographing from Corey Yuen Kwai (*X-Men*, *Kiss of the Dragon*), the fantasy film tells the story of a young soldier who teams up with a monk and the apprentice of an ice queen to defeat an evil blood demon before it destroys the world. The abundance of visual effects in the film's action sequences would inspire films like *The Bastard Swordsman* (1983) and *Holy Flame of the Martial World* (1983), two over-the-top *wuxia* films that are considered last-ditch efforts by the Shaw Bros to stay in the game.

In 1990, Tsui Hark teamed up with Ching Siu-Tung, King Hu, and another critically-acclaimed director, Ann Hui (*Romance of Book and Sword*, *The Boat People*), to make *The Swordsman*. The film featured a super-convoluted plot involving a number of parties who are after the famed Sacred Scroll and a naïve swordsman who gets caught in the conflict. The film featured lots of wire-assisted combat courtesy of Ching Siu-Tung and also amped up the supernatural *qi* (spiritual energy) attacks performed by the players. The film was successful enough that it opened the door for dozens of *wuxia* films over the next five years. However, the rules of the game were now changed: Advances in the use of wires in fight choreography permitted that people not trained in martial arts participate in these films. Thus, a lot of the movies made during this period featured a lot more bankable stars that weren't necessarily trained fighters, like Tong Leung Chiu-Wai (*Butterfly and Sword*, *Ashes of Time*), Maggie Cheung (*Flying Dagger*), Tony Leung-Ka

Fei (*Flying Dagger, New Dragon Inn*), Brigitte Lin (*The Swordsman II, The East is Red*), and Leon Lai (*Sword of Many Loves*). Moreover, not only did these films cast lots of pretty-faced popular actors, but they became more multi-genre exercises, mixing slapstick humor, convoluted storytelling, intense graphic violence, tragedy, and over-the-top "wire-fu" action all in one film. It was during this period that *wuxia* practically became synonymous with *flying* swordsman. The best examples of the early 1990s *wuxia pian* are *Blade of Fury* (1993), *Ashes of Time* (1994), *Kung Fu Cult Master* (1993), and *The Blade* (1995).

The box-office failure Tsui Hark's downbeat and somber masterpiece, *The Blade*, marked the end of the so-called "wire-fu" boom in the mid-1990s. It would take a slight hiatus for a few years, after which the genre would appear as a very different creature. In 1998, director Andrew Lau adapted a famous Chinese comic book, *Feng Yun*, to the big screen. The film, *The Stormriders*, was a box-office success and brought some new tendencies to the genre, mainly in the form of extensive digital effects. In the film, pop stars Aaron Kwok and Ekin Cheng play Cloud and Wind, two martial artists who have to team up to defeat Lord Conqueror, played by Japanese actor Shinichi "Sonny" Chiba. There is lots of wire-assisted swordplay courtesy of action director Dion Lam, who would go on to work in Hollywood on films like *Doom* (2005) and *Spider-Man* 2 (2004). However, there are lots of digital effects to used for energy attacks, making the film seem like a combination of the *wuxia* films earlier that decade and video games like *Mortal Kombat*. Andrew Lau's two follow-ups, *A Man Called Hero* (1999) and *The Duel* (2000), would follow the same template.

It was in 2000 that the *wuxia* genre would get a final makeover, this time making it suitable for mainstream audiences all over the world. Director Ang Lee, who had won critical praise for films like *The Ice Storm* and *The Wedding Banquet*, decided to make a big budget *wuxia* film with famous actors, genre veteran Yuen Woo-Ping as the action director, and people like Yo Yo Ma and CoCo Lee (known at the time as the "Asian Christina Aguilera") to work on the soundtrack. The end result was *Crouching Tiger, Hidden Dragon*, an enormous worldwide success that rejuvenated the genre in such a way that its effects can still be felt today. All of a sudden, the *wuxia* genre became something a little more prestigious, something that could appeal to not only Chinese audiences, but audiences all over Asia. Thus, a number of directors who had previously nothing to do with the genre got into the game and started making big-budget historical fantasies with elaborate, wire-assisted action sequences, beautiful cinematography, elaborate sets and costumes, and actors whose appeal spread out over all of Asia. These films are a far cry from the *wuxia pian* of the previous decade; they are serious affairs, often dealing with themes like treachery and unrequited love, stripped of the schizophrenic shifts in tone that defined a lot of *wuxia* films of the early 1990s in order to appeal to a wider audience. Moreover, the action in these films, while elaborate and often breathtaking, is decidedly less "crazy" than that of its predecessors, since things like *qi* blasts and burrowing swordsman would be more than a mainstream Western viewer could take, their suspension of disbelief already stretched to the limit by the flying swordsman. The best films of this recent batch are easily *Crouching Tiger, Hidden Dragon* (2000) and *Hero* (2002), the latter of which was directed by Mainland Chinese director Zhang Yimou (*Raise the Red Lantern*).

III.   The Gospel of Modern Kung Fu Cinema According to Shaw (1970 – 1984)

Despite having a development not too much unlike most other kung fu films of its day, the Shaw Bros studio is such an entity unto itself and has such a cult following that we feel it appropriate to follow their history apart from the martial arts films produced by other studios during the same period. The Shaw Bros were a studio that was run by two brothers, namely Run Run and Runme Shaw. The Shaw Organization was founded in 1924 and was primarily a distribution company for films in Southeast Asia (the company worked out of Singapore). In 1930 the Shaw Brothers Studio was founded under the moniker South Seas Film, producing films out of Malaysia.

In 1957, the Shaw Brothers moved their operations from Singapore to Hong Kong, and the opening of their studio in Clearwater Bay in 1961 was what helped the studio establish a certain dominance over the Hong Kong film industry during the next two decades. The Shaw Brothers dominated the *wuxia* genre during the 1960s with the success of films like *The One-Armed Swordsman* and *Have Sword, Will Travel* (see previous section).

In 1970, the Shaw Brothers Studio produced what would become known as the first modern kung fu film: *The Chinese Boxer*. What we mean by "modern kung fu film" is that empty-hand fighting was emphasized, instead of swordplay, in this film. The film is considered a classic, although the choreography is a bit crude by modern standards. Many fans refer to *The Chinese Boxer* as a "Basher" film, in that the style of fighting used by the actors de-emphasizes actual technique in favor of choreographed arm flailing, (often) sloppy kicking, and occasionally the use of knives in combat. This sort of onscreen fighting would dominate the genre for the first half of the decade, both inside and out of the Shaw Brothers studio.

Jimmy Wang Yu, who had starred in a number of successful *wuxia* films for the Shaw Brothers in the 1960s and in *The Chinese Boxer*, had a falling out with the studio in 1970 and would go out on his own. Thus, the slack was left to actors David Chiang and Ti Lung, who were the main Shaw Brothers stars for the first part of the 1970s. Chiang and Ti would star in a number of a films directed by Chang Cheh, including the *Vengeance!* (1970) and *Duel of the Iron Fist* (1971), which are considered classic "basher" films. Another actor who would get his start during the era was monkey kung fu expert Chen Kuan-Tai, who would star in the memorable *Boxer from Shangtung* (1973), a classic film which features a bloody climax in which Chen takes on an entire gang while slowly bleeding to death from a hatchet wound. Another popular martial arts film made during this period was *Blood Brothers* (1973), a tale of brotherhood and treachery among three military officers during the Taiping Rebellion[14].

In 1974, Lau Kar-Leung, who was one of director Chang Cheh's principal action directors, suggested that Chang improve the action in his films by focusing on traditional

---

[14] - The Taiping Rebellion was a revolt by a group of Christian rebels that lasted from 1850 to 1864, during which time the rebels were able to seize control of a significant portion of the country, subjecting up to 30 million people to their rule. They carried out a large number of social reforms, including the temporary abolition of traditional Chinese religions in favor of a modified form of Christianity, in which the movement's founder, Hong Xiuquan, was considered to be the younger brother of Jesus. The resulting war between the rebels and the Qing army resulted in the death of somewhere between 20 and 30 million people.

kung fu, especially the Southern Styles like *wing chun* and *hung gar*. Chang agreed and together they made *Five Shaolin Fighters*, which starred regulars Ti Lung and David, up-and-coming actor Alexander Fu Sheng, newcomer Chi Kuan-Chun, and Meng Fei, who had doing films for other studios since 1972. The film focused on the themes of brotherhood and loyalty, two themes that Chang Cheh held dear in practically all of his films, and focused on the conflict between Shaolin-trained martial artists and the Qing government. The film was a huge success and started what fans refer today as Chang Cheh's "Shaolin Cycle" of films. Chang Cheh would go on to direct a number of a films about Shaolin kung fu, such as *Heroes Two* (1974), *Men from the Monastery* (1974), *Disciples of Shaolin* (1975), and *Shaolin Temple* (1976).

In 1975, Lau Kar-Leung, who had been choreographing Chang Cheh's films since the mid-1960s, broke off from Chang and started directing (and choreographing, of course) his own movies. The difference between the films that Lau Kar-Leung would go on to make and those that Chang Cheh has made (and would continue to make throughout his career) is often described in the following way: Chang Cheh made kung fu movies, while Lau Kar-Leung would make movies about kung fu. In other words, Chang Cheh made movies in which kung fu was the means in which to push his usual themes of brotherhood, loyalty, and friendship. On the other hand, Lau Kar-Leung's films were often a dissection of kung fu itself, analyzing the differences between different styles and how one style's strengths could be used to exploit another's weaknesses. We can see this in films like *Executioners of Shaolin* (tiger vs. crane), *Heroes of the East* (Chinese martial arts vs. Japanese martial arts), *The Martial Club* (Southern kung fu styles vs. Northern Kung Fu styles), *Fist of the White Lotus*[15] ("hard" styles vs. "soft" styles), and a number of others. Moreover, Chang Cheh's films were usually violent, bloody affairs with nihilistic climaxes while Lau Kar-Leung's films often ended with the characters resolving their conflict without killing each other.

In 1978, Chang Cheh's "Shaolin Cycle" had run its course and, after a number of actions films tackling various subjects, including Chinese literature (*The Brave Archer*) and immigrant gangs (*The Chinatown Kid*), Chang Cheh would settle into his last great "cycle" at the Shaw Brothers studio: the Venom Mob cycle. The Venom Mob was a troupe of five actors trained in different martial arts and weapons who starred together in more than a dozen films from 1978 to 1982. The name "Venom Mob" comes from the first film that they all worked on together, *The Five Deadly Venoms*. They were Philip Kwok, Lu Feng, and Chiang, who were Peking Opera trained and thus skilled in different styles, acrobatics, and weapons; Sun Chien, who was trained in *tae kwon do* and thus was a proficient kicker; and Lo Meng, who was trained in the *chow gar* style and was the hand technique expert and the brawniest of the bunch[16]. The plots of their films covered everything from adaptations of *wuxia* novels to tales of Shaolin-trained fighters fighting the Qings to conflicts between warlords during the Republic Era of the early 20th century. What separates their films from most of Chang Cheh's earlier films is that the quality of

---

[15] - *Fist of the White Lotus* was actually directed by Lo Lieh, and is a follow-up/remake of *Executioners of Shaolin*, but Lau Kar-Leung's influence on the story is quite apparent.
[16] - There was a sixth, Wei Pai, who appeared in three Venom Mob films: *Kid with the Golden Arm*, *Five Deadly Venoms*, and *Invincible Shaolin*. He left the Shaw Brothers to work for their rival, Golden Harvest. Another actor, Wang Li, is considered to be the seventh Venom for having participated in important supporting roles in a number of Venom Mob films, often as one of the protagonists.

the action rose up several notches from his earlier films, thanks to the ever-inventive choreography of the Philip Kwok, Lu Feng, Chiang Sheng, and Robert Tai, the latter of whom was a Peking Opera compatriot of the other three.

By the end of the 1970s, the Shaw Brothers were under a lot of pressure by the success of people like Jackie Chan and Sammo Hung and the growth in popularity of the kung fu comedy that the success of the former's *Snake in the Eagle's Shadow* and *The Drunken Master* brought with them. Thus, filmmakers like Chang Cheh and Lau Kar-Leung found themselves having to insert more humor into their films. A good portion of Lau's work from 1980 onward, excepting his downbeat *Eight Diagram Pole Fighter* (1984), were kung fu comedies. The best of those are generally considered to be *My Young Auntie* and *The Martial Club* (both from 1980), while the consensus on some of his other ones, like *Cat vs. Rat* and *Lady is the Boss*, is heavily towards the negative. Chang Cheh's Venom Mob films mixed some humor with the usual his usual brotherhood themes and ultra-violent action, notably *Shaolin Rescuers* and *The Magnificent Ruffians* (both were produced in 1979).

However, not content to have their biggest directors go on with business as usual while inserting comic bits into the proceedings, the Shaw Brothers produced a number of lower-budget films that more or less followed the so-called "Seasonal Formula." The "Seasonal Formula" refers to the general plotline used by most kung fu comedies during the time period: Some young, arrogant martial artist gets into trouble until he is humbled, either by getting beaten down by the main villain or losing his master and/or someone close to him. He then trains with an even more talented master and must take on the main villain again. This plot was used in the two Jackie Chan films mentioned in the preceding paragraph and was copied by dozens of films made at that time. These films could be produced for a lot cheaper than a lot of the classier *wuxia* and kung fu films they were making at the time. Some of the films that came of this were *The Five Superfighters*, *The Fighting Fool*, *Stroke of Death*, *The Master*, and *Coward Bastard*. These films starred lesser-known (at the time) actors like Mang Yuan Man, Yuen Wah, and Yuen Tak, all of whom were colleagues of Jackie Chan; Tony Leung Siu-Hung, who'd go on to be a respected action director in American films; and Ching Siu-Tung, whom we mentioned earlier was a big figure in the development of the *wuxia* genre.

In 1982, it was the clear that the period piece kung fu films and *wuxia pian* were on their way out. That year saw some of the last great classics from both genres from not only the Shaw Brothers studio, but from some of the best talent outside the studio as well. By 1983, it was clear that Golden Harvest, the Shaw Brothers' rival, was moving on to something new in the form of action films set in the modern day, highlighted by stunt-based action and the physical talents of Jackie Chan and Sammo Hung and their respective stunt teams. Unfortunately, the Shaw Brothers continued to churn out kung fu films set in period and *wuxia pian*, which contributed to the studio's downfall. There were some good films produced, like *Shaolin* Intruders (1983), *Opium and the Kung Fu Master* (1984), and *Disciples of the 36th Chamber* (1985), but these did little to save what was essentially a sinking ship. Furthermore, in 1984, Alexander Fu Sheng, one of their greatest stars, lost his life in a car accident, casting an even darker shadow over the studio. The negative energy built up by what was going on around them was channeled into one of Lau Kar-Leung's *Eight Diagram Pole Master*, one of the most pessimistic films ever produced by the studio. By the middle of the decade, the Shaw Brothers studio had shut down its movie production department and would focus its energies on television for more than a decade.

The Shaw Brothers made an attempt at a glorious comeback in 1997, with a big-budget remake of their 1973 classic *The Boxer from Shantung*. The film, *Hero*, was directed by acclaimed director/choreographer Corey Yuen and starred Takeshi Kaneshiro, a Sino-Japanese actor on his way to stardom; Yuen Biao, a colleague of Jackie Chan for whom the film was supposed to be a career-booster; and former Shaw Brothers actor/choreographers/stuntmen Yuen Tak and Yuen Wah were on hand for supporting roles. The film received praise all around for its action sequences, but was a box-office disappointment and failed to revive the studio. Five years later, the Shaw Brothers made a final attempt to recapture their lost glory with *Drunken Monkey*, a return to the old school kung fu film directed and choreographed by Lau Kar-Leung. The film starred Shaw Brothers veterans Gordon Liu, Lau Kar-Leung himself, and Chi Kuan-Chun as the villain, not to mention Mainland Chinese actor Wu Jing, who, as of 2003, had yet to establish himself as a bankable actor in Hong Kong. Like *Hero*, the film received praise from fans for its back-to-basics fight scenes, but was enough of a failure that it became the proverbial nail in the coffin for the once-powerhouse studio.

IV.   The Gospel of Modern Kung Fu Cinema According to Everybody Else (1970 – Present)

We already mentioned that the first modern kung fu film came about in 1970 with the release of Jimmy Wang Yu's *The Chinese Boxer*. The film set the standard for choreography for the next few years, creating the "Basher" style of screen fighting in which punches and kicks came across as choreographed arm-flailing more than anything else. The film also established a strong anti-Japanese sentiment[17], and a great deal of movies made during the 1970s would capitalize on the then-natural dislike of the Japanese by Chinese audiences. Well, Jimmy Wang Yu left the Shaw Brothers soon after *The Chinese Boxer* but would go on to make a number of well-known "basher" films during that time period, despite the fact that he really wasn't that great of an onscreen fighter. There were a number of other actors who would make this sort of martial arts film during the time period, like Chang Yi, Jason Pai Piao, Cheng Sing, Yasuaki Kurata, and Bruce Leung Siu-Lung. Not many of these films are considered classics, since the fighting was often sloppy and overlong, the production values low, and the plots rudimentary at best. Nevertheless, they represent an integral part of the genre.

Now, though the "basher" films of the early 1970s constituted the prevailing style of martial arts film during said period, they did not constitute the so-called "cream of the crop". The best martial arts films of the early 1970s were produced by Golden Harvest, the biggest studio in Hong Kong, second only to the illustrious Shaw Brothers, and starred Bruce Lee and Angela Mao. Bruce Lee really need not much of an introduction. His films were wildly successful all over the world and featured a style of quick, precise, and realistic action direction that wouldn't be equaled until Jackie Chan and Sammo

---

[17] - This dislike stems from the ill feelings caused by the Japanese occupation of China during the Second World War, and the number of atrocities committed by Japanese Imperial Army during that period, such as the Rape of Nanking.

Hung would revolutionize the genre in the early 1980s[18]. Angela Mao was Golden Harvest's starlet, often referred to as the Female Bruce Lee. Her films were a lot like Bruce Lee's in terms of storyline and her fighting style came very close to matching the intensity of "The Little Dragon"[19], thanks to the superior fight choreography of a young Sammo Hung.

Unfortunately, Bruce Lee died of an allergic reaction to marijuana in 1973, leaving a great void in the world of Hong Kong martial arts films. However, there were a lot of studios hoping to cash in on his name and legacy, and thus began the sub-genre known by fans as "Brucesploitation". From 1973 until the late 1980s, a number of actors would assume monikers like Bruce Li, Bruce Le, Dragon Lee, Bruce Lai, etc. and appear in low budget films, often imitating Bruce's distinctive style of fighting, in hopes of making a quick buck. The most famous of these was Jimmy Ho Chung Tao, who assumed the stage name of Bruce Li. Bruce Li's most famous films deal directly with his inspiration, including *Exit the Dragon, Enter the Tiger* (1974), in which Bruce Li investigates the death of Bruce Lee; *Bruce Lee: A Dragon Story* (1974) and *Bruce Lee: The Man, They Myth* (1976), which are unauthorized biopics; and *Bruce Lee's Deadly Kung Fu*, which features an early appearance by onscreen super kicker Hwang Jang Lee. Despite having a strong cult following, Brucesploitation films tend to be cheap, sleazy affairs with sub-par fight direction, terrible acting, and often take very exploitive attitudes towards women.

By the mid-1970s, the Shaw Brothers studio were enjoying a lot of success with Chang Cheh's Shaolin-themed films and Southern Chinese martial arts seemed to be the "in" thing for kung fu movies[20]. It was in 1976 that Ng See-Yuen, one of the main producers and directors at the independent studio Seasonal Films, had a great idea: make a movie in which a fighter whose specialty is kicking team up with another fighter who was trained in hand-based styles. The film *The Secret Rivals* was the first to implement that idea and its success not only created a small sub-genre of similar films, but it also made fancy kicking popular again, paving the way for lots of talented kickers further down the road.

It was Seasonal Films that would end up revolutionizing the genre again in 1978 when an unknown actor named Jackie Chan was loaned to the studio by producer/director Lo Wei, who was sick of working with him to no avail. Chan teamed up with Ng See-Yuen and action director Yuen Woo-Ping, who was beginning to gain recognition in an already-saturated genre, and together they produced two kung fu comedies, *Snake in the Eagle's Shadow* and *The Drunken Master*. The films were tremendously successful, the latter breaking the record established by Bruce Lee's films five years earlier. Jackie Chan became an instant star and would go on to make several more kung fu comedies before abandoning the genre and moving on to something different. Yuen Woo-Ping quickly became known as one of the great old school directors and choreographers and would go on to produce a number of genre classics, including *The Magnificent Butcher, The Buddhist Fist*, and *Legend of a Fighter*. More importantly though, the kung fu comedy

---

[18] - See the chapter on Jeet Kune Do for a more detailed discussion on Bruce Lee and his films.
[19] - Bruce Lee's Chinese name is Lei Siu-Lung, which means "Little Dragon Lee".
[20] - Apparently, Shaolin was also the "in" thing, judging by the number of films that "feature" Shaolin in the title and yet have very little to do with the Shaolin Temple or even Shaolin martial arts.

became a genre staple and soon dozens of films were being made trying to ape the success of Chan's films, mixing comic pratfalls with intricate kung fu action design.

We consider 1982 to be the last great year for the old school kung fu movie, despite the fact that the genre would continue for about four more years[21]. In 1982, Sammo Hung, who had been directing his own films since 1977, made his swan song to the genre, *The Prodigal Son*, which is considered by many to be one of the greatest kung fu movies ever made. Jackie Chan too his last old school movie, *Dragon Lord*, in which it was clear that he was more interested in pushing the boundaries on stunt-based fighting rather than fighting based on traditional kung fu techniques. Corey Yuen, who had studied Peking Opera with Jackie Chan and Sammo Hung, released his first directorial effort for Seasonal Films, *Ninja in the Dragon's Den*, which was quite successful. Yuen Woo-Ping continued to find success with his *Miracle Fighters*, which mixed intricate kung fu choreography with wizardry and special FX. Finally, 1982 was the year that Mainland China finally entered the game, producing the successful film *Shaolin Temple*, which starred an 18-year old Jet Li and featured an entire cast of *wushu*-trained Mainland actors.

The first modern action films that really made an impact on the Hong Kong box office during the early 1980s were the first *Aces Go Places* (1982), *Winners and Sinners* (1983), and *Project A* (1983). The former was something of a caper film, about a high-tech thief and the elaborate ways he'd steal stuff and then get away with it. The film spawned four sequels and a cross-over film. *Winners and Sinners* was an action comedy directed by and starring Sammo Hung, about a group of ex-cons that tried to go straight but ended up getting involved in a conflict between rival crime families. The movie featured some large-scale stunts courtesy of Jackie Chan and some great fighting that would win it the Hong Kong Award for Best Action Design that year. *Project A* was Jackie Chan's great contribution to the genre: a stunt-based action film in which Jackie Chan, Sammo Hung, and their respective stunt teams find as many ways to make the audience cringe while fighting pirates in turn-of-the-century Hong Kong. It has become one of the gold standards for measuring Hong Kong action films.

By the mid-1980s, there two major lines of action movie being produced. The first, which will not get any attention in this book, was the "Heroic Bloodshed" film, in which the conflict between cops and triads (or even triads and triads) was glamorized and the action consisted of stylized gun battles, often referred to by fans as "Bullet Ballet". Director John Woo (*Face-Off, Mission Impossible 2*) and Chow Yun Fat (*Crouching Tiger, Hidden Dragon*) are responsible for this genre.

The other line of action film was the type of stunt-based action film that Jackie Chan and Sammo Hung were churning out at the time. Those films featured set pieces that hinged on people falling from high places, breaking things, using found objects as weapons, and a more freer style of fighting often referred to as "kickboxing", since it eschewed traditional movements for more practical and economical (but still flashy) punches and kicks. One will notice that these films in general will not get as much attention here in this book, since our focus is on traditional styles, although we should

---

[21] - Independent studios from Taiwan, Hong Kong, and South Korea would continue to make "traditional kung fu", as would Mainland China and the Shaw Brothers. Some of these movies would be successful in various parts of Asia, not to mention the cult following that many would get in Western countries. Ultimately, it was Golden Harvest and their modern action films that would dominate the local box office.

note that some action directors like Frankie Chan and Tony Leung Siu-Hung did make an effort to throw some traditional techniques into their films. Some of the greatest action films of all time, like *Eastern Condors* (1987), the first two *Police Story* films, *Righting Wrongs* (1986), and *Yes Madam!* (1985) belong to this time period.

Another product of the 1980s, and kind of a sub-group of the modern kickboxing film, is the "Girls n' Guns" sub-genre. As the name implies, these films feature female protagonists (and antagonists, too) getting into brutal fights and gun battles. This particular sub-genre has called the attention of a lot of Western viewers and has been the reason that a lot of Westerners have gotten involved in the genre. Actresses like Yukari Oshima, Moon Lee, Cynthia Khan, and of course, Michelle Yeoh, were among the fighting femme fatales who were most popular at the time. The girls n' guns genre started dying out in the early 1990s, being relegated to cheap Filipino films[22] by the middle of the decade and then shot-on-video films by the beginning of the new millennium.

The success of such "wire-fu" fantasy and *wuxia* films like *A Chinese Ghost Story* (1987), its 1990 sequel, and *The Swordsman* (1990) re-ignited public interest in period piece martial arts films, starting in 1991 with Tsui Hark's *Once Upon a Time in China*, whose success propelled Jet Li to stardom and guaranteed the production of dozens of kung fu films set in period for the next several years, much like their *wuxia* counterparts. Some fans often refer to this period between 1990 and 1995[23] as the Hong Kong "New Wave"[24]. The "New Wave" was marked by an increase in the use of wires to enhance the abilities of the performers and to allow over-the-top fights to be filmed that would be very difficult, if not impossible to film under regular conditions. While some actors from the old school period found work in supporting roles in a number of a films, there was a shift in emphasis from Peking Opera styled-acrobatics and Southern Chinese styles to the more flashy Mainland *wushu* techniques, giving actors like Jet Li, Donnie Yen, Vincent Zhao Wen-Zhuo, and others a chance for fame.

This was the period in which actor Jet Li would make a name for himself, playing seemingly every single Chinese folk hero in existence, from Wong Fei-Hung (the *Once Upon a Time in China* series) to Hong Xiguan (*New Legend of Shaolin*) to Chen Zhen (*Fist of Legend*), the character popularized by Bruce Lee in *Fist of Fury* (1972). Yuen Woo-Ping, who had been so prolific during the old school period but had little to do during the height of popularity of modern action films, came into the spotlight once again as a go-to guy for quality wire-assisted action, which reputation led to his hiring on films like *The Matrix* (1999) and *Crouching Tiger, Hidden Dragon* (2000). Conversely, Sammo Hung, who had been so prolific during the 1970s and 1980s, suffered a severe fall in popularity and, as a result, his output declined sharply, as did his recognition as an action director at the Hong Kong Film Awards – he only got nominated twice during an

---

[22] - Filipino films were often considered to be lowest point to which a Hong Kong actor could descend.

[23] - 1995 is generally considered the last year of the New Wave, with the mammoth commercial failure of Tsui Hark's *The Blade* signaling the close of the genre. However, there were still a few period piece kung fu films made in following years, like *Iron Monkey 2* (1996), *Tai Chi II* (1996), and *Once Upon a Time in China and America* (1997). Only the latter met with success in the box office, though.

[24] - There is some debate as to what the "New Wave" actually refers to. Keith Allison, professional writer and movie critic at the Teleport City website, maintains that the New Wave referred to the fantasy and action films of the 1980s, with the wire-fu craze of the early 1990s simply being the tail-end of something bigger. For our purposes, however, the "New Wave" refers to the boom in period piece films in the early 1990s, with the fantasy and *wuxia* films of previous decade being precursors to it.

eight-year period, for his work on *Ashes of Time* and *Once Upon a Time in China and America*.

By the second half of the 1990s, Hong Kong cinema was facing a lot of competition from the growing horde of big-budget, FX-filled Hollywood blockbusters, both in the domestic and foreign markets, not to mention a loss in profits due to the ever-growing threat of piracy and Triad interference in the movie business. Thus, Hong Kong filmmakers started making films that could compete on the international market with good-looking stars (even those who didn't possess much physical talent), glossy cinematography, and more special FX than films made before. As a result, the action films ended up coming across as being more dumbed down than before, as the actors involved had to be given simpler routines by the action directors, not to mention the use of doubles and wires to make up for the lack of martial arts prowess. Moreover, the physical decline of such great actors like Yuen Biao, Jackie Chan, Sammo Hung, and many others due to age and injury started to show in their films as well.

As stated earlier, the box office receipts generated by *Crouching Tiger, Hidden Dragon* made historical martial arts films popular again, although most of the subsequent films were decidedly in the *wuxia pian* genre and not the kung fu genre. Nonetheless, audiences were blessed with two superior biopics as a result, namely *Fearless* (2006), which tells the story of Huo Yuanjia, who founded the Jingwu Martial Arts Academy in Shanghai in the early 20th century; and the more recent *Ip Man* (2008), which tells the story of the wing chun master who became Bruce Lee's teacher. However, the rush to make historical action films for domestic and international audiences did lead to a number of epic battle films being produced, such as *The Warlords* (2007), John Woo's *Red Cliff* (2008) films, and *Battle of Wits* (2006), to name a few. Those were influenced as much by Hollywood blockbusters like *Gladiator* (1998) and *Troy* (2004) as they were by *Crouching Tiger, Hidden Dragon* and *Hero*.

The greatest revelation to the kung fu film in the new millennium has been actor/choreographer Donnie Yen. To be honest, his rise to success hasn't been so much a revelation as a sigh of "It's about time!" Donnie Yen had entered the industry at the tail-end of the old school period and then gone on to appear in some of most beloved action films of the 1980s, *Tiger Cage 2 (1990)* and *In the Line of Duty IV* (1989), under the direction of Yuen Woo-Ping. His career showed promise during the "New Wave" era after appearing in successful films like *New Dragon Inn* (1992) and *Once Upon a Time in China II* (1992), not to mention less-successful, but still fan-acclaimed, films like *Iron Monkey* (1993). After failing to establish himself as a director in the late 1990s and as a force in Hollywood in the early 2000s, Donnie went back to Hong Kong to give audiences a taste of the 1980s-style action with a twist: he incorporated MMA (mixed martial arts), notably jiu-jitsu and ground fighting techniques, which had grown in popularity because of the Ultimate Fighting Championship. Donnie has since become the go-to man for any film that needs a martial arts master in its cast, as well as having become one of the most acclaimed action directors in the business.

V.   The Purpose of this Book

The focus of our book is to give attention to the films and fight scenes that best depict the various kung fu styles in existence. Thus, each chapter will focus on a specific style and two or three films (or in some cases, four or more) that feature a specific fight scene that does the style depicted justice. Although the focus is on Chinese martial arts, we do recognize that other styles founded outside China have always had a special place in Chinese cinema, and thus we did include chapters about fighting styles from Japan, Korea, Thailand, and India. As you will see, we have dedicated good portion of the book to weapons from Chinese martial arts, not to mention some Japanese weapons, too. Not every Chinese martial arts style will be represented in the book, considering that there are hundreds of styles in existence, including family and regional variations of the same style. Some of the lesser-known styles will receive attention in one of the book's appendices.

With a few exceptions, most of the chapters will follow the same general format. In the chapter introduction, a brief history of the style (or weapon) will be given, followed by a description of the style and its techniques. There will then be a brief history and catalogue of the style's appearance on film, mainly in Chinese cinema, although we will do our best to include examples of the style in world cinema where possible. At this point, we'll introduce the film and the fight therein. For each fight, we will talk a little about the film's context in the history of the genre, the fight's context within the film, a description of the fight, and followed by an analysis of the performance(s) of the lead(s), including a comparison of how the lead uses the style and how the style is used in a real fight. Finally, we will analyze and evaluate the choreography of the film. Where possible, we will include a rundown of the careers of the actors and action directors involved, including commentary about the context of the film in the career of the person and the history of the genre as a whole.

The criteria for the selection of the individual fight scenes are based on equal parts accuracy and presentation. A fight has to portray the style in a fairly accurate manner, showing the viewer how the style is (theoretically) applied in a fight and including as much as possible the most accurate movements and techniques associated with the style itself. A fight that includes a totally distorted portrayal of the fight will most likely be disqualified, although we may mention it in the chapter introduction. Good examples of this criterion in action may be the *wing chun* style, which has gotten some very inaccurate portrayals in film over the years, including films like *Shaolin Martial Arts* (1974) and *Wing Chun* (1994). Now, must recognize that some artistic liberties will almost always be taken while choreographing a fight scene and that a lot of actors are trained in various styles, so the style being used may not always be "pure".

Despite the importance of accuracy in our criteria, we are in no way sticklers for realism. After all, no fight in real life would ever last ten minutes or more with synchronized acrobatics and flashy kicking. Moreover, despite the often flowery movements that we see whenever someone performs a set, the application of such movements is almost always a lot more direct. No fighter would ever consciously drag out a real-life fight; he/she would take the quickest route possible to neutralize, disarm, injure, or even kill an opponent or attacker. Thus, most fights in Chinese films are unrealistic by nature. Nonetheless, we don't really care about realism in our films and thus will not use it as a specific criterion for selecting any fight.

Now, presentation to us is just as important in making a fight entertaining as the accuracy of the style itself. Performing a style onscreen and using it real life fights on in tournaments are two different things. This rule often applies to people who are real-life masters of a style, but not experienced actors. Compare the monkey style performed by Sammo Hung in films like *Encounter of the Spooky Kind* and *Knockabout*, with *Monkey's Fist*, starring Grandmaster Chan Sau Chung. The latter may be a lot more realistic, but not as entertaining as the former. Thus, a fight not only has to be (reasonably) accurate, but entertaining and fun to watch, too. A lot of this will depend on the choreographer, who bears the burden of balancing technique with the more aesthetic side of action direction, including wire stunts, acrobatics, use of one's surroundings and objects, etc.

One criterion that we will not be using is the duration of the fight itself. Length does not always equal quality. There are fights that end right as things are getting interesting and fights that go on for so long that they exhausting. On the other hand, a good choreographer can either make a 20-minute fight seem like a few minutes long, or film a three-minute that's just as satisfying as it needs to be. For the most, we will mention what the length of each selected fight is, although we want the reader to know that it's not a deciding a factor.

For those readers who are already fans of the genre: Keep in mind; a recommendation to a certain fight scene does not necessarily indicate a recommendation to a certain film as a whole. There are lots of otherwise bland and/or formulaic films that just happen to have one or two awesome fight sequences in them. On the other hand, the absence of some fan favorites does not mean that we the authors hold any dislike to those films; we simply could not fit a detailed description of every single fight scene showing off a given fighting style into the book. We admit up front that there is a certain degree of subjectivity involved in our selection, but just because we don't put in one fight doesn't mean that we harbor any ill feelings towards it or the film it's in. Moreover, there are a number of classics that simply don't meet the criteria to be in our book, including a lot of action films set in the modern day and a number of the wire-fu films made during the 1990s.

We hope that the book will prove a great learning experience for our readers, our objective being that they come away with a greater appreciation for Chinese martial arts cinema, looking past old stereotypes and seeing the effort that filmmakers have put in to showcasing different martial arts styles in the most entertaining ways possible. We also hope that the reader will come away from this experience desiring to seek out the films mentioned and show support for the genre. Finally, it is our desire that reader learn something new about Chinese history and culture, and the martial arts in general.

Part 1: Southern Kung Fu Styles

Dragon Kung Fu

The dragon style is one of the five animal styles of Southern Shaolin martial arts and the only style that is based on an entirely mythical animal[25]. The style was developed in 1565 at the Shaolin Temple in Hunan. There are quite a number of legends about its creation, one being that it was founded by the famous nun Ng Mui, who is also associated with the legend of the creation of *wing chun* kung fu. Another legend states that it was founded by a monk who had contemplated the twisty movements of the dragon and integrated it into his kung fu. The original dragon style is now known as the Southern dragon style; there is a Northern dragon style[26] that was developed in 1680.

At the beginning of one's training, there are a number of blocks, strikes, and claw techniques that pupils of the art will learn. Like other Southern kung fu styles, the attacks associated with the Dragon style tend to be short and snappy. There is little kicking in the dragon style and the footwork resembles the zigzag motion of a dragon—the goal of the practitioner is to keep himself at a 45° angle to his opponent. The dragon style is perfectly suited to combat situations in which severely crippling or even killing one's opponent is a necessary course of action.

Once a practitioner enters the advanced level of style, however, one will see that he has little in common with a beginner. The dragon style is considered to be a "high" style, in that a master of the style will eventually dispense all hard techniques, including blocking, and go for a more evasive and parrying style of fighting. A master of the style will try to make an opponent tire himself out rather than take him on directly. Thus, it becomes important that a dragon stylist learn to cultivate his *chi*, or internal energy, as brute strength is replaced with fluid movements meant to redirect the force of an enemy's attacks or simply to avoid it completely.

The dragon style (both Northern and Southern) is rarely seen onscreen not accompanied by the other animal styles. Thus, a lot of early Sammo Hung and Jackie Chan films will feature the style, if only briefly. The same applies to Lau Kar-Leung's classic films. One of the better demonstrations of the dragon style is that performed by Frankie Chan in *The Prodigal Son*, especially in his fight against Lam Ching-Ying[27]. Chan would briefly parody this style in the modern action film *Burning Ambition* (1988). Old school super-kicker Tan Tao Liang uses some dragon hand techniques in the Taiwanese film *Challenge of Death* (1977) to compliment his *tae kwon do* kicking. Legendary super kicker Hwang Jang Lee would do a something similar in Joseph Kuo's *Dragon's Claws* (1979). Independent "star" Elton Chong does some dragon at the climax of *Fist of the Golden Monkey* (1983), and we can see some dragon being performed in *Dragon on the Shaolin Tower* (1980) during the film's big climax.

---

[25] - There are some styles that have named their techniques after other mythological animals, namely the phoenix and the unicorn. The dragon, however, is the only mythological creature to have an entire style devoted to it.

[26] - The difference between the Southern and Northern Dragon styles is that the footwork in the latter is a lot more wide and sweeping, as opposed to the short, complex leg movements of the Southern dragon style.

[27] - See chapter on *Wing Chun*.

Dragon Fist (1979)

Despite the fact that many of Jackie Chan's earlier efforts suffered from a lack of box office draw, many of them were, in fact, above-average kung fu movies, often being just as entertaining as the Shaw Bros and Golden Harvest films made at the same time. By 1977, Jackie Chan was choreographing most of his own films and his knack for putting together a good action sequence was evident even at that time. His own skills were just as sharp as those of his more-successful contemporaries, and he often is not given the credit he deserves as a martial artist because of his later films' emphasis on combining fighting with slapstick comedy. Although not his best film that he made with director/producer Lo Wei, *Dragon Fist* does feature some of Jackie Chan's most intense fighting of his classic kung fu period.

In the book Jackie Chan: Inside the Dragon, author Clyde Gentry III states that this film was closest film in tone and execution to a Bruce Lee film that Chan ever made. It is indeed a very serious affair, with a dark revenge plot and lots of brutal martial arts on display. Jackie Chan shows off some his quicker handwork in this film, especially in a fight against co-star James Tien in the middle of the film. Jackie Chan and James Tien get into a little scuffle, as James Tien is part of the clan whose master had murdered Jackie's master at the beginning of the film. The two start fighting and Jackie soon shows himself to be Tien's match. Despite the fact that their fight is very short, Jackie Chan gets in some very good moves and gives the dragon fist style a solid showcase for people who want to know what it looks like in combat.

Hong Kong Poster for *Dragon Fist* (1979).

Jackie Chan provides us with some his quicker and more direct choreography for his earlier films here. His handwork is quite quick, switching between short, powerful punches (a lot of underhand strikes) and more complex blocking and parrying techniques. Jackie's stances are, generally speaking, high and narrow, although he does some lower stances, too (none of them very wide, though). He throws in some nice kicks, including a few roundhouse kicks and a jumping round kick. But other than that, the emphasis is on the fantastic handwork.

The action direction duties were handled by Jackie himself, of which he does quite a good job in this particular fight. The choreography is very complex, but very quick. The complexity isn't due so much to usual surplus of Peking Opera acrobatics, as was common at the time, but because the movements of the dragon style itself are complex. Chan does his best to keep himself at an angle to James Tien, instead of attacking in a straight line. James Tien provides an effective foil to Chan in this fight, although this isn't one of his better fights.

We chose this one over the other fights, including the 15-minute finale, because this fight really gives Chan a chance to shine and show off a little-seen fighting style. The finale has some good moments, including a few good kickers and a pretty good (if way too drawn out) crutch/tonfa fight. However, this fight between Jackie Chan and James Tien is 70 seconds of pure dragon goodness that viewers rarely get to see in any other place.

Kung Fu Cult Master (1993)

It's almost disheartening to consider the fall that Sammo Hung suffered during the late 1980s and most of the 1990s. For most of the 1970s and 1980s, Hung had enjoyed quite a bit of success as an actor, action director, director, and producer of many quality kung fu, modern action, horror, and comedy films. He was one of the top five action directors[28] for the better part of those two decades, being the man responsible for some of the great individual fights of all time. However, due to a number of factors, including a public outcry against his then-relationship with action starlet Joyce Mina Godenzi and a number of box-office disappointments, his career suffered a number of blows that took more than a decade for Sammo to bounce back from.

The sad part about all this is that his career really sunk during the early 1990s, right smack dab in the middle of the "New Wave" resurgence of historical martial arts films. Considering that his old school kung fu movies are all considered classics, his limited participation in the glut of period pieces produced from 1990 to 1996 is lamentable indeed. He did dabble in the genre a little, even getting himself two nominations for Best Action Design for *Ashes of Time* (1994) and *Once Upon a Time in China and America* (1997). However, by this time Sammo's career was almost a shadow of its former self. Nonetheless, the films he did work on did show that Sammo strived to put in the element of physicality that many of the wire-fu films of that era lacked, including the historical fantasy-epic, *Kung Fu Cult Master*.

Kung Fu Cult Master is an epic story compressed into a 90-minute film about a boy (eventually played by Jet Li) whose parents are forced to kill themselves by a number of kung fu schools. He trains in a number of fantastic styles in order to get his revenge, but finds himself involved in an even greater plot than he had imagined before. One of the styles he learns is called "The Great Solar Stance", which allows him to not only shoot fireballs a la *Street Fighter II*, but it allows him to adapt to learn the styles of others in a question of minutes. In one fight scene, he challenged by a Shaolin monk (Cho Wing) after accusing the monk's master of being a traitor for the Yuan dynasty[29]. The

---

[28] Who do we consider to be the other top action directors? Those would be Yuen Woo-Ping and his family, Lau Kar-Leung, Jackie Chan, and the Venom Mob.

[29] Yuan Dynasty (1271 – 1368 A.D.) – Dynasty in which China was ruled by Mongol invaders, the most famous being Genghis Khan. The sheer size of the Mongol empire at the time allowed for the dissemination of many foreign influences into Chinese culture, such as crops (carrots, turnips, melons,

monk starts using the Dragon style against Li, who eventually is able to learn and perform the style himself.

Sammo Hung had previous worked with the dragon style in his masterpiece *The Prodigal Son* (1982), which style was used by villain Frankie Chan. Here, Cho Wing is obviously channeling the same fighting style, although obviously with a number of wire-assisted flourishes not present in the earlier classic. Cho`s dragon style is very similar to the tiger style, with a number of clawing and grabbing techniques present among the handwork. However, if you compare the stances between the dragon and tiger styles, you'll notice that Cho's stances are not as low and wide as say, the tiger style seen in a typical Carter Wong or Chen Sing film.

Although heavy kicking is bit uncharacteristic of the dragon style, Cho Wing does throw in a quite a bit of legwork in this scene. He performs mainly roundhouse and spin kicks, with a few aerial kicks thrown in for good measure. He establishes a good rapport with Jet Li while trading kicks, especially in the second half of the fight.

Being a 1990s period piece, there is a bit of wire-assisted technique thrown into the fight because it was the vogue at the time. Sammo Hung was never as adept at extensive wire use as were his contemporaries Ching Siu-Tung, Corey Yuen, and the Yuen Clan. Most of the wire use in this particular fight is limited to assisting both Jet Li's and Cho Wing's jumps from one platform to another. There is an interesting, if a bit awkward, wire-assisted move that Cho Wing performs where he jumps in the air, kicks at Jet Li with both his feet, and then with both his hands, and then with his feet again, with his body staying the same place the entire time. Jet Li performs the same move at the end of the fight.

Speaking of Jet Li, don't expect a whole lot from him in this fight, since he's mainly fighting on the defensive. He does get in some solid footwork, including a nice, high spinning kick. However, most of his wushu skills are used for blocking and evading Cho Wing's attacks until he can assimilate Cho's dragon style into his own repertoire.

Sammo does a neat job with the choreography, giving it a fairly traditional feel in spite of the wires and effects. Things stay fast, but retain the intricacy of an old school kung fu brawl. The fight itself is not very long, which is understandable considering that the fight doesn't have a really important part in the (convoluted) narrative of the film itself. However, as Northern *wushu* was a very important of the New Wave of historical martial arts films in the 1990s, it's always a treat to see traditional animal styles get some attention, making this fight a lot more notable than it would have been had it been made 15 years earlier.

---

cotton, etc.) and ideas (cartography, astronomy, etc.), all of which came from the Middle East. It was also the dynasty during which Marco Polo visited China.

Southern Tiger Kung Fu

One of the most popular of the Shaolin Five animal styles is the Tiger style. It is also a rather more complex idea, as Tiger can refer to a specific style or a large family of different styles. As an individual style (and the one that we will focus on in this chapter), the Tiger style most often seen on film is the Southern Tiger style[30]. The style is one of the more brutal and powerful kung fu styles. Power is the key to the Tiger technique, with its quick, short kicks and punches that are meant for breaking bones and crippling one's opponent. The hand techniques, which generally find the fingers in the form of claws, focus on ripping through the skin and tearing apart the tendons and muscles of one's opponent.

The Southern tiger style is part of the Tiger family of kung fu styles. The Tiger Family is a group of "low" styles, which are based on "earthly" animals and are dependent on brute force, as well as destroying one's opponent's structure. Some styles included in the Tiger family include the crab, leopard, eagle, drunken boxing, and pak mei ("white eyebrow") styles. There are a number of other sub-styles that bear the name tiger, including hong tiger, s'hu tiger (a weapons-based system), white tiger, imperial tiger, and snow tiger. Also included in the Tiger Family is *hung gar*, which was developed by Hung Shi-Kwan combining elements of the Tiger and White Crane styles.

In martial arts cinema outside of Hong Kong and Taiwan, the tiger style is not very often seen, although it has popped up in a few films here and there. The Chinese stylist in Jean-Claude Van Damme's *The Quest* (1996) uses the tiger style in one of his fights. Bolo Yeung plays a tiger claw-fighting serial killer in the aptly-named *Tiger Claws*, alongside American B-movie queen Cynthia Rothrock. Jackie Chan briefly uses the tiger style in his fight against Jet Li in *The Forbidden Kingdom* (2008). There's a brief parody of the tiger style in the independent classic *The Six-String Samurai*, as well.

The tiger style isn't usually shown pure in most traditional kung fu films. Most of the time, the tiger style being shown is either as an integral part of *hung gar* or in conjunction with the other Shaolin animal styles. A lot of Jackie Chan's earlier films like *Shaolin Wooden Men* and *Spiritual Kung Fu* feature the tiger style, as do Sammo's classic films like *Iron-Fisted Monk* (1977) and *The Magnificent Butcher* (1979). Most films choreographed by Lau Kar-Leung made after 1974 will feature the tiger in one form or another, such as *5 Shaolin Masters* and *Executioners of Shaolin*. Carter Wong, a Taiwanese martial arts mainstay, usually throws in some tiger style as a result of his *hung gar* training, as does Don Wong Tao, notably in the film *Along Comes a Tiger* (1977). Like most Southern Shaolin styles, the Tiger style got little attention onscreen after the death of traditional kung fu cinema. However, in one of the more memorable fights of Jet Li's masterpiece *Fearless* (2006), Jet Li fights a tiger claw master on a small platform 40 feet above the ground.

---

[30] - There is a Northern Shaolin style known as the "Black Tiger", which is characterized by kicks, acrobatics, and some Tiger claw techniques. It occasionally shows up in films, notably performed by Philip Kwok in *Shaolin Rescuers* (1979) and *The Killer Army* (1980).

Fatal Flying Guillotines (1977)

Although we didn't mention him in the chapter introduction, the most prominent tiger stylist in Chinese cinema is a man named Chen Sing. Chen Sing was a short, stocky guy whose build made him perfect to practice the tiger style and whose mustache and ugly sneer made him a go-to guy for playing sleazy villains for most of his career. Chen Sing was appearing in kung fu movies as early as 1970, where he starred as one of the three main villains in Jimmy Wang Yu's *The Chinese Boxer*. He played a hero in a couple of early chopsockey films, and would even play some interesting historical figures like San Te, Huo Yuanjia, and Tamo (Bodidharma), but most of his career revolved around him ruthlessly tearing people apart his tiger claw technique, which he used a good portion of his films. Once in a while he would throw in some snake or crane to diversify things, but you could always depend on Chen Sing to work his claw skills onscreen. Some of his more notable showcases include *The Himalayan* (1975), *Heroes of the Wild* (1978), *Mantis Fist Boxing* (1979), and *The Iron-Fisted Monk* (1977). However, one of his all-time great performances is this independent Taiwanese kung fu epic.

In *Fatal Flying Guillotines*, Chen Sing plays a rogue kung fu master who lives in a hidden valley separated from the outside world by a cave full of poisonous gases. In his solitude, he has constructed a deadly weapon called the flying guillotine, which is a motorized blade at the end of a chain that Chen throws at his adversaries to decapitate them with. When he isn't lopping their heads off, Chen is tearing them to shreds with his superior tiger style. It is near the end of the film that the protagonist, played by Carter Wong, confronts Chen in his retreat, leading to a bloody duel between them. It is preceded by another fight in which Chen is confronted by a number of armed fighters from different schools, who have come to confront him to prevent him from siding with the Ching government.

Chen Sing's tiger style is very good here and is not visibly diluted with other styles as the tiger tends to be in other films. His handwork consists of mainly the tiger claw itself, with fingers slightly curved and moving in clawing motions. As with a lot of his films, his handwork is relatively simple, but effective and brutal. Chen does perform a few kicks, but nothing flashy (the closest he comes to being flashy is a back kick to the midsection). He moves fast and is appropriately brutal.

The use of the flying guillotine here is rather interesting. In other films, the flying guillotine looks something like a wire-mesh that fits over the head has several curved blades at the opening. The guillotines used here are more bulky, looking like large metal helmets with anachronistically motorized blades that spins both on the inner and outer rims of the device. The use of wires to control the movements of the weapon are admittedly awkward, but the sight of Carter Wong running around the valley being relentlessly chased by Chen Sing's two-fisted guillotines, which apparently can defy gravity, is just too awesome to dismiss.

Although Chen Sing is ultimately the highlight of this fight, he does get some really solid support from Carter Wong. Carter Wong, who uses *hung gar* in this fight as he does in most movies, is often accused of being too stiff in his movements (probably on account of his height and muscular build). Wong also starred in a staggering number of independent Taiwanese films, many of which were too impoverished to hire any talented choreographer. Wong gets some strong back-up from the film's action director, genre veteran Chan Siu-Pang, and puts in one of his career best performances here. And, for using *hung gar* in this film, we end up getting two tiger styles for the price of one.

Carter Wong is arguably better in the film's climax, which is also a well-choreographed duel between Wong and Chen Sing. Chen Sing's performance in that fight, however, is a bit muted compared to their first showdown. This can be explained by the fact that his character gets blinded, and thus doesn't fight as effectively as he did in previous scuffles.

Poster for *Fatal Flying Guillotine* (1977).

This is easily one of Chan Siu-Pang's best gigs as action director, which he had many of during more than 20 years of work. Chan Siu-Pang actually started choreographing films as early as 1960, working on a number of swordplay films in the 1960s before focusing on kung fu in the following decade. Although he appeared in a number of big studio films as an extra or stuntman, his main body of work was in independent Taiwanese films. He worked on a number of independent classics under acclaimed director Joseph Kuo, such as the *The 18 Shaolin Bronzemen* (1976) and *The Blazing Temple* (1976), both of which are loved by fans and both of which star Carter Wong. Chan Siu-Pang keeps the fight moving fast and furious, both through the simple movements of the actors and some very dynamic camerawork. The camera moves almost as fast as the actors themselves, without ever feeling shaky or nauseating. The one-against-many choreography is well done and flows quite well, never seeming unnatural or overly staged.

Executioners of Shaolin (1977)

Executioners of Shaolin was one of the first films that Lau Kar-Leung made after breaking off from director Chang Cheh in the mid 1970s. The filmmaking philosophy of the two men was quite different: Lau preferred to analyze the *martial arts* themselves in his films while Chang tended to explore themes like brotherhood and loyalty. So when Lau Kar-Leung made a movie about the Chinese folk hero Hong Xiguan (Hung Hey-kwun), *Executioners of Shaolin,* his approach to the material was a lot different than in Chang Cheh films like *Heroes Two* and *Men from the Monastery*.

Hong Xiguan is a Chinese folk hero best known for his opposition to the Manchus during the Qing dynasty, not to mention one of the first non-monks to study at the Shaolin Temple. According to one of the legends of Hong Xiguan, he founded the *hung gar* style of kung fu after he merged the tiger style he had learned at Shaolin with the White Crane style that his wife, Fong Wing Chun, had taught him. Nonetheless, he was eventually killed. The culprit, depending on the legend, was either ex-Shaolin monk Pai Mei (White Eyebrow), or Ma Ling-Yee, another layman at the Shaolin Temple who defected to the side of the Qings. As the story goes, the murderer was a master of the "iron vest" style and Hong was killed when he was unable to find its weak point. Afterward, Hong's son Wentai, was able to find the weak spot using his mother's white crane technique and killed the man.

The theme of this film is that Hong Xiguan, played by Chen Kuan Tai loses because of his reluctance to adopt his wife's style, being dependent on the tiger style. In the film, the main villain is Pai Mei, played by Shaw Brothers veteran Lo Lieh in one of his most memorable roles. Near the end of the film, Hong storms Pai Mei's estate and takes out his bodyguards before challenging Pai Mei to what will be his final match. Although he is able to kill one of the Shaolin traitors, Hong is unable to find Pai Mei's weak spot and is eventually killed in the scuffle.

The tiger claw demonstrated in this particular fight is just magnificent—the best tiger style seen this side of a Sammo Hung-choreographed film featuring Chen Sing. Chen Kuan Tai moves quickly and keeps his techniques simple and hand-based, as the tiger style really is. In his first, brief exchange with actor Kong Do, who plays a Shaolin traitor, you can see him tear through the sleeve of his tunic with his fingers and disabling the man's arm. That is the essence of the tiger style. He uses the tiger claw technique throughout the fight, although he occasionally does a few one-knuckle punches when he's searching for Lo Lieh's vital point. Chen's kicks are kept low and to minimum, mainly used when Chen is trying to kick Lo in the groin and strike him in the face simultaneously.

Lau Kar Leung gets a pretty good performance out of Lo Lieh, who was never a master martial artist, but was fairly good at doing anything the action director asked him to do. Pai Mei was one of the most memorable roles of Lo Lieh's career, even so much that he partially resurrected the character in this film's sequel/remake *Clan of the White Lotus* (1980). Lo Lieh does some solid southern techniques here, and thankfully keeps himself fairly animated despite the fact this character is virtually indestructible. His portrayal as Pai Mei here is a lot more realistic than it would be as the White Lotus chief in the aforementioned sequel.

The choreography here is quite good. Lau Kar-Leung was always a stickler for purity…well, most of the time. With regards to Southern Shaolin styles like the five animals techniques and *hung gar*, Lau Kar-Leung was the man to go to for authentic fighting and real life applications of the techniques. Thus, you can trust that the tiger style on display is about as true to the real life style as we're going get on film. We liked that, when multiple attackers gang up on Chen Kuan-Tai, Lau Kar Leung steered clear of the whole "a crowd of attackers attacks one-by-one" situation and instead showed how the tiger style could fend off multiple fighters. As we mentioned here, Lau Kar Leung stays true to the spirit of Southern kung fu and keeps the flashy kicks, which were becoming popular at the time because of people like Hwang Jang Lee and John Liu, out of the picture.

This is easily the best fight in the movie. The finale is actually something of a let down and is rather anti-climatic. Wong Yue's character is, according to the script, not that good at the tiger style and thus comes into the final fight already at a disadvantage. He wins simply because of a trick his mother (played by Lily Li Li-li) had taught him, and not because of superior kung fu. Thus, that fight is not the place to look for some good tiger style. Here, on the other hand, is a far better example. It even features an important theme that will come up in some of the better martial arts films: Hong Xiguan loses the fight because of his lack of flexibility. He puts all his trust in one style and thus remains subject to the style's faults. Had he been more open-minded, he could have covered those faults with the virtues of another style and maybe wouldn't have lost.

White Crane Kung Fu

There are two different styles that bear the name "White Crane": Tibetan White Crane and Fukien White Crane.

The Tibetan Crane style[31] is the older of the two; it's founding being traced to 14th century Tibet. Interestingly enough, the Crane style was not founded by the Shaolin monks, but rather by the Tibetan lamas. The most famous legend is that there once was a Tibetan lama who used to go out to a pond to meditate. One day, he saw a crane being attacked by a gorilla. Thinking that the much stronger gorilla would tear the crane to pieces, the man was surprised to see the crane using its beak and wings to defend itself and strike the gorillas vital points. Pondering this incident, the old man adapted the movements he had seen into a style of fighting.

Poster for *One-Foot Crane* (1979).

The Fukien White Crane style was founded in 18th century China in the Fukien province. There was a family of martial artists with the surname of Fang. One day, the patriarch's daughter was outside doing her chores when she saw a crane on the patio. She started swinging her broom at the bird, but it was able to avoid all of her blows and even pecked at her in defense. The young girl was so impressed that she studied the crane's movements and adapted it into a fighting style. The Fukien White Crane style was eventually combined with the Tiger style to form the *hung gar* style[32], and was also incorporated into a number of Japanese *karate* styles[33].

The Crane style is known for being a defensive style, using long-range strikes and evasive footwork to keep one's opponent at bay or to exhaust him. There are two main hand strikes, one being the crane's beak, which consists of the thumb joining together at the four fingers; and the other is wing, which is a finger rake used for parrying the opponent's blows. More than the other four animal styles associated with Shaolin kung fu, the Crane style utilizes diverse kicks, including high kicks, which are less common in the other styles.

---

[31] - There is also a "Black Crane" style, which combines elements of the white crane, snake, and tiger styles, and has an emphasis on *Chin na*, or joint-locking techniques.

[32] See *Hung Gar* chapter.

[33] - See the film *The Karate Kid* (1984) for a pretty clear-cut example of crane techniques in Japanese martial arts.

The Crane style was fairly common in martial arts films up until the mid-1980s, when the traditional chopsockey film died out. After that, it would only make a few appearances, although it was rarely in its pure form. The crane style is often seen in conjunction with the other animal styles. In a number of Jackie Chan's early films, like *Shaolin Wooden Men* (1976) and *Spiritual Kung Fu* (1978), Jackie performs the five animal styles, including the crane. Independent actor Meng Fei does some solid, if not memorable, crane style in the Taiwanese film *Snake and Crane Secret* (1977). In *Executioners of Shaolin* (1977), Lily Li plays Fong Wing Chun, a white crane master who married Hung Hey Kwun, founder of *hung gar*. There is some magnificent crane demonstrated in the final fight of *Heroes of the East* (1978), which is used by Gordon Liu to counter Yasuaki Kurata's crab technique. During the 1990s "New Wave" era of historical kung fu films, lip service was paid to the crane style in films like *Last Hero in China* (1993), *Iron Monkey* (1993), and *Burning Paradise* (1994).

The Crane Fighters (1979)

One of the queens of hard-hitting kung fu is a little lady named Chia Ling (known in many of her films as Judy Lee). Chia Ling was a beautiful woman who was equally good at being both fierce and playful, depending on the film. Chia was Peking Opera-trained, studying at the same school as Angela Mao and other famous people. Together with Angela Mao and Polly Shang Kuan Ling Feng[34], Chia Ling is part of the triumvirate of 1970s fighting female action queens, despite being a bit lesser known than her two colleagues. In her first big role, *Queen Boxer* (1972), she showed off a certain ferocity in the climatic set piece that pit her against more than fifty attackers armed with knives that has really only been equaled by Angela Mao. She made around 60 old school kung fu movies and even won the Golden Horse Award[35] for best actress at one point. Most people will point to four films as being her overall best: *Queen Boxer* (1972), *Iron Swallow* (1978), *Against the Drunken Cat's Paw* (1979), and this film. This film, especially the final fight, benefits from being the best showcase for the crane style (individually) on record.

In this film, Chia Ling plays the daughter of a Shaolin monk who is on the run from the Qing soldiers. When her father and uncle are captured, she and another kung fu fighter (Raymond Lui) mount a rescue mission and are successful. They decide to get married, but shortly after their wedding the Qings show up and they go on the run. After a series of escalating fights, Chia Ling and Raymond Lui are forced to face the main villain: an invincible master of Shaolin kung fu played by Kam Kong.

As expected, the calling card here in Judy Lee and her crane style. We already mentioned that crane style rarely appeared in fights where it wasn't being combined with other styles, so it's actually kind of novel to see Judy Lee and co-star Raymond Lui show off that much crane. The emphasis here is on the hand techniques associated with the crane style, especially those using the crane's beak hand position. There is some kicking from Lui and Judy, although it's kept to a minimum. This is good news to those that think that modern martial arts cinema has put too much emphasis on flashy kicking. Here, we

---

[34] See the chapter on Korean Open-Handed Fighting for more information about Angela Mao Ying and the chapter on Japanese Open-Handed Fighting for more information about Polly Shang Kuan Ling Feng.
[35] The Golden Horse Award is the Taiwanese equivalent to the Oscars.

get seven minutes of almost pure handwork, which a lot of purists should enjoy. Judy Lee and Raymond Lui are both very fast and precise in their movements.

There is some solid villainy here courtesy of Kam Kong. Kam Kong was a rather big, muscular fellow who made a career out of playing either the villain or an oafish sidekick to the film's protagonist. He main training was in *tae kwon do*, although he appears to have been trained in a number of other styles, considering how diverse his work was over the years. Kam Kong is best known for his turns as a villain in a lot of Jackie Chan's earlier films, but even more so for appearing as the titular character in Jimmy Wang Yu's *Master of the Flying Guillotine* (1975). Here he plays an evil Ching warlord, who is apparently trained in Shaolin kung fu. His style here is a mixture of Southern animal systems, notably the tiger and dragon styles. His work is quite powerful and brutal here.

Raymond Lui, who directed the film, also handled the action direction. Raymond Lui was a Taiwanese actor, director, and choreographer who worked on several independent martial arts films during the 1970s. Besides this film, his other notable film is *Fatal Flying Guillotines*, which starred Carter Wong and Chen Sing and featured one of the best performances from the former[36]. Raymond is assisted here by So Kwok-Leung, a little-known and moderately talented action director and stuntman. Interestingly enough, So had also handled the choreography on another crane style showcase, *One-Foot Crane* (1979).

The choreography here is quite good, especially by Taiwanese movie standards (see explanation in the following discussion on *The Goose Boxer*). There is some acrobatics tossed in, but Raymond Lui and So Kwok-Leung wisely focus on the technique part of the action. Lui himself throws in a little bit of snake fist for variation. The brutality of Kam Kong's tiger style is emphasized here, as our heroes are bloodied up quite a bit by the conclusion. As Kam Kong's character is supposed to be a master of the legendary "Iron Vest" technique, it's refreshing to do see him "on his feet" throughout most of the fight, only standing still and allowing himself to intentionally be hit for a brief moment. The location of his weak spot is pretty easy to see coming, doesn't make a whole lot of sense, but still makes for compelling viewing once our heroes start making a mad dash effort to hit it.

The great crane techniques on display, the expert choreography not generally seen in most other Taiwanese films, and the great combination of Judy Lee, Raymond Lui, and Kam Kong make this set piece one not to be missed.

The Goose Boxer (1979)

We often say that the reason Taiwanese martial arts films are so bad is because they suffer from terrible budget restraints, causing quite a bit of problems in casting, costumes, building sets, etc. They will often spend a large portion of their budget to hire some washed up Hong Kong star and are then left with little money for anything else, including hiring a decent action director. There are a few solid action choreographers to come out of Taiwan. Robert Tai, who started off as a successful action director at the Shaw Brothers studio, came to Taiwan with the promise of good pay. Chan Siu-Pang was

---

[36] See previous chapter.

able to do a lot of decent Taiwanese films over the years. Alan Chui, best known for his supporting roles in dozens of independent classics, was a solid choreographer. However, most fans of the genre will agree that the best Taiwanese choreographer was a man named Gam Ming, aka Tommy Lee.

Like many of the best action directors, Tommy Lee was Peking Opera trained and thus was familiar with quite a number of different kung fu styles, in addition to weapons and acrobatics. Tommy's main contributions to the genre were the films he made with director Lee Tso-Nam, including *The Hot, the Cool, and the Vicious* (1976) and *Challenge of Death* (1977); *The Secret Rivals* (1976), which practically began the super-kicker sub-genre. His style of choreography could be best described as "realistic traditional." Tommy Lee typically eschewed the use of heavy wires (although he did use them on occasion), undercranking, and the overuse of acrobatics and mannered choreography that became popular with the advent of both Jackie Chan and the Venom Mob. Thus, his fights felt like they were ground in the real world, but still featured the traditional movements associated with the various Southern systems and *tae kwon do* that he incorporated in the films he did.

Surprisingly enough, *The Goose Boxer*, which was nothing more than an attempt to ride on the coattails of Jackie Chan's success, features some of Tommy Lee's best work as a choreographer. It was something of a departure for Tommy in terms of style, as the fighting on display in this film is more in tune with the kung fu comedies that Jackie Chan was making, in the sense of being slightly over-choreographed, rather than the (relatively) realistic kung fu dramas that Tommy Lee had done with Lee Tso-Nam. We want to direct your attention to the superb work Tommy Lee did in choreographing a battle midway through the film between lead actor Charles Heung and genre veteran, the great Philip Ko.

The gist of the film is that Charles Heung is a nobody who can't actually fight, but wins a number of bouts on accident and thus everybody thinks he can. He eventually is reluctantly recruited to be the student of a murderous Crane Fist master, played Lee Hoi-San. His fame begins to grow and he calls the attention of another kung fu master (Philip Ko), who's on the trail of the crane stylist who's been committing a number of murders in the area. Thinking that Charles Heung is the killer, Ko challenges him to a duel.

Their three-and-a-half minute duel features some really good crane fist on the part of Heung. You can see early on that he's including the complex and graceful footwork associated with the actual crane style. He keeps his hands in the crane beak position throughout the fight, which he uses to try to strike Ko's various pressure points. Midway through their duel, Heung switches to some "secret" crane moves in which he fights with one hand behind his back, only to spring into a surprise crane beak strike at a given moment. The film itself represents what is arguably Heung's best martial moment, although he may be more recognized by fans of Hong Kong cinema for his role as the bodyguard in the *God of Gambler* films[37] and for being a presenter of quite a few important films in Hong Kong.

---

[37] The *God of Gamblers* films were a series of four films (with some spin-offs) that were huge box office successes in Hong Kong, particularly the first and fourth entries, which starred Chow Yun-Fat (*The Killer; Crouching Tiger, Hidden Dragon*). The second and third entries in the series are notable for being early comedy vehicles for popular Hong Kong actor Stephen Chow Sing-Chi (*Shaolin Soccer, Kung Fu Hustle*).

Philip Ko is one of the unsung heroes of the traditional chopsockey era and participated in a number of the greatest onscreen fights of that time period. Here he doesn't use any identifiable style, but we the audience can easily tell that he's using a mix of Southern styles, as defined by the heavy handwork and deep stances. Both he and Heung are very fast and crisp here, which is impressive considering that the choreography is a lot more intricate than the other films that better define Tommy Lee's output. If you said that Sammo Hung or Jackie Chan choreographed this fight, we'd almost believe you. And for a man like Tommy Lee whose name will never be recognized by the general public, that's as good as a compliment as an independent action director will get.

The films are a good example of the multi-genre film that Hong Kong used to make during the 1980s and 1990s, mixing violent action (kung fu and gunplay), slapstick comedy, and sleight-of-hand gambling tricks.

Snake Style

The Snake style is one of the oldest-known Shaolin styles. As the name implies, the movements, done primarily with the hands, mimic the defensive and offensive movements of different types of snakes, including the viper and cobra. The idea of the style is to strike pressure points on the body as quickly and accurately as possible, leaving little room and necessity for blocking. Thus, it is very much like the internal *hsing-I* style[38]. To tell the truth, the movements of the Snake style have been incorporated into a number of other styles, such as *wing chun, choy li fut, hung gar,* and *pa kua*.

An offensive style, there is very little actual blocking incorporated into the style; most defensive techniques are evasive moments. The offensive techniques are fast and often circular in nature. Finger and open-hand strikes are used for striking nerves and pressure points, as well as veins and arteries in order to cause hemorrhaging. There is very little kicking in the Snake Style, most of which is aimed at the foot and shins, although leg sweeps are occasionally used. Unlike other animal styles that have low horse stances as a fundamental posture, snake practitioners tend to use more upright stances.

The Snake Style is often seen in kung fu movies, although it usually seen used in conjunction with the other four Southern animal styles. A lot of movies about Southern Shaolin martial arts and *hung gar* will probably feature some demonstration of the snake at one point or another. *The Magnificent Butcher* (1979), *Enter the Fat Dragon* (1978), *The Iron-Fisted Monk* (1977), *Shaolin Wooden Men* (1976), *Five Shaolin Masters* (1974), and a host of others are just a few that feature the snake style along with other animal styles.

Finding movies that only feature the snake style are a bit more difficult to come by, although they do exist. Jackie Chan used predominately the snake style in his classic films *Snake and Crane Arts of Shaolin* (1977) and *Snake in the Eagle's Shadow* (1978). Taiwanese career villain Chang Yi used some snake style in the lackluster *Monkey Fist, Floating Snake* (1979). Another Taiwanese favorite, the great Don Wong Tao, used the snake fist against Chang Yi in *Challenge of Death* (1978). Tino Wang Chiang, best known for appearing a number of films with Legendary Super Kicker Hwang Jang Lee, tried to do in our favorite super-kicker with the snake style in *Hitman in the Hand of Buddha* (1980), but with little success. One of best films to feature a snake style variation, mainly the viper, is *The Five Deadly Venoms* (1978), where Poison Clan student #2 is played by Wei Pai.

So with all of these examples, where do we end up finding our best examples of the Snake Style? Well, from a gentleman named Wilson Tong.

Snake in the Monkey's Shadow (1979)

Wilson Tong is an interesting figure in the realm of classic kung fu cinema. As an actor, he has appeared in a number of classic films for both the Golden Harvest and Shaw Brothers studios, generally as a supporting villain. His credits include memorable roles in Sammo Hung's classic *The Victim* (1980) and the classic Lau Kar-Leung masterpieces *Dirty Ho* (1980) and *The 36ᵗʰ Chamber of Shaolin* (1978). He directed a number of

---

[38] See chapter on *Hsing-I* in the Internal Styles section.

independent films, mainly classic kung fu, but also a few in the horror and modern action genres as well. The man is an expert martial artist and has been known for pulling off some astonishing footwork in a number of his films, notably in the aforementioned *The Victim* (his character's name is the "Foot Doctor") and *Dirty Ho*. However, here we will recognize Wilson Tong as the best choreographer of the snake style in the history of genre.

Tong's first important film about the Snake fist was *Snake in the Monkey's Shadow*, made in 1979. As its name implies, the film is something of a remake of the Jackie Chan blockbuster *Snake in the Eagle's Shadow*, made the year before. The plotlines of the two are indeed similar: a guy learns kung fu, gets beaten by the main bad guys, and then learns another style to incorporate into what he already knows in order to win. The main difference between this one and its predecessor is that the snake style is the style of the villains, not the protagonist.

Let's take a look at the fight in question is between Wilson Tong, Charlie Chan, and Pomson Shi. Pomson Shi, a lesser-known supporting actor in Hong Kong cinema, plays a monkey fist master who disgraces Charlie Chan's snake fist master at the beginning the film. Later in the film, Chan returns with another colleague, played by Wilson Tong, in order to teach Shi a lesson. The result is a two-on-one snake vs. monkey fight that'll set the stage for the final fight between the two villains and the hero (who, for the record, is played by John Cheung).

Charlie Chan and Wilson Tong unleash the snake fury in *Snake in the Monkey's Shadow* (1979).

We chose this fight over the final fight, which is generally the best fight in most of these films, mainly because the snake stylists get to win in this one. By the final fight, hero John Cheung is a master of both the monkey and drunken fist styles, so the finale is really his show. But here, where the two villains are almost undoubtedly going to win, we get a better showcase for the snake style.

The snake work put on by our two villains, Chan and Tong, is quite good. There are lots of lightning-fast open-hand strikes on display, all done with a "hissing" sound effect to invoke feelings of a real snake fighting. It's pretty clear that Charlie and Wilson are going for the more "soft" parts of Pomson's body, including the solar plexus and eyes. Yes, by the end of the fight, Pomson will have been blinded by their attacks, which is pretty common in the cobra sub-style[39].

As we know, four minutes of Wilson Tong and Charlie Chan pelting Pomson Shi with their fingers will probably grow thin pretty quickly. So, action director Wilson Tong decides to spruce things up with a bit of Peking Opera acrobatics. Tong and Chan do a number of acrobatic, up/down formations, trying to hit their target in a number of different spots. There a number of somersaults to be seen, which is par for the course for a kung fu comedy made in the late 1970s. One move that Charlie Chan does that can be seen in other snake-themed kung fu movies is where Chan jumps through the air, spinning bi-laterally, with his hands out and fingers together. It looks like a powerful move and is done well here. There are some liberties taken here: some of their kicking is a bit high for traditional Southern snake fist, but that's small beans.

What really sells this fight is the unison in which Charlie Chan and Wilson Tong fight. Almost every move they perform is done together with an astonishing degree of exactness. Their movements are synchronized, which may give some the feeling of the fight being over-choreographed, but it also contributes to the feeling of how screwed their opponent really is. After all, how does one effectively defend himself from so many deadly strikes coming in different directions with such deadly accuracy and breakneck speed? It's a great moment for fans of the snake style everywhere.

For fans of traditional animal kung fu styles, *Snake in the Monkey's Shadow* is a good movie to take your chances on. Some excellent style is complimented with some excellent monkey fist kung fu, not to mention some of the better drunken fist boxing you'll see outside of a Jackie Chan movie. And the best thing is that Wilson Tong would later outdo himself the following year, in terms of some nice serpent fighting.

Snake Deadly Act (1980)

Whereas *Snake in the Monkey's Shadow* stuck relatively close to the traditional styles it purported to be showcasing, *Snake Deadly Act* allowed director, star, and action choreographer Wilson Tong to take advantage of the barriers of traditionalism that Jackie Chan was breaking down at the time and exercise more creativity in fight direction. While the story and acting are rather pedestrian, the fight sequences rank up with there with the work of Yuen Woo-Ping and Sammo Hung of the same era: intricate, creative, fast, and hard hitting.

In the film's final fight, young Kuo (Ng Kun-Lung) has finally been trained and prepared to fight against who he thinks is his worst enemy: his own father (Wilson Tong). This is all part of an elaborate plot by Kuo's teacher, played by Fung Hak-On, to get revenge on Wilson Tong's character for raping his wife years before. By this point, young Kuo's snake style has surpassed that of even his father's. However, when his father starts unleashing his secret weapon, the dreaded lobster style(!), he'll need the help of Fung Hak-On to survive the encounter.

The fight is set up in something of a four-act structure and lasts for nearly ten minutes. In the first part, Ng Kun-Lung takes on Wilson Tong, both men using the snake

---

[39] The Cobra is a substyle of the Snake style. In the Cobra substyle, the aim is to strike and puncture an opponent's eyes or throat and then grip the region until the opponent is dead.

style. In the next part, Wilson Tong switches over to the lobster style and starts to get the upper hand, giving Ng a thorough thrashing. Fung Hak-On eventually steps in and the two are able to turn the tables on Wilson Tong. Finally, all is revealed and Ng Kun-Lung is forced to face his own master in mortal combat.

Ng Kun-Lung appears to be a very talented individual, very much in the Yuen Biao mold. There was a certain specter of Yuen Biao's *Knockabout* (1979) hanging over the proceedings. Like Yuen Biao, Ng Kun-Lung fights using a mixture of Southern styles (Ng using the snake fist instead of *choy li fut*) and some nicely executed *tae kwon do* kicking, notably Ng throwing multiple high kicks without lowering his legs. Like many actors in kung fu comedies made during the late 1970s and early 1980s, Ng Kun-Lung does get to show off some nice acrobatics as well. It's actually kind of a shame that this is his only film credit.

Fung Hak-On acquits himself well in this fight, using the usual mixture of snake fist and acrobatics. Fung had actually made a name for himself in classic kung fu films as a mantis stylist, so it's nice to see him do something a little different. You can see a little bit of his mantis style showing through at a few moments, but for the most part he's fighting with 100% Southern Snake fist.

Wilson Tong does a tremendous job as a superior fighter trained in both the snake style and the made-up lobster style. Since the lobster style is obviously fictional, there really are bounds and limits with which to judge his performance. Thus, he's able to go over the top without having to worry about traditional techniques. In his lobster style, his pointer and middle fingers, together with the thumb, form "pincers" with which he tears at his son's clothes and clenches his skin in painful ways. There is a lot of acrobatics involved, some of it mildly wire-assisted, but it looks fresh and convincing.

The snake fist showcased in this fight is pretty much on par with the snake style that Wilson Tong directed in *Snake in the Monkey's Shadow*, but with more flourishes and sprucing ups to keep things interesting. Pay attention to a lot of the sidestepping footwork that is characteristic of the style. The fight runs a bit long, but there are some really good pay offs if you stick around for all of it. There's a lot to take in, being nine minutes of non-stop hand-to-hand kung fu, but it's a high point in the careers of both Ng Kun-Lung, whose career never quite took off, and Wilson Tong, as both an actor and an action director.

Panther (Leopard) Kung Fu

The panther, or leopard style, is one of the five animal styles in Southern Shaolin kung fu. The style is based on the movements of the panther, which, unlike the tiger, derives its lethal power from its speed and not brute strength. Thus, the goal of the panther technique is to defeat one's opponent with a barrage of speedy strikes in such a way that blocking or any defense would be unnecessary. The panther fist can be described as a half-open fist and the practitioner will strike with either the ridge if knuckles formed by the fist or with the palm of the hand. Moreover, there's a strike in the panther style known as the "phoenix eye", which is the panther fist with the index finger extended for striking the eyes or temple. Panther stylists are trained for close-quarters combat, and thus will use their knees, shins, and elbows in addition to their feet and fists.

The panther style is rather rare in martial arts movies, rarely being used as a solitary style. An actor or actress who is using all five of the animal styles in a single film or set piece usually performs the panther. It's usually identified by the familiar panther fist more than anything else. Jackie Chan uses it in *Spiritual Kung Fu* and *Shaolin Wooden Men*. Sammo Hung uses it in *Magnificent Butcher*, *Iron-Fisted Monk*, and *Enter the Fat Dragon*. Chi Kuan-Chun performs it very briefly in *5 Shaolin Masters* and *Shanghai 13*, which also features Sonny Yu performing the style. We can also see it being performed, albeit quite briefly, in *Spiritual Boxer* and *The Martial Club*, too. Actor Tino Wong often used the panther style in his films, notably *Secret Rivals II* (1977) and *Dragon on Fire* (1979). African-American kempo stylist Carl Scott got to perform some solid panther in the kung fu western *Sun Dragon* (1979). As we said, in most of these films, it's being used in conjunction with the other five animal styles rather than by itself (*Shanghai 13* being the exception).

Surprisingly enough, modern viewers got a taste of the panther style in the recent Donnie Yen film *Wu Xia* (2011), where he kills an assassin with a rapid burst of panther punches, similar to what he did with *wing chun* in *Ip Man*.

Tino Wong Chung (left) prepares the leopard fist in *Secret Rivals 2* (1977).

Tigress from Shaolin (1979)

When it comes to martial families that stand out in Chinese cinema, there are two clans that stand out: the Yuen clan and the Lau clan. The former, which includes Yuen

Woo-Ping, Yuen Cheung-Yan, and Yuen Shun-Yi, are considered to be among the greatest action directors of all time, even though as actors, they've mainly kept themselves in supporting roles. The latter family includes Lau Kar Leung, one of the greatest choreographers of pure kung fu of all time; Lau Kar Fei (Gordon Liu), one of the great martial arts actors and known in the United States mainstream for his duel roles in the *Kill Bill* films; Lau Kar-Wing, a solid kung fu actor, director, and action director; and the lesser-known Lau Kar-Yung, who was solid martial arts actor, even though he never reached the same level of fame as his famous uncles. Like the other Laus, Lau Kar Yung was trained principally in the *hung gar* style of kung fu and used it and other Southern styles in most of the films he appeared in.

As we watch the climax to this film, it becomes clear that the action directors are making a concentrated effort to showcase the Panther, or Leopard, style of kung fu. This is indeed a good thing, considering how little the style is ever shown without being in conjunction with the other four animal styles. However, the great irony is that the Panther style showcased here is not called the Panther style, or even the Leopard style. It is referred to in the film as the "Leper Fist", as if the style had been invented by someone suffering leprosy. This may be partly explained by the fact that at the time the film was produced, kung fu comedies were hugely popular and made-up styles were a big part of the sub-genre. But the Lau clan, being the sticklers for purity that they were, probably just insisted on using the leopard style and changed the name of it to make it sound like a funny style, even if it wasn't.

The film's final fight revolves around the hero, Ah San, taking on a horde of spearmen and then a pair of Tibetan villains, played by the film's action directors, Huang Ha and Chan Dik-Hak. During the initial scuffle, Ah San is joined by Xiao Hong, played by Shaw Bros diva Kara Hui Ying-Hung. She too uses the panther style, although her participation in the climax itself is surprisingly limited, considering the film's English title.

The style of the choreography on display is the same type of intricate, mannered fighting that defined period kung fu movies following the success of *The Drunken Master*[40] the year before. The goal of this type of choreography is to showcase both the styles in question and show the full range of the actors' physical talents, and not to simulate an actual fight. The choreography is solid; if you like films like *The Magnificent Butcher* and *Drunken Master*, then the level of choreography on display will definitely please you. Huang Ha has had quite the career as an action director, although he doesn't get a whole lot of credit for it. His most important contribution to the genre has been his work on *The Challenger* (1979), in which he was able to do something that Lau Kar-Leung, one of the greatest action directors of all time, could barely do: Huang Ha made actor David Chiang look like an absolute kung fu master[41]. That in and of itself should be enough to catapult the man to the level of the Yuens.

---

[40] - For the record, action director Huang Ha had had a supporting role in *The Drunken Master* as the fellow who challenges Jackie Chan at his father's school.

[41] - That's really another story. David Chiang was a much-beloved actor working for the Shaw Brothers from the late 1960s until the early 1980s, notably as one of Chang Cheh's leading men during the early 1970s. Despite the fact that he was a good actor with a lot of charisma, he was not all that good of a martial artist and in his later films, that became blaringly evident. Thus, we have nothing but the highest praise for Huang Ha having made him look good in *The Challenger*.

In any case, the star of this fight is the leopard style performed by Lau Kar Yung. He really just does it all in this fight. We commented that the leopard style is adapted for close-range combat and what do we get here? Close range combat, complete with forearm and elbow strikes. Lau Kar Yung keeps his hand in the leopard fist position throughout the duration of the fight, which he continually uses to strike at his opponents with the ridge of knuckles. He does use the palms and backs of his hands to hit from time to time, which is perfectly valid in the style. Lau even does some leopard claw attacks near the end of the fight, which, unlike the tiger or dragon claws, looks simply like a half-closed fist with the fingers slightly raised. His attacks are generally fast and Lau strives for the essence of the style, going for multiple punches in brief outbursts.

Kara Hui Ying-Hung is on hand to provide a little bit of leopard boxing here, although her performance is severely muted and she quickly gets taken out by Chan Dik-Hak. This is unfortunate, as she has shown us in other films that she's just about as talented as any other kung fu diva from the 1970s.

Our villains are some real strange characters. Huang Ha plays the somewhat typical white-haired villain. He does the usual blend of Southern styles (nothing really specific) with some kicks tossed in for good measure. Chan Dik-Hak, however, is something else. His character is a Tibetan, but he's wearing a wig that makes him look like a Rastafarian(!) Chan does some pretty good kicks, in addition to the generic Shaolin eagle style that appears in so many films. They're both solid villains, although they're nothing special. That's okay, however, as we wouldn't want them taking away from the best onscreen leopard kung fu in the genre.

Hung Gar

One of the most popular and widely-used kung fu styles is the famous *hung gar* or *hung kuen*. The name means "Hung's Fist", and is named after its founder, the famous Chinese folk hero Hong Xiguan (Hung Hey-Kwun in Cantonese). The story of its founding goes back to 18th century China. Hong Xiguan was a merchant who was opposed to the Qing (Manchurian) rulers in China. Hong Xiguan eventually went to the Fukien Shaolin Temple where he became one of the first laymen to study kung fu there. According to legend, he became an expert in Shaolin martial arts, most notably the Tiger style and the pole. Following his departure from the temple, Hong Xiguan married a female martial arts practitioner named Fong Wing Chun, who had mastered the White Crane style. The Hung Gar style was the fusion of the tiger and crane techniques. The style was used by a number of other important figures in Chinese folk history, like Fong Sai-Yuk, Luk Ah-Choy, Wong Kei-Ying, and Wong Fei-Hung, who has had literally hundreds of films made about his life over the years.

There are a number of different forms and techniques in the *hung gar* style. The four main ones are the Tiger form, Tiger-Crane form, Five Animals form, and the Iron Wire Fist. Much like the Tiger style itself, *hung gar* is a brutal style and is perfectly capable of reducing one's opponent (or his weapon) to shreds using a variety of quick, brutal attacks and clawing attacks. One of Hong Xiguan's most well-known techniques was the "iron forearm", in which his forearms were so strong that his blocks and strikes were interchangeable—a block could cause as much damage as a punch to the same area and a punch was so powerful that it could stop an opponent's strike as well as any block could. Much like other Southern styles, *hung gar* uses a lot of low stances and features more hand-based attacks than kicks, although they aren't completely excluded, considering the presence of the crane style in *hung gar*'s origin.

From 1974 to 1986, *hung gar* got more attention in movies than just about any other style in Chinese kung fu. Most Peking Opera-trained actors were knowledgeable of the style, and used it in a number of ways in films. Moreover, once the kung fu comedy became popular in the late 1970s, *hung gar* was usually one of the major styles that would get a bit of "tweaking" in order to be passed off as a new (often comedic) style. There were a lot of other actors who had major training in *hung gar*, mainly the Lau Clan (Lau Kar Leung, Lau Kar Wing, Lau Kar Fei, and Lau Kar Yung) and Shaw Bros favorites Chi Kuan Chun. Other Shaw actors like Alexander Fu Sheng and Chen Kuan Tai used the style extensively in a number of classic films about Hong Xiguan and Fong Sai Yuk. Taiwanese actors Don Wong Tao, Carter Wong, and Alexander Lo Rei also used *hung gar* quite a bit in their movies, Don Wong Tao being the best out of the three.

Hung gar got less and less attention after the fall of the traditional chopsockey film, being used mainly in films featuring members of the Lau clan, most notably Lau Kar-Leung. Tsui Hark, who directed the wire-fu classic *Once Upon a Time in China*, wanted to set himself apart from the films of old and thus started focusing on Mainland Chinese *wushu*, which would become something of the norm for most period piece kung fu films made after 1990.

While not quite a resurgence, *hung gar* has popped up recently in a few mainstream film, notably *Ip Man 2* (2010), where Sammo Hung (also the film's action director) plays an aged *hung gar* master who fights Donnie Yen during the film's first half. Donnie Yen himself has incorporated elements of *hung gar* into his other recent films *Wu Xia* (2011) and *14 Blades* (2009).

Disciples of Shaolin (1975)

When it comes to onscreen *hung gar*, there is no better place to turn to than the Lau Clan, principally Lau Kar-Leung. Lau Kar-Leung and his family learned *hung gar* from his father, Lau Charn. Lau Charn, in turn, had been the student of a rather well-known exponent of the style, Lam Sai-Wing. Lam Sai-Wing was a butcher in Fushan who was portrayed in a number of films, including Yuen Woo-Ping's *The Magnificent Butcher* and *Once Upon a Time in China*. Lam Sai-Wing was a student of the famous Wong Fei-Hung, the Chinese folk hero and *hung gar* expert. Thus, the genealogy of the Lau family *hung gar* is a proud one.

Lau Kar-Leung worked as an action director for the Shaw Bros for quite a number of years, generally under director Chang Cheh. One of the first films they made together was *The One-Armed Swordsman* (1967), a ground-breaking martial arts film starring Jimmy Wang Yu. For next eight years, Lau Kar-Leung would be one of Chang Cheh's main action directors (the other one being Tong Gaai). Lau Kar-Leung has stated in an interview that in 1974, he was talking to Chang Cheh one day and Chang asked him how he could improve the quality of the action in his movies. Lau suggested that they start using pure Southern styles, most notably *hung gar*. Chang agreed and the two worked together on the film *Five Shaolin Masters*, which feature some *hung gar* performed by both Alexander Fu Sheng and Chi Kuan-Chun, the latter emphasizing the Five Animals technique.

The movie was a great success and the opened the door to *hung gar* and Shaolin Temple films for the next decade. Lau Kar-Leung would go on to work with Chang Cheh in quite a number of Shaolin-themed films, including *Heroes Two*, *The Men from the Monastery*, *Shaolin Martial Arts*, and this film. Chang Cheh would also make films featuring the style, including *Shaolin Temple* and *Shaolin Avengers*, with other action directors. All of these films featured Alexander Fu Sheng as the *hung gar* exponent, and Fu Sheng quickly became one of the most popular kung fu actors of the period, owing to his physical prowess and boyish good looks. Nonetheless, out of all of these films that Chang Cheh, Lau Kar-Leung, and Alexander Fu Sheng worked on together, the best choreography and physical performance from Fu Sheng belong to *Disciples of Shaolin*.

In this fight, Alexander Fu Sheng confronts a gang of ruffians working for a rival dye factory, run by Kong Do. The fight is Alexander Fu Sheng using his *hung gar* to tear a hole through his attackers in the most brutal way possible. While fighting, Fu Sheng is injured, but nonetheless he continues to fight, even though he is bleeding to death (at this point, the film becomes black-and-white, probably to dull the edge of the gore to avoid censorship). At the end of the fight, Fu Sheng succumbs to his injuries and dies.

Fu Sheng is absolutely wonderful in this fight. He comes across as an unstoppable force, a hurricane of Southern Shaolin martial arts skill. The "iron wire" and "iron forearm" techniques are in evidence as regular blows and strikes from poles seem unable to faze him. He even shakes off strong blows to his legs early on in the fight. He's so powerful that his forearms can smash through the poles his enemies wield, breaking them in two. That is an example of the hardness and external force that *hung gar* is known for.

Fu Sheng uses most hand techniques throughout the fight. He uses mainly punches, and quite a bit of jumping punches, which are generally uncommon in movies. He uses his elbows quite a bit, which are also common in *hung gar*. Being the "Tiger-Crane" style, there are a number of moments where's it's evident that Fu Sheng is using the tiger claws to rip through the peoples' clothes, weapons, skin, and even through their faces. While fighting briefly against Kong Do, we see Fu Sheng use the crane style briefly as he goes for Kong Do's throat.

The best part about the fight is how animated and agile Fu Sheng is compared to the other films where he used *hung gar*. In a lot of films made the previous year, Fu Sheng seemed to be a bit slower and the choreography seemed to be slower, less dynamic, and missed the balance between being technically correct and entertaining, too. This was especially true in *Heroes Two*, which boasted fifteen-minute final fight that seemed to drag on forever during it. Here, it seems that Lau Kar-Leung and Fu Sheng are a lot more comfortable in what they're doing and thus the fight flows smoother and quicker. It's simply a marvelous one-vs-many fight, ranking up there with the dojo fight from *Fist of Fury* (1972) and the finale to *Boxer from Shantung* (1972). It's certainly one of the best fights filmed in the first half of the 1970s.

The Martial Club (1980)

One of the sad things about Lau Kar-Leung's career is that the man was simply a genius when it came to portraying kung fu on film. We have stated before that being a master of a style in real life doesn't mean a whole lot when it comes to fighting in front of the camera. Nor does it guarantee that if one opts to be a fight choreographer, that he'll be just as successful. After all, Chen Kuan-Tai was a master of the monkey style and a champion and his portrayals of the style practically pale in comparison to other actors. On the same token, how many Mainland kung fu films featuring choreography by Wushu stylists don't hold a candle to Mainland productions that had Hong Kong talent working behind the camera?

Thus, the sad thing about Master Lau's career is that, following the decline in popularity of the traditional film, it seems that his work practically became obsolete. Lau Kar-Leung only directed one modern-day action film during the 1980s, *Tiger on Beat*, and co-starred in a few others, including *The Pedicab Driver*, *The New Kids in Town*, and *Operation: Scorpio*. When the wire-fu boom of the 1990s brought period pieces back into popularity, one would think that Lau Kar-Leung would've ridden the snake back to spotlight, but sadly, that didn't really happen. He was the action director for *The Barefooted Kid* (1994) and directed most of the all-time classic *Drunken Master II* (1994). He tried (but failed) to make a more traditional kung fu film with *Drunken Master III* (1994) and that about summed up his contributions to the genre for that decade.

In any case, one of Lau Kar-Leung's most ingenious moments in his career as director and choreographer came in the 1980 film *The Martial Club*, in which Lau Kar-

Leung had to come up with a novel idea on how to film your typical Southern style good guy vs. Northern style bad guy, which had been done dozens of time before. Lau Kar-Leung seemed to raise the bar for himself and decided to take the difficult road: film the fight in an alley that slowly becomes narrower with each twist and turn. After all, filming a fight in a tight spot often requires very tight angles, which in turn obscures the movements of the actors themselves. Thus, Lau Kar-Leung put himself in a position where he had to not only choreography an entertaining fight in a tight spot, but also film it in such a way that everything could be seen and enjoyed. Needless to say, Lau came out victor on this fight. That is his genius.

The final fight of the film has our hero, Wong Fei-Hung (Gordon Liu/Lau Kar-Fei) taking on a Northern master, played by Johnny Wang Lung-Wei. Johnny Wang Lung-Wei was one of the best villain actors of the old school period, a stocky but imposing figure with a menacing stare and a mustache that wasn't sleazy, but had "no-nonsense" written all over it. The fight has both of our players unleashing a barrage of techniques and styles on each other, each one switching styles to exploit the other's weaknesses. It's kung fu heaven for most fans.

In the beginning of the fight, Gordon Liu uses the five animals form against Johnny Wang. He starts with a bit of tiger and panther and goes onto the snake style. Interesting about the snake style is how Wang counters it: he uses the mantis fist, which consists of the index finger pointed forward and the other fingers curled in, to separate the fingers of Liu's snake fist and thus break the rigid, but strong snake head strike. Gordon Liu switches up quickly to the crane style and is able to get in a good hit before Wang counters with his Eagle's Claw to catch Liu's crane's beak. It's a really neat application of animal styles and how one animal can be used for both offense and defense. This part of the fight ends with Gordon Liu using the dragon technique and striking Johnny Wang and knocking him into a clearing.

In this next part, Johnny Wang switches to kicking techniques and demonstrates a flexibility that he normally never showed in his films. His kicks look quite good, although they are muted a bit by the confines of the alley, which is admittedly sort of the point of the fight. Gordon Liu is sort of compelled to fight in kind, although his *hung gar* is better adapted for tight fights. Nonetheless, he responds with some legwork of his own, mainly low kicks, leg locks, and other techniques.

Gordon Liu's fundamental posture, the horse stance, comes in mighty handy during the final segment of the fight. In *hung gar*, it was important to have a horse stance so powerful that it was nearly impossible to break, and that helps Liu to trap Wang's blows during a good portion of this sequence. The final bit becomes a duel between Liu's low stances and short blows and Wang's kicking and hand techniques. Moreover, Liu goes back to the snake and crane styles in order to find and exploit Wang's pressure points, which is a true application of those two styles.

The photography of the fight is simply wonderful and you can see everything that's going on, despite the cramped setting. To be honest, the only other fight in a similar setting that he comes close to being well-filmed as this fight in the final fight between Jet Li and Michael Ian Lambert in *Unleashed* (2005). That is why Lau Kar-Leung is such a genius, he was able to make a technically-correct kung fu fight, set it in one of the most difficult places you could set a fight, and just goes forward and creates a classic fight.

What's even more classic about this particular duel is the ending: the hero doesn't win. The last laugh technically belongs to Johnny Wang Lung-Wei, who gets the final kick in. And yet, by the end of the fight, both fighters have come to respect each other and thus the fight ends with not only nobody dying, but neither of the two are even seriously injured. To really bring home that message of respect and peaceful resolution, one of the final shots has Johnny Wang trying to mimic Liu's *hung gar* postures. It's a great moment and an excellent way to end an excellent fight.

My Young Auntie (1980)

We've talked in great length about Lau Kar-Leung's contributions to the genre as far as making *hung gar* one of the most important kung fu styles in old school chopsockey films. Now, one of the most important things that Lau Kar-Leung ever did was separate himself from director Chang Cheh to become a director of his own films. One of the reasons for that is not just because of the artistic freedom, but also he was able to cast himself as the lead protagonist (or one of them) in a number of films and show the world just how powerful his own kung fu was. The best of these were *Legendary Weapons of China* (1982) and this film, especially for its showcase of the Lau family *hung gar*.

The set-up of the final fight between Lau Kar-Leung and perennial villain Johnny Wang Lung-Wei is pretty simple: Lau and Wang play brothers who are disputing ownership of the kung fu school their brother left when he died. The school was left to the master's young bride (played by Kara Hui Ying-Hung) and she was eventually kidnapped by Johnny. So, Lau Kar-Leung, his pupil (played by Hsiao Ho), and a number of other fighters have to storm Wang's household and fight through numerous martial artists in order to rescue her before she's forced to sign the school over to Wang. The main event amidst all of the fighting is the showdown between brothers.

Their fight is actually relatively short; it takes up about three minutes of the final set piece's 12-plus minute running time. There are about two minutes dedicated to a brief duel between Hsiao Ho and Johnny Wang and Lau Kar-Leung and Yuen Tak, who plays Johnny's son. There's a lot of quick handwork here and some acrobatic falls by both Hsiao and Yuen, but it's only a warm-up for the showdown between the duel masters.

Their fight is three-minutes of pure bliss when it comes to fast handwork. There is very little kicking in their duel, it is mainly some of the fastest exchange of blows that you'll see in an old school film, ranking up there with the best of Sammo Hung's films and *The Master Strikes*. There is also no Peking Opera acrobatics thrown in to spice things up; it is pure technique all the way.

Lau Kar-Leung uses quite a number of techniques from his *hung gar* repertoire. He uses a bit of panther, some dragon and tiger, a bit of Shaolin monkey, and the more traditional *hung gar* fist and palm strikes. It's all performed with quite a bit of panache, that's to be sure. In one great moment, Lau Kar-Leung's panther fist is caught by Johnny Wang's Eagle claw, which Lau simply switches into a finger lock. The Shaolin monkey performed here is the *tai shing men* that is most oft associated with monkey kung fu, but a variation of *hung gar* that is an integral part of the Lau Gar family style. The dragon and tiger is used not for show, but to showcase how it is applied: Lau rips into Wang's arm, leaving deep scratches and rendering the arm useless for fighting. It's some great stuff on display, made more impressive by the fact that Lau was in his late 40s when he filmed this.

Johnny Wang Lung-Wei makes the perfect foil for Lau, considering that the man was so sure of his skills that he once expressed his desire to take Bruce Lee on personally. Johnny Wang uses primarily the Eagle claw, although it seems that he's using the Southern Shaolin Eagle variation, instead of the Northern *ying jow pai*, as evidenced by the lack of kicking and acrobatic movements. He fights quite well and matches Lau move for move.

The choreography is complex, yet fast, though it's obvious that some undercranking is used to speed things up. We also should point that that Lau Kar-Leung pays homage to some of his other films, more notably *Heroes of the East* (1978) in a brief sequence where Lau performs a bit of crab boxing. While that may sound a bit silly, there once existed an actual crab style, which was part of the Tiger family of kung fu. The goal of the style was to pinch and cut off the nerves and blood vessels, rendering different parts of the body useless. It was eventually absorbed, partially at least, into the tiger style.

My Young Auntie is, no bones about it, one of Lau Kar-Leung's ultimate showcases when it comes to some good ol' fashioned *hung gar* and here he shows us that he was just as capable of doing in front of the camera what he had told other actors to do from behind it.

Five Animals (Dragon, Tiger, Crane, Snake, and Leopard) in Unison

Ironically, the Five Animals technique is most associated with Southern Shaolin martial arts, most notably *Hung Gar* and *Choy Li Fut*, even though the style was founded in the Northern Shaolin Temple in the Hunan province. The story is that a Shaolin monk named Jueyuan, a master of the 18 original techniques of Shaolin, met a martial arts master named Li Sou, who taught him the hongquan ("Red fist") style, which Jueyuan used to expand his techniques from 18 to 72. Li Sou introduced Jueyuan to another man named Bai Yufeng, who helped Li Sou expand his repertoire from 72 to 180 techniques, which were divided into five animals: the Leopard, the Tiger, the Snake, the Crane, and the Dragon. Nonetheless, in Northern Shaolin martial arts, the five animals have never existed as an individual set. Today, if a person says that hey have studied the five animals technique or know the five animal styles, they are probably referring to the five animals as practiced by Southern Shaolin stylists.

Most of the Five Animals techniques seen in kung fu movies are the ones taken from *hung gar*. It's very common to see these five animals used in conjunction in most kung fu movies from the 1970s, especially the mid-1970s when Southern Shaolin styles were at the apex of their popularity. People like Sammo Hung, Jackie Chan, Chi Kuan-Chun, Carter Wong, and Lau Kar-Leung have used the Five animal styles in many of their early films. We will make a number of references to these films in other chapters, so we'll focus here on the best films to feature the five animal techniques.

The Magnificent Butcher (1979)

It was probably inevitable that following the international success of Jackie Chan's *Drunken Master* (1978), which focused on the misadventures of Chinese folk hero Wong Fei Hung, that a movie would be made about the (fictitious) exploits of all those associated with Master Wong, including one of his most famous students, Lam Sai-wing. Lam Sai-Wing was a butcher in Fushan who studied *hung gar* under Wong Fei-Hung. One of Butcher Wing's students was Lau Cham, who was the father of Lau Kar-Leung and Lau Kar-Wing. Ironically, the best movie about Butcher Wing was not made by any member of the Lau clan, but was a joint effort of the two other top choreographers of the era: Sammo Hung and Yuen Woo-Ping.

The Magnificent Butcher follows the exploits of Lam Sai-Wing as he gets into trouble with Master Ko (Lee Hoi-San), a rival of Lam's master Wong Fei-Hung. Following the murder of his brother, Butcher Wing kills Master Ko's lecherous son, bringing upon him the ire of Master Ko himself, who's the master of the 5 Element style and the deadly Cosmic Crimson Palm. With the help of his other teacher, Beggar So (Fan Mei-Shan), Butcher Wing is able to counter each of Ko's elemental styles with one of the five animal styles.

It becomes evident just in the synopsis how much this fight seems like a rehash of the final fight of Yuen Woo-Ping's *The Drunken Master*. In both final battles, the protagonist is assisted by his master (Beggar So in both films), who tells him which technique to use to counter the technique the antagonist is using. The fundamental difference is the styles used in this fight. Just switch Drunken Boxing with the Five Animals (and *hung gar*) and Hwang Jang Lee's *tae kwon do* with Lee Hoi-San Five Elements style.

In the beginning of the fight, Lee Hoi-San uses the Gold element against Sammo. Sammo responds with the Panther style, which is done quick and clean. He had done some Panther in his directorial debut *The Iron-Fisted Monk* (1977), but the technique is a lot crisper here with less undercranking, too. When Lee Hoi-San can't defeat Sammo with the Gold Technique, he switches to the Wood technique. Sammo responds by using the Snake style, which is simply wonderful in this sequence. Sammo uses the snake fist and moves his arm as if it were a separate entity from the rest of his body. The photography of this sequence is phenomenal, focusing entirely on the hand techniques of the two fighters and how each fighter's hand reacts to the other's movement.

Following the snake vs. wood fight, Lee Hoi-San switches the water technique, which uses a lot of palm strikes and softer, tai chi-looking movements. After taking a few blows, Sammo's teacher tells him that, "A Dragon can control water", signifying for Sammo to switch techniques again. Sammo does some interesting dragon kung fu here, especially with a number of quick and agile kicks. The rest of the hand-based dragon techniques are both complex and fast. Like most other films in which the dragon style is performed, the style is marked by Sammo's hands being in the form of claws and being in a position that looks like a person holding a ball at the top and bottom.

After Sammo's demonstration of the dragon style, the fight enters the more comedic second phase, in which Sammo does everything in his power to keep himself from being hit by Lee Hoi-San's "Cosmic Crimson Palm." Sammo performs a bit of acrobatics and there's quite a bit of physical humor here, including some painful falls from high places. We must note here that the idea of a deadly palm strike that can slowly kill a person after being hit is an old favorite of kung fu movies. A number of old school classics like *Two Great Cavaliers* (1978), *Phantom Kung Fu* (1978) and *Fist of the White Lotus* (1980) feature deadly palm techniques. Yuen Woo-Ping paid homage this film in *Iron Monkey* (1993), in which the villain (played by Yen Shi-Kwan) fights using the poisonous "King Kong Palm" (which was then parodied in *Charlie's Angels*).

Entering the third act of the climax, Lee Hoi-San switches the Earth element technique, which Sammo counters with the Crane style. Finally, Sammo uses the tiger and snake styles to disable Lee Hoi-San's arms and leave him crippled. It's a comparatively brutal scene, as the Tiger style is used to rip and strike at Lee's joints. Some of the powerful fist strikes used in Sammo's final barrage of attacks are *hung gar*.

There's no doubt to Sammo Hung's physical skills, which are full display in this fight. Lee Hoi-San, a Sammo Hung regular, also gets one of his best showcases to his skills. However, this is also a triumph for Sammo Hung and director Yuen Woo-Ping as the fight choreographers. Although Yuen Woo-Ping is best known for his wire-fu action direction, he was one of the more creative action directors in terms of grounded, technique-based kung fu during the late 1970s. This is one of his most pure films in terms of showcasing Southern animal styles. Yuen Woo-Ping and Sammo keep the choreography as intricate as it had been in Yuen Woo-Ping's previous comic hits, although it is a lot faster and hard-hitting than in those movies. It is one of his last pure kung fu movies, as most of his 1980s films were sorcery films and his period pieces in the 1990s would use large quantities of wires in them. Basically, this fight represents the best work of three people involved.

Drunken Fist Boxing

Drunken Fist Boxing (*Zui Quan* in Mandarin) is a very popular and iconic style of martial arts. Most people will recognize it as being one of Jackie Chan's signature fighting styles as well as a style used by characters from a number of fighting games. Drunken Fist Boxing, however, is not so much an actual style as it is a series of techniques and principles that are applied to other styles. Thus, styles like *choy li fut*, praying mantis, snake, etc. can have their drunken techniques, as can a number of weapons like the pole and sword.

As you can imagine, the techniques of Drunken Fist Boxing are based on the movements of a drunken person: staggering, falling, and unpredictable outbursts of attacks. Drunken Fist practitioners are required to be flexible, strong, and have a good sense of balance. People often recognize the style not only because of the practitioner's staggering movements, but because of the handwork: drunken fist boxing is known for strong wrist strikes and finger-based attacks, usually in which the hand looks like it is holding a small cup.

Drunken Boxing has its roots in Taoist folklore. In film, the style is often referred to as "Eight Drunk Fairies[42]". The said "fairies" are immortal beings that inspired the Drunken Style. Each set of movements is based on one of these immortals. The fairies in question are:

Lu – "The Drunken with Inner Strength"
Crippled Li – "The Drunk with a Strong Right Leg"
Fat Han – "The Drunken Man holding a Pot"
Tso – "The Drunk with a strong Throat Lock"
Lan – "The Drunk with a sudden Wrist Attack"
Flute-Playing Han – "The Drunken Man playing the Flute"
Chang – "The Drunk with Double Kick"
Angel Ho – "The Drunken Woman Flaunting her Body"

The best-known actors associated with this style of fighting are Jackie Chan and Simon Yuen Siu-Tin, patriarch of the Yuen Clan. The latter became an icon to the genre after playing the legendary Beggar So Hat-Yee (known to many fans as "Sam Seed") in *The Drunken Master* (1978). Beggar So was a martial artist in southern China who was part of a group of martial artists known as "10 Tigers of Guangdong", who were known for their efforts in fighting against bandits and protecting the people. After the huge success of that film, Simon Yuen spent the last few years of his career either reprising his role in movies like *World of the Drunken Master* and *Story of the Drunken Master*, or playing very similar roles in movies like *Ol' Dirty Kung Fu*.

---

[42] - "Fairy" is commonly replaced with "God" or "Immortal" in different films.

Other actors have taken to the bottle to provide fans with some good ol' fashioned kung fu entertainment. Independent actor Meng Fei did some drunken boxing in the sub-par *Kung Fu of Eight Drunkards*. Judy Lee (Chia Ling) became one of the only women to perform this style in *Against the Drunken Cat's Paws*. Venom Mob member Philip Kwok did a little of drunken boxing in *The Kid with the Golden Arm* (1979). During the 1990s "Wire-Fu" boom, stars like Jet Li and Donnie Yen put their own twists on the style in movies like *Last Hero in China* (1993) and *Heroes Among Heroes* (1993).

Some other variations of the style have been seen on film, too. In Jet Li's breakthrough film, *The Shaolin Temple* (1982), Li gets to use drunken pole in one fight scene. In Sammo Hung's epic *Blade of Fury*, villain Zhao Changjun does some drunken sword. In *Dance of the Drunk Mantis* (1979), the unofficial sequel to *The Drunken Master*, Hwang Jang-Lee mixes his trademark kicking with drunken mantis techniques.

There have also been a number of spoofs and comic takes on the style, which is already pretty comic to begin with. In *Invincible Shaolin Thunderkick* (1984), third-tier actor Benny Tsui gets "drunk" after drinking a lot of water. In *Shaolin Popey 2: The Messy Temple*, one of the child actors performs drunken boxing after breastfeeding from a woman in a super-hero costume. More recently, Yuen Biao got to do some drunken forms in the Chinese-Japanese co-production *No Problem 2* (2002).

However, none of these actors have come even close to matching Chan's work in his two *Drunken Master* movies, which are the pinnacles of onscreen Drunken Fist Boxing.

Drunken Master (1978)

It is almost common knowledge among films of Hong Kong filmdom that fame and fortune did not come easily to Jackie Chan. For the greater part of 1970s, Chan toiled away as a stuntman (in both big and small movies), an action director, and an actor in low-budget, poorly-promoted films with Lo Wei, who had directed Bruce Lee's first films, that, while entertaining on their own merits, did not serve to build his image with the public. Now don't think for a moment that it was because of a lack of vision or anything like that. While working Lo Wei, Chan did his best to convince Lo Wei to let him make a kung fu comedy. Unfortunately, Lo Wei was too busy trying to make Chan the next Bruce Lee in lackluster films like *New Fist of Fury*.

It was only when Lo Wei had "lent" Chan out to Seasonal films that Chan's fortunes changed for the better. Producer Ng See-Yuen knew talent when he saw it and paired Jackie Chan with action director Yuen Woo-Ping, who also was starting to get the recognition he deserved for his talents. Their first film together was *Snake in the Eagle's Shadow* (1978), which was Jackie's first box-office success. Their next film, *The Drunken Master*, broke box-office records in Hong Kong and put Chan on the road to international stardom.

This fight is the pinnacle of Chan's traditional "chopsockey" days, in terms of choreography, opponents, and showcase for Chan's physical skills. Earlier in his career, Chan had fought people like the tiger-clawed Chen Sing and the master of the flying guillotine himself, Kam Kong. But in this fight he got to take on Hwang Jang-Lee, who, if you have been paying attention to this book, was one of the greatest onscreen kickers of all time and easily the greatest kung fu movie villain of all time. Chan also gets a great showcase, finding the perfect balance between both the martial aspects of his "Eight Drunk Gods" and its comic potential.

After a fast-paced beginning scene in which Chan drinks himself silly while acrobatically avoiding Hwang's attacks, we get to the meat of the fight. So Jackie first shows us the strength of God Lu. All the while, Chan's character's master, Sam Seed (played by Yuen Siu-Tin), gives Chan tips on how to counter Hwang's moves. For example, when their legs get locked, Yuen tells him to use the Crippled Li technique and soon Chan is taking on Hwang using some good ground kicks. Fingers, wrists, feet, and even Chan's head are used to get the upper hand on Hwang.

However, after this initial demonstration of the drunken boxing, Hwang Jang Lee switches his style to a more hand-based style called "Shadowless Hands" (the style was created for the purpose of the film). Chan finds himself powerless to dodge and outmaneuver Hwang's handwork in this portion of the fight. Even the combined work of the Flute Han, Drunken Tso, and Chan's Double Kick is less than a match for Hwang. We give kudos to Hwang in this sequence for his fast and intricate handwork, showing us that he was more than simply a great kicker.

Jackie Chan is *The Drunken Master* (Seasonal Films, 1979).

It is at this point that the fight reaches its comic apex, when Chan mixes together seven of the eight drunk gods to create his own style for Angel Ho, whose technique his character had been too lazy to practice. We then get funny movements like a slapping technique "Putting on her make-up" and "The Widow with a Lover." Hwang Jang Lee unleashes one of his trademark kicks, a double flying dragon kick, but it's too little, too late for him; Chan is on a roll here. This is one of the few fights where a solitary fighter beats Hwang Jang Lee and makes it look fairly believable. Usually, Hwang Jang Lee would lose in a fight only because he was double-teamed or because of some trick. Usually if an action director tried to sell the protagonist as being better than Hwang, he'd fail miserably, making us in the audience say, "Aw! Come on!"

So Jackie Chan and Hwang Jang Lee get great showcases here. Chan is at the top of his game and cinematic drunken boxing here wouldn't be equaled until 1994 with *Drunken Master 2*. His acrobatics, comic timing, and crisp drunken techniques are a joy to watch. While not Hwang's best performance, he does as well here as he'd done in any other movie. As we already mentioned, his kicks are well-showcased, but choreographers Yuen Woo-Ping and Tyrone Hsu Hsia don't forget to show us that Hwang was no one-trick pony.

Drunken Master marked the point in which Chan would really start evolving his style of screen fighting and move out of the bounds of traditional kung fu. While his drunken boxing is certainly authentic, he balanced it out with his wacky acrobatics and comic touches. In his next movie, *The Fearless Hyena*, he'd forego most traditional styles and stick with made-up styles that'd accentuate the comic side of the fight. Then he'd go onto *The Young Master* (1980) and simply choreograph set-pieces made up of physical comedy, leaving traditional kung fu even further to the wayside. By *Dragon Lord* (1982), he had practically moved the emphasis from kung fu fighting to choreographed stunt work and acrobatics. As it stands, this fight represents the "traditional" Jackie Chan at his best.

Drunken Master II (1994)

In spite of the immense popularity of the "wire-fu" movies made during the New Wave period of Hong Kong cinema during the first half of the 1990s, Jackie Chan had almost no participation in the sub-genre. He continued to crank out his usual modern-day action comedies (and one crime drama) like *Police Story 3: Supercop*, *City Hunter*, and *Crime Story* the same way he had done back during the 1980s. It wasn't until 1994, when the popularity of New Wave period piece movies was beginning to wane, that Chan stepped in and made his contribution. The film was *Drunken Master II*, the sequel to the film that kick-started Chan's career and much like that movie, this movie would in time become the Gold Standard of martial arts films and be considered by many as Chan's all-time greatest films.

In a movie populated with memorable fights, the last fight is one of the most staggeringly exhausting fights ever choreographed. While the previous fights had been choreographed by the legendary Lau Kar-Leung, the film's director, Chan and Lau had had a falling out before they had finished filming and Chan ended up firing Lau. Thus, the burden of staging the final fight fell on Chan. It took him three months to film this scene. Needless to say, he really outdid himself with this one.

The fight is divided into three parts: Chan's short duel with Caucasian actor Vincent Tuctan, his subsequent fight with your typical band of nameless thugs, and his final showdown with super kicker Ken Lo and cohort Ho Sung-Park. In the first part, Tuctan is portrayed as a rock-hard bodybuilder type whose techniques are simple, but gets away on sheer brute strength. In this fight, Tuctan is armed with a chain. Chan easily dispatches him using a number of attack combinations based on drunken boxing, although his character is not drunk yet. The scene is notable for a moment where Chan's foot is pushed against the brick wall of a furnace and his shoe catches fire.

In the next scene, Jackie goes further into the foundry where he confronts Ken Low and Ho Sung-Park, who send their lackeys to fight Chan. The men, who belong to Sing Ga Ban (Jackie Chan Stuntman Association), are armed with metal poles and hooks and other weapons. Thus begins a one-vs-many fight that Jackie has always excelled in staging. He trades blows and blocks and kicks and sweeps with multiple attackers with the rhythm and speed that few choreographers have ever equaled. Making the fight more interesting is the presence of Ken Low and Ho Sung Park, who are dropping heavy buckets of dirt and throwing flaming streams of methanol at Chan as he fights the others, making the fight so much more complex than it would've been otherwise. While some drunken techniques can be seen in this sequence, Jackie's style here is the same "everything-goes" style that he uses in most of his modern-day films.

After dispatching the hired goons, Jackie takes on Ho Sung-Park in a rather short fight. Park had originally been hired to be the film's main villain. Park, who is best known as playing Liu Kang in the *Mortal Kombat* video game, is a Korean tae kwon do expert and a very talented fighter. However, according to Chan, Park seemed unable to keep up with the speed and intensity of Hong Kong choreography. Chan complained that Park would complain of the pain of trading real blows and want to stop the take after only a few movements. Park's role was thus relegated to a supporting role and Ken Low, Chan's personal bodyguard, became the main villain. Hong Kong action cinema is richer for it.

It is in their duel that Chan starts unleashing his drunken boxing skills. The beginning of the fight belongs to Low, who spends the first few moments throwing out numerous kicks without ever putting his foot down. Chan, still sober, tries to fight back with his drunken boxing but is ultimately unsuccessful. In this superb display of *muay thai* kicking, Low ranks himself with Hwang Jang Lee, Tan Tao Liang, John Liu, and others as one of the great onscreen kickers. The crowning moment of the first half of their duel is when Low kicks Chan into a bed of hot coals. Chan really did allow himself to be kicked onto the coals, even filming the take *twice* after feeling that he didn't fall right the first time!

Beaten, burned, and bloody, Jackie's character is now desperate to super-charge his drunken technique. It is here that he starts consuming methanol (wood alcohol) in a last-ditch attempt to get truly drunk. He does get drunk, and goes literally bonkers for the last part of the fight. We are treated to a brutal crash course in drunken fist boxing as Chan unleashes all of Eight Drunk Gods in rapid succession. Double jump kicks, Angel Ho's eye poking, wrist attacks, throat grabs, acrobatic head-butting—it's all there. It is an awesome scene.

When it comes to drunken fist boxing, Jackie Chan will always be your go-to guy. Many other actors have performed the style, as we mentioned already, and some of them have done a rather good job and doing so. But Jackie Chan's philosophy of improvisation in fight choreography (Chan compared his style to Jazz music on one occasion), mixing comedy with the action, love of dangerous stunts and anything-goes attitude mixed with his physical and acrobatic skills give him so much more of edge over other actors that have attempted to perform the style. The *Drunken Master* films are the supreme examples of this strange, yet consistently entertaining way of fighting.

Choy Li Fut

Choy Li Fut is considered to be one of the three principal Southern styles of kung fu, next to *Hung Gar* and *Wing Chun*. The style was officially founded by Chan Heung in 1836 in King Mui village in Southern China. During his younger years, Chan had trained with two masters of Southern Shaolin kung fu, Chan Yuen-Woo and Li Yau-San. From them he learned the Five Animal (Snake, Dragon, Tiger, Crane, and Panther) techniques, as well as the short, powerful hand-based strikes that are generally associated with Southern Shaolin styles. After progressing rapidly, he went up to a mountain to learn kung fu with Choy Fook, a Shaolin Monk. From Choy Fook he learned Northern Shaolin techniques, including fast footwork and long, circular hand techniques. He synthesized all of the techniques he had learned into *choy li fut*, whose name pays homage to Chan Heung's teachers.

Choy Li Fut is best known for its variety of hand techniques, ranging from sweeping, circular punches to shorter, more direct strikes. There is kicking in *choy li fut*, most of which comes from the style's Northern roots—powerful sweeping kicks are common as well. Moreover, *choy li fut* makes heavy use of pressure point striking and joint locks (*chin na*). One thing that this style is very well-known for is its diverse weapons training: there were originally 40 principal weapons taught in *choy li fut*; today there are 52.

Choy Li Fut does not appear commonly in Chinese kung fu movies. Yuen Biao uses the style, mixed with other styles, in the classic films *Knockabout* (1979) and *The Magnificent Butcher* (1979). *Choy Li Fut* can be seen briefly in the tournament sequence of Sammo Hung's epic *Blade of Fury* (1993). In the all-time classic *Drunken Master II*, there's a short sequence where Jackie Chan is challenged by Felix Wong, who plays a *choy li fut* stylist. There's an independent kung fu movie from 1979 called *Choy Lee Fut Kung Fu*, starring independent actor Cliff Lok. However, that movie, while featuring some good choreography for an independent film, dilutes the style with a bit too much Peking Opera-inspired acrobatics and other things like umbrellas and queues being used as lashes. The best film to feature the style is actually probably the first movie to feature it.

Recently, some well-meaning filmmakers including former Jackie Chan stunt team member Sam Wong made a film called *Choy Lee Fut*, which aspired to do for the style what *Ip Man* had done for *wing chun*. Unfortunately, instead of pitting leads Sammy Hung and Kane Kosugi against dozens of fighters, all of whom might be destroyed by a pure display of the titular fighting style, the filmmakers try to glorify *choy li fut* by having the characters say *"choy li fut"* every few lines. Moreover, choreographer Sam Wong throws in too many *tae kwon do* and *wushu* kicks into the fights, which goes against the spirit of the art. Guys, we're grateful you tried, but you sort of missed the point.

New Shaolin Boxers (*aka* Grandmaster of Death)(1976)

When we talk about movies produced by the Shaw Brothers studio, there are three major choreographers that define the studio's best output. The first is Lau Kar-Leung, who started working at the studio in the late 1960s doing swordplay films and would become one of the greatest choreographers of traditional Southern styles in the history of the genre. The second is Tong Gaai, who worked alongside Lau Kar-Leung during the late 60s and early 70s, but then found his calling as an action director in *wuxia* films and showed a preference for exotic weaponry. The third is the Venom Mob, including Robert Tai, who were able to mix weaponry, Southern styles, and Peking Opera style acrobatics to great effect.

The impressive thing about *New Shaolin Boxers* is the film was not only choreographed by people other than those mentioned in the previous paragraph, but the choreographers are relative unknowns in the world of action direction. Those are Hsieng Hsing, Chan San Yat, and Chen Jih-Liang. Nonetheless, they seem to pull off a marvelous feat in this film: they make the final fight into not only one of the best showcases for the star, Alexander Fu Sheng, but they give the *choy li fut* kung fu style its best showcase.

The final fight between Alexander Fu Sheng and villain Johnny Wang Lung Wei begins as a challenge between a good man and a gangster. Fu Sheng, upon discovering that Wang Lung Wei was responsible for the death of his first kung fu teacher, is seething with desire for revenge. Leading Wang to his old school, the two begin to "throw down" with traditional kung fu styles.

Fu Sheng gets to perform a wide variety of *choy li fut* techniques with great speed (for the time the film was made) and accuracy. He uses both long and short punches, in addition to some limited kicking. You can see the influence of Southern Shaolin in Fu Sheng's moves, as he uses what appears to be both tiger and dragon techniques (pay attention to his open-handed strikes). His low stances and footwork are all very impressive.

Spanish-language poster for *New Shaolin Boxers* (Shaw Brothers, 1976).

In the last part of the fight, Johnny Wang Lung Wei arms himself with an iron claw, to which Fu Sheng responds with the *shuangdao* (double saber). Fu Sheng uses lots of authentic techniques here and the weapons choreography in this sequence is better than that of a lot of films made during the same era. There a bit of violence here—this is a Chang Cheh film after all—but it is less graphic than most other films by the same director.

Our main gripe[43] about this fight has nothing to do with the action direction itself. However, there are lot of "flashbacks" to Fu Sheng's training. We see Fu Sheng performing a technique in black and white, and then we see him doing the same move in the fight. This is an effective technique for showing how traditional styles can be applied in a fight, but this film simply overdoes it.

---

[43] - Our other complain about the movie itself is the presence of a brief, but inexplicit, rape scene. The scene exists to drive home the film's theme about the consequences of letting people commit crimes in order to save one's own skin, but rape in any context is repugnant to us.

Action directors Hsieh Hsing, Chan San Yat, and Chen Jih-Liang worked with Chang Cheh after Lau Kar-Leung parted company with Chang to direct his own films and before Chang Cheh started making films with the Venom Mob. Hsieh Hsing and Chan San Yat provided the choreography to films like *Marco Polo* (1975), *Shaolin Avengers* (1976), and *The Shaolin Temple* (1976). They were decent choreographers in their own right, but this film easily features their best action direction of not only the films they did with director Chang Cheh, but of the independent films they worked on both before and after this, which include two of Jackie Chan's earlier films: *The Killer Meteors* (1976) and *To Kill With Intrigue* (1977).

Wing Chun

Wing Chun is one of the three principal Southern systems of kung fu, having gained popularity in recent decades for being the style that Bruce Lee had studied before founding his own *Jeet Kune Do*. The style was founded in the 17th century by a woman, Yim Wing Chun, who had studied kung fu from a Shaolin nun, Ng Mui. According to legend, Wing Chun was betrothed to a certain Leung Pak-To. However, another suitor, a local warlord, appeared wanting to force her to marry him. Wing Chun then fled to Shaolin to train in kung fu to defend herself from the man. Yim Wing Chun eventually married Leung Pak-To, who passed the style on to his posterity.

Wing Chun is primarily a hand-based style. Strikes and punches are very short and very fast—a *wing chun* master is capable of delivering dozens of strikes in a matter of a few seconds. Practitioners encourage an "economy of movement" in striking and most punches are directed toward the "center line", giving the style some similarities to *hsing-i*. Some principles of *wing chun* include simultaneous strikes and blocks and the so-called "sticky hands", which is a technique where a practitioner places his hands on his opponent's hand or wrist, and is able to follow it wherever the person moves it. Stances in *wing chun* tend to be closed and higher than the stances of *Hung Gar* and *Choy Li Fut*, the other two principal Southern kung fu styles. Kicks rarely go above the mid-section. Some weapons that are commonly used by *wing chun* stylists are the pole and the butterfly swords.

Wing Chun comes up fairly often in cinema and has done so ever since the days of Bruce Lee in the early 1970s. As Bruce Lee had originally trained in *wing chun*, a lot of movements he uses in his films are taken directly from *wing chun*. There are some good examples of this in his fight against Chuck Norris in *Way of the Dragon* (1973) and in his fight against Bob Wall in *Enter the Dragon* (1973). Bruce Lee imitator Ho Chung Tao (aka "Bruce Li") was also trained in *wing chun*, and thus most Bruce Li films feature demonstrations of *wing chun*, although they are often let down by the lack of talent of the choreographers.

Another actor who trained extensively in *wing chun* is Shaw Brothers actor Ti Lung. Although he started off making *wuxia,* or swordplay, movies, he made a number of movies in the later part of the 1970s and early 1980s that showcased his wing chun training, including his prowess with the pole. Some of the best films to showcase his skills are *The Savage Five* (1975), *The Shaolin Heroes* (1980), *Opium and the Kung Fu Master* (1984), and *The Shanghai 13* (1984). Recently, he had a cameo appearance in *Star Runner* (2003) as a *wing chun* master who tutors lead actor Vaness Wu.

Although not his first style, actor Donnie Yen trained in *wing chun* and has used it in several of his movies. There are some strong *wing chun* overtones to his fighting style in modern action films like *In the Line of Duty IV* (1989) and *Crystal Hunt* (1991). Moreover, his later low-budget period piece films like *Iron Monkey II* (1996) and *Shanghai Affairs* (1998) would show off even crisper *wing chun* techniques than his earlier films.

Peking Opera brothers Sammo Hung and Yuen Biao would be among the foremost *wing chun* practitioners in the industry, especially the former, who could easily be called the greatest choreographer of the style ever. Sammo has appeared in and choreographed a number of classic films featuring *wing chun*, including *Warriors Two* (1978) and *The Prodigal Son* (1982), which we will get into more detail later in the chapter. Moreover, Sammo Hung's homages to Bruce Lee, *Enter the Fat Dragon* (1978) and *Skinny Tiger, Fatty Dragon* (1990) also feature the style. One of his best *wing chun* moments was in *The Gambling Ghost*, where he defeats a thai boxing Billy Chow and James Tien with the style. The villain in the Sammo-directed and choreographed *Once Upon a Time in China and America* (1997) shows off some super-fast *wing chun* handwork in the final fight against Jet Li. Yuen Biao has performed *wing chun* and played the role of legendary master Leung Tsan in *The Prodigal Son* and the TV series *Real Kung Fu* and *Wing Chun*.

Despite a number of films that portrayed the style accurately, there are number of films that haven't quite got it right. One of the earlier films to show off "wing chun" is *Shaolin Martial Arts* (1974), a Shaw Brothers film directed by Chang Cheh. In this movie, Chi Kuan Chun learns *win chun*, although it is mostly close-range finger jabbing that he does. More accurate is Wei Pai's *wing chun* in the Venom Mob film *Invincible Shaolin* (1978). Choreographer Robert Tai commented that Wei Pai didn't have much of a martial background, so he had Wei Pai perform some basic *wing chun* movements. Two movies that tried to tell the story of Yim Wing Chun were *Stranger from Shaolin* (1978) and *Wing Chun* (1994), although the *wing chun* in those movies was more on the fantastic side. *Descendent of Wing Chun* (1978) was another film that attempted to tell the story of Leung Tsan, but featured more generic movie kung fu instead of authentic *wing chun*.

The Prodigal Son (1982)

By 1982, there had been no definitive *wing chun* movie. That's not to say that it hadn't been seen in movies, because viewers had been seeing *wing chun* demonstrations in movies ever since the early 1970s. However, a lot of the films that dealt with the history and philosophy of the style had come up short in one area or another. *Shaolin Martial Arts* didn't feature anything remotely resembling *wing chun*. *Invincible Shaolin*'s training was too fantasy-based. Other movies featured inadequate casting, such as Korean *tae kwon do* expert Casanova Wong as a wing chun expert in *Warriors Two* (1978).

Nonetheless, it was Sammo Hung who eventually did for *wing chun* what Lau Kar-Leung had done for *hung gar*: He made the definitive *wing chun film*. *The Prodigal Son* (1982) was Sammo Hung's last traditional kung fu film before moving on to modern day action and is also one of his most-revered masterpieces. The casting was on target: Lam Ching-Ying and Yuen Biao were trained in *wing chun*; the choreography, courtesy of *Hung Ga Ban* (Sammo Hung's Stuntman Association), was accurate and thrilling; and the philosophy was spot on without going off into the more esoteric territory that previous films about *wing chun* had done.

If you read enough reviews of this film, you'll notice that there are a lot of differing opinions on which is the best fight in the movie. A lot of people point to the final duel between Yuen Biao and villain Frankie Chan. It certainly is a brutal fight and one of Yuen Biao's more intense moments. Other people really enjoy the training sequence between Lam Ching-Ying and Yuen Biao on top of the table. That scene has a lot of technically-correct *wing chun* and gives special emphasis to the closed-quarters fighting that is essential to the style's philosophy.

The fight we are going to talk about is the fight between Lam Ching-Ying and Frankie Chan. It is a short fight—about two minutes long. It is however, a wonderfully accurate portrayal of the style with little embellishments like fancy kicks or wires to make things interesting. Lam Ching-Ying fights Frankie Chan with pure *wing chun* and shows off some of the fastest handwork in any traditional *kung fu* movie made up to that point. Frankie Chan's dragon claws compliment Lam's super-intricate handwork perfectly. Lam Ching-Ying keeps his kicks low and economical. His stances are low only when they need to be; he keeps them high most of the fight. Look quick for a brief moment in which Lam uses the snake style, which style had some movements incorporated into *wing chun*.

This fight stands as one of the great showcases for Lam Ching-Ying, who up this point had spent most of his career as either a stuntman or as a supporting villain. Here he shows us that he had what it took be a leading man and would eventually get that chance a few years later when the *Mr. Vampire* series jumpstarted his career as a kung fu-fighting Taoist ghost buster. Many of those films wouldn't showcase his physical skills very much, though. As a result, this film stands on its own as the pinnacle of Lam Ching-Ying's martial skills.

Portuguese-language VHS cover for
***Stranger from Shaolin* (1978)**

The choreography here is simply stunning, especially by "old school" standards. Few men could match the velocity in choreography as Sammo Hung. Sammo Hung and his crew, made up of Lam Ching-Ying, Yuen Biao, Billy Chan, and others show us that "intricate" and "slow" do not need to go hand in hand. The year after this film was made, the Hong Kong Film Association would introduce the "Best Action Design" award to their annual film award roster. *The Prodigal Son* would go on to win the first award for Best Action Design, beating out Jet Li's *The Shaolin Temple*, Jackie Chan's *The Dragon Lord*, Lau Kar-Leung's *Legendary Weapons of China*, and Corey Yuen's *Ninja in the Dragon's Den*.

Ip Man (2008)

By the beginning of the new millennium, Donnie Yen was seen by many as the great hope for Chinese cinema. With people like Jackie Chan, Yuen Biao, Jet Li, and Sammo Hung getting older and losing a lot of the ability they had once possessed due to age and injury, not to mention Hollywood, Hong Kong was faced with a certain dearth of talent. Vincent Zhao Wen-Zhuo had tried, but failed, finding success on television. Wu Jing, who made his first movie with Yuen Woo-Ping in 1996, would not find true success for nearly a decade. While there were a lot of younger actors who were fortunate enough to appear in some decent action films, the credit belonged to talented action directors like Ching Siu-Tung, Yuen Bun, and Stephen Tung Wei than to the actors themselves.

Donnie Yen had started his career in the early 1984 as a protégé of Yuen Woo-Ping, appearing in cult classics like *Drunken Tai Chi* and *Tiger Cage II* (1990). He appeared in a number of successful "New Wave" films during the early 1990s and by 1997, Donnie was trying to establish himself as a director and action choreographer. Although success wasn't immediate, a few high-profile action-directing gigs like *The Twins Effect* (2003) and *Blade II* (2002) put Donnie on the road to success. He helped bring back the glory of Hong Kong's 1980s action with *Kill Zone* (2005) and *Flash Point* (2007), not to mention star in a number of high-budget period piece films like *Seven Swords* (2005) and *Hero* (2002).

When *Ip Man* (2008) was made, it was only natural that Donnie Yen play the role of the man who had taught *wing chun* to Bruce Lee. Donnie Yen had a *wing chun* background; he himself had previously appeared in the highly-successful 1995 TV series *Fist of Fury* playing the role of Chen Zhen, that Bruce Lee had played in 1972; and he was one of the remaining true martial arts talent in Hong Kong. The job of action director went to the best possible choice: Sammo Hung. Sammo had previously worked with Donnie on *Kill Zone* and, as we have already established, has consistently been the best guy to go for accurate screen *wing chun*.

In the fight in question, Ip Man is taking on General Miura, who has been trained in Japanese *karate*. The fight is a formal match set on a platform, like so many tournament fights in *kung fu* cinema. Like the fight we discussed in *The Prodigal Son*, this one is not that long—it clocks in at around 2:30. Therefore, Sammo Hung does not waste time with posturing or fancy moves. He keeps everything grounded and fast, with dozens of punches and strikes be traded at almost record speeds for a cinematic fight. Sammo Hung and director Wilson Yip do one thing that isn't done very often anymore in martial arts films: they show flashback footage of Ip Man's training to show how techniques are applied in a real fight.

Donnie Yen looks great in this fight, giving us the best *wing chun* demonstration of his career. Once deemed by Hong Kong film scholar Bey Logan as "the fastest man in Hong Kong", Donnie gets to unleash those flurries of short-range punches that *wing chun* is known for. Yen has generally been known for his trademark aerial kicks adapted from *wushu* and *tae kwon do*, but it keeping with the spirit with the style, keeps his kicks to the midsection and below. This is easily his best martial performance of 2008, beating out his other films *Painted Skin* and *An Empress and the Warrior*. This scene, and the others that precede it, put Donnie alongside Lam Ching-Ying and Sammo Hung as the best actor to perform *wing chun* in front of the camera.

Ikeuchi Hiroyuki manages to keep up with Donnie Yen for the most part in this scene. As a *karate* stylist, he uses mainly reverse punches and lateral chops, in addition to roundhouse and side kicks that are characteristic to the style. Ikeuchi Hiroyuki, a television actor in his native Japan, has ample judo and sword fighting training in real life, although only the former gets a workout here.

Donnie Yen and Ikeuchi Hiroyuki face off in *Ip Man* (2008).

Jeet Kune Do

Jeet Kune Do (which means "Way of the Intercepting Fist") is a style founded by the legendary Bruce Lee. It was his response to traditional Chinese kung fu, which he criticized heavily for depending too much on traditional forms and not on practicality. Bruce felt that martial arts should be adapted to practical use in real combat, or, as he put it: "Be shapeless, like water…" Bruce Lee has also referred to his art as "the style of no style."

Jeet Kune Do has, as a foundation, the Southern Chinese style known as *wing chun* (*yongchun* in Mandarin). Wing Chun was the style that Bruce had studied in Hong Kong prior to moving to the United States. In addition to wing chun, which was based on fast and short hand strikes and short, low kicks; Bruce incorporated other styles into Jeet Kune Do. Those included *jiu-jitsu*, which specialized in ground fighting; escrima, or Filipino stick fighting; kicking adapted from Northern kung fu styles; and Western boxing. As a martial art geared toward actual hand-to-hand combat, Bruce urged direct punches, kicks that never went higher than the mid-section, simultaneous blocks and strikes, and attacks that doubled as blocks.

Now, because Bruce Lee taught that Jeet Kune Do was a "formless" martial art, then the martial art could, in theory, be simply any fight style that takes the best of all worlds in an attempt to increase effectiveness in real world combat. Some of his students teach that theory: that Jeet Kune Do should always evolve, and thus have incorporated styles into their teaching that Bruce had not studied in his lifetime. On the other hand, some of his students continue to teach Jeet Kune Do the way Bruce had taught them, emphasizing the wing chun foundation and then encouraging the students to follow their own paths.

With regards to Jeet Kune Do on film, the best examples you'll see are in Bruce Lee's own movies. Most "Brucesploitation" films don't feature Jeet Kune Do; many of them feature a number of Southern styles, traditional forms, hapkido, and other styles, but most of the fights in these movies are choreographed in a way that Bruce wouldn't have approved of, considering his attitudes towards practicality and form. A few Bruce Li films, like *Story of the Dragon* and *Bruce Lee: The Man, The Myth*, have decent imitations of Bruce's screen fighting style and try to teach the same philosophy that Bruce taught. The best Bruce Lee imitator has always been Sammo Hung, who performed flawless imitations of Bruce in *Enter the Fat Dragon* and *Skinny Tiger, Fatty Dragon*. Bruce Lee references have also permeated most of comic actor Stephen Chow's films. The martial arts actor who has best applied Bruce's teachings in screen fighting has been Donnie Yen, who has created a distinctive screen style incorporating elements of boxing, Northern wushu, Tai Chi chuan, Wing Chun, Tae Kwon Do, and Brazilian Jiu-Jitsu.

Way of the Dragon (1973)
(a.k.a. Return of the Dragon)

During the early 1970s, the general style of choreography could be described as flailing arms, no traditional techniques, and, in extreme cases, interminable fights with little power in each blow. In stark contrast to this style of screen fighting, a young star named Bruce Lee had other ideas about how to choreograph a fight. His philosophy of fighting was to break away from classical form and go for practicality. He preached quick and efficient moves, that simplicity was the key to winning a fight. When he started making movies, Bruce Lee wanted to bring these sensibilities to film.

Bruce Lee vs. Chuck Norris in *Way of the Dragon* (Golden Harvest, 1973)

To demonstrate the difference between Bruce Lee's style of fighting and the contemporaneous "basher" style, watch *Fist of Fury* or *The Big Boss* and compare Bruce's fights to those of his co-star James Tien. James Tien is firmly rooted in the "basher" style of fighting while Bruce is taking everyone out with simple, but strong, kicks and strikes. Bruce's style brought a reality to movie martial arts that hadn't been seen before and wouldn't be seen for another decade.

The final fight to *Way of the Dragon* would not only give viewers another opportunity to see Bruce Lee in action, but would carry with a number of other significances. The first was that it would give Bruce Lee a worthy opponent: Chuck Norris. Chuck Norris, a relative unknown at that point, was a Middleweight Karate Champion (record: 65-5) and a master in Tang Soo Do, Shinto-Ryu karate, Brazilian Jiu-Jitsu, and Tae Kwon Do. He had a spinning-back kick that would help catapult him to legend status in certain internet circles 30 years later, the which gets ample time for demonstration in the first half of this fight. He was certainly a better opponent for Bruce Lee than Han Ying Chieh or Riki Hashimoto.

As powerful as Chuck's kicks are, they are no match for the rapid kicks that Bruce unleashes on him. Chuck can try to make a movement, but by the time he's halfway to his target, Bruce's foot is already connecting with Chuck's face. Lee's roundhouse and spinning kicks are faster than his opponents. Lee's speed is spell-binding, especially in his famous kicking combination: one kick to the legs, another to the stomach, and three to head, all in rapid succession. This combination would be used by the character Jackie, a proponent of Jeet Kune Do, in the Sega game *Virtua Fighter*.

An interesting observation about Bruce Lee's kicks: Bruce's original style, Wing Chun, uses few kicks and most of them are low kicks adapted to close-quarters combat. In teaching practicality, Bruce believed that high kicks were not ideal for actual fights. However, time and time again audiences have shown a love for flashy moves and thus Bruce incorporated such kicking into his movies. His kicks are from Tae Kwon Do, which he learned with Tae Kwon Do master Jhoon Rhee. It is said that Chuck Norris himself encouraged Bruce Lee to use high kicks in their fight, although Bruce had been using flashier kicks since *The Big Boss*.

Besides his famous kicking combination, the most memorable combination we'll see in this fight is a demonstration of pure Wing Chun. In close quarters, Bruce and Chuck trade a few blows, with Bruce being able to trap Chuck's arms. What follows is a five-punch combination performed in about *one second*. That's right, he punches Chuck Norris five times in one second, following it with a roundhouse kick to the head. It's an awesome moment, and Sammo Hung would pay homage to this sequence in his 1990 film *Skinny Tiger and Fatty Dragon*.

Their duel in the Roman Coliseum would set the standard for all one-on-one fights for all years to come. Not only that, it would establish the glorious tradition of Hong Kong filmmakers importing foreign martial artists for their films, generally as the villains. People like Jeff Falcon, Richard Norton, Bill "Superfoot" Wallace and Benny "the Jet" Urquidez owe a big part of their careers to the Bruce Lee-Chuck Norris Showdown. It truly is a classic moment in martial arts cinema.

Game of Death (1978)

Before his unexpected death in 1973, Bruce Lee had filmed only a handful of scenes to his pet project: *Game of Death*. In 1978, *Enter the Dragon* director Robert Clouse was contracted to finish the movie, and did so with the help of some Bruce Lee imitators, Sammo Hung as a choreographer, and a few script re-writes that changed the script to be something completely different than from Bruce Lee's vision. The film culminated in the fight scenes that Bruce had originally filmed, although they were heavily edited to fit the context of the film. Nevertheless, these fight scenes stick out and are easily superior to a lot of the kung fu fights made during that decade, so let's go forward.

There were three fights that Bruce Lee was able to film for this scene. The first is a duel against Dan Inosanto. Inosanto was an escrima, or Filipino stick fighting, expert. Inosanto is probably most known in Bruce Lee fandom for having taught Bruce how to fight with the *nunchaku*, Bruce's signature weapon. The fight begins with Bruce entering the first level of the building and confronting Inosanto, who's armed with two sticks. Bruce himself is armed with a bamboo cane. After a few taunts, Bruce strikes out with lightning-fast blow and has soon carved a little "x" into Inosanto's forehead. Then the two of the grab their *nunchaku* and they start to demonstrate their prowess in front of each other. Bruce's strategy is remarkable, as he gets Inosanto so involved in the *nunchaku* displays that he doesn't see Bruce's blows or roundhouse kicks coming.

On the next floor, Bruce Lee confronts Chi Hon Choi, a *hapkido* stylist. The hapkido style is known for its locks, throws, and breaks, which is precisely what Chi starts pulling on Bruce. After a few throws and take-downs, Bruce shows that he has sufficiently analyzed the style and begins to exploit its weaknesses, turning Chi's attempts at throwing and striking Bruce into successful throws and kicks on Bruce's part. There's even a short bout of ground fighting thrown in good measure.

The third and final fight that Bruce had filmed is between him and basketball player Kareem Abdul-Jabbar. Jabbar had been Bruce Lee's student and stood a towering seven feet in height, compared to Bruce's 5`7". The fight becomes a literal David and Goliath martial arts showdown, and the perfect opportunity for Bruce Lee to show how adaptable his *jeet kune do* style was. Immediately, Kareem appears to be at an advantage, and is able to make up the distance between him and Bruce and go in for the hits with relative ease. So Bruce retaliates by closing the distance and staying as close to Jabar as possible.

The logic is that if your opponent is better-adapted to fighting at a distance, then don't let him maintain his distance. Bruce gets to use his punches a lot more there than in the previous two fights, which is keeping in with the whole close-quarters combat strategy. Notice how Bruce Lee never tries to simply roundhouse kick Jabbar, but hits him first to bring both Jabbar's head and guard down, and then unleashes his lightning-fast kicks with all of the snap you'd expect out of him. Besides that, Lee also throws in some ground fighting techniques and some *jiu-jitsu* to give the fight an extra dose of realism.

One important aspect of these fights in particular is that they symbolize Bruce Lee's philosophy as far as fighting is concerned. His fighting style is a lot simpler and economical than that of Jackie Chan, Jet Li, and others, but he once again brings a measure of realism to his fights that would never be seen in any other movie made during the 1970s. His *jeet kune do* style was based on the philosophy of being "free form" and here we get to see him use a variety of techniques in order to beat his opponents. While his opponents are bound by the styles they use, Bruce is able to adapt and thus exploit their faults and beat them. This would be a major theme of the Jet Li film *Fist of Legend*, a tactic that would help Jet Li's Chen Zhen character beat Billy Chow in the end.

Bruce Lee's performance is one of the greatest of his entire career. He handles the choreography and allows the other fighters to show off their skills, but the entire sequence belongs to him. His kicks are executed with speed, snap, and height, in spite of his shying away from anything really showy. There is one showy-looking kick where Bruce is struggling to keep Jabbar from shoving his head into a pot shard and, supported by his hands, throws his legs over his back and hits Kareem in the head. However, if you look closely at the context, you'll see that the movie was both practical and effective in that context. His punches are all powerful. The use of jiu-jitsu is something that would never be used often in Hong Kong and American cinema until recent years when Donnie Yen re-started the trend in *Kill Zone* (2005) and *Flash Point (2007)*. Bruce gives us yet another excellent demonstration of the *nunchaku* as well. The fight is really a 12-minute lesson on why Bruce Lee was such an important figure in martial arts cinema.

Another great aspect of this fight (and of the film itself) is John Barry's score. Barry is best known for scoring most of the *007* films and the score is reminiscent of those films. Nonetheless, it is a fast-paced score and really brings the viewer in the fights. It is one of the best fight themes ever composed.

This fight has been subject to a lot of parodies, rip-offs, and homages during the past 30 years. Probably the most notable influence is the yellow track suit that Bruce Lee used in this scene. That track suit has been used and re-used in a variety of mainstream films like *Shaolin Soccer (2001)*, *Kill Bill Vol. 1* (2003), and *High Risk* (1995). Another idea that would be the inspiration for numerous other films was the idea of having our hero fight a guy that was a lot taller than him. In *Enter the Game of Death*, Bruce Le (Huang Kin Lung) takes on a number of taller black fighters outside of pagoda, as opposed inside of it. In *Supercop 2* (1993), Michelle Yeoh takes on seven-foot Caucasian fighter and even takes a kick to the chest that leaves a boot-print on her chest. Probably the most affectionate homage was in Jackie Chan's *City Hunter* (1992), where Jackie takes on two tall black fighters in a movie theater that is actually playing the fight between Bruce Lee and Kareem Abdul-Jabbar. In further homage to this scene, Jackie copies a few of Bruce Lee's moves in order to get the upper hand in the fight.

Bruce Lee had originally planned to have two more fights in the pagoda sequence of the "original" game of death. One was to have Bruce take on Taky Shimura, who was a student of Bruce's and also a *karate* stylist. After taking on both *hapkido* and *escrima* stylists, a *karate* master would add to the variation and allow more comparisons between Bruce's art and other styles. The other fight was to feature Whang Inn-Sik, a *hapkido* expert who had had a small role in *Way of the Dragon*.

In 2002, a group of documentary filmmakers were able to restore the original fight scenes from the *Game of Death* footage that Bruce had filmed before his sudden passing. Using the footage and his notes on the scenes, the fight scenes that had totaled twelve minutes in the Robert Clouse film had gone up nearly forty, including fights between Bruce Lee's three adversaries and two other fighters. One of those other fighters was frequent Bruce collaborator James Tien, who can be seen briefly near the beginning of the Clouse version of the film. More of Bruce Lee's *jeet kune do* philosophy was on display and the other fighters got a better showcase for their skills than in the edited version. It's an awesome sequence either way, and really deserves its place at the top of Chinese action cinema.

Monkey Kung Fu

Monkey kung fu is one more the movie-friendly styles of kung fu, in large part because its practitioner's imitation of an actual primate is amusing in and of itself. Interestingly enough, there are more than one style that are known as the monkey style in English, each of them with its own vision of how to incorporate a monkey's movements into the style. One of the oldest is *houquan*, or "monkey fist". The monkey fist style exists today and is taught in most Mainland wushu schools. The goal of the style is for the person to become the monkey, in such a way that the stylist's movements, expressions, and gestures are indistinguishable from that of a real primate. Flips, somersaults, walking on all fours, and handstands are inherent in this style.

The other, more popular style that has been dubbed as "monkey kung fu" is the *tai shing men* style. The story behind this style is that there was a martial artist named Kau Sze who was sentenced to prison during the 16th century. While serving his sentence, Kau observed a number of monkeys who played the forest outside the prison. After observing them for some time, he began to incorporate their movements into his own kung fu, which he called *tai shing men*, or the "Great Saint Style", named in honor of Son Wukong, the Monkey King. Included in the style are techniques called Drunken Monkey, Stone Monkey, Lost Monkey, Wooden Monkey, and Standing Monkey, which incorporate everything from iron body techniques to pressure point strikes to tumbling and falling movements.

Scene from *Monkey Fist, Floating Snake* (1979).

The monkey style was fairly common in classic kung fu movies, although it got less attention in movies after the decline of chopsockey films in the early 1980s. One of the earliest films to feature *tai shing men* is *Monkey Fist* (1974), starring *tai shing* grandmaster Chan Sau Chung, who would later appear in *Duel of the Seven Tigers* (1978) to show off some pure *tai shing men*. One of Chan Sau Chung's disciples is fan favorite Chen Kuan Tai, who would show off the style in a more serious way in films like *Iron Monkey* (1977) and *Invincible Monkey Fist* (1978). The Sammo Hung masterpiece *Knockabout* (1979) features some *tai shing men* courtesy of Sammo Hung and Yuen Biao, but it was spoiled by a bit too much acrobatics. Some independent films like *Monkey Fist, Floating Snake* (1979) and *Snake in the Monkey's Shadow* (1979) feature the style prominently. Despite the titles, Lau Kar-Leung's *Mad Monkey Kung Fu* (1978) and *Drunken Monkey* (2002) don't feature actual *tai shing men* as much as it features a monkey variation of *hung gar*.

Houquan pops up occasionally in Mainland kung fu films and films feature wushu-trained actors. There are some monkey fist fights and training sequences in *Betrayal and Revenge* (1985), a Mainland film about the Taiping rebellion. *Young Hero of Shaolin* (1985) features some *houquan* briefly during the tournament sequence. Other films like *The Drunken Master* (1979), *Phantom Kung Fu* (1979), and *The Seven Grandmasters* (1979) feature some brief exhibitions of *houquan*. In *The Inspector Wears Skirts* (1987), Caucasian actor Jeff Falcon performs the style in the brief climax.

Stroke of Death (1979)

It sounds almost like an oxymoron to associate wire-fu maestro Ching Siu-Tung with traditional, FX-free martial arts. By 1980, Ching was well on his way to establishing his reputation as the auteur of wire-enhanced swordplay that he is best known today. It was just one year before that Ching Siu-Tung choreographed and starred in this film, one of his few major starring roles before he focused his efforts behind the camera. Interestingly enough, while Ching Siu-Tung shows us that his knack for action direction came somewhat naturally to him, there's almost nothing in this film, especially the final fight, that would hint at the work he would produce in films like *The Swordsman* (1990) and *A Chinese Ghost Story* (1987) several years later.

One of the interesting things about *Stroke of Death* is that the film is one of those few films that even kung fu movie enthusiasts accuse of having just too many fight scenes. Nonetheless, quantity *and* quality are the order of the day, with the best fight being left for the final duel against Kuan Feng. Ching Siu-Tung plays an escaped convict who is looking for a kung fu manual and is trained in the Gibbon Fist style of martial arts. Zhou (Hau Chiu Sing), another pupil of the style, is also hot on the manual's trail. Following them is a gangster, Tung (Kuan Feng), who also after the manual. As expected, this leads to a series of fights culminating in a final showdown between the two protagonists and Tung, accompanied by three henchmen, in an open field.

The monkey style on display here is *tai shing men* enhanced by a bit of Peking Opera acrobatics that are expected for most of these late 1970s kung fu comedies. Yes, there are quite a bit of cartwheels and flips on display in this particular fight, but they do not make up the bulk of the action (as opposed to *Knockabout*). Interestingly enough, the "Lost Monkey" routine, with its very low stances and rolling movements, is used very little. The actors running on all fours and talking in dubbed-in monkey calls are nowhere to be seen here. Despite the fact that the film is a kung fu comedy, the monkey style is played rather straight.

Most of the techniques belong to the Drunken Monkey and Standing Monkey variations of *tai shing men*. Ching Siu-Tung stays in a regular, upright position throughout most of the fight, attacking with his monkey claws (which faintly resemble a crane's beak), his wrists, and fists. He even throws in a few elbows here and there for effective close-range fighting. Hau Chiu-Sing uses the Drunkey Monkey variation of *tai shing men* in the first part of his fight against Kuan Feng—look close for the staggering footwork in the beginning of his scene. Few kicks are used from either fighter, as *tai shing men* is a Southern style.

The choreography here is very good, as it is basically eight minutes of non-stop kung fu, with little time thrown in for exchanges of taunts or anything else. Like many other fights from the era that, if you cut out the acrobatics and goofing around, have very little actually happening in them, it's obvious that Ching Siu-Tung, Hau Chiu-Sing, and Tony Leung Siu-Hung (who plays one of the henchmen and was one of the action directors) are dead-set on packing as much authentic monkey style as possible into the fight. While Ching Siu-Tung has often been considered one of the top five action directors in Hong Kong cinema over the years because of his endless imagination in putting together over-the-top, fantasy-oriented action scenes, his work here is enough to make you wonder why he didn't do more traditional kung fu and modern kickboxing than he ended up doing over the past four decades.

Kuan Feng practically steals the show in this fight as the pole-wielding villain. He wields a metal pole with quite a bit of prowess here, and does wonders for the weapon. He's quite agile with the weapon, at one point he jabs the pole at Hau Chiu-Sing's neck, misses, and simply twirls it around the back of Hau's neck and pulls it back on the other side. He gets some solid support from Chiang Cheng, Tony Leung and Waan Fat, who play his three henchmen. Of note is Tony Leung, who throws in some solid kicks here.

A lot of this film's cast made another film with director Lo Mar that same year, which is known as *Five Superfighters*. Kuan Feng plays the spear-wielding villain. Hau Chiu-Sing plays the old master who does some wicked drunken saber at the end. Tony Leung Siu-Hung plays one of the high-kicking students. That film also features some excellent martial arts, although the choreographer of that one was genre veteran Tyrone Hsu Hsia (the "King of Sticks" from *The Drunken Master*).

As we mentioned a few paragraphs back, this was one of Ching Siu-Tung's few major starring roles. His other major role was in *The Master Strikes* (1980), in which he got to show off some solid handwork and acrobatics, much like in this film. Those two films are fan favorites and are two pinnacles of action direction for a kung fu comedy outside of the best work of Jackie Chan, Sammo Hung, Yuen Woo-Ping, and Lau Kar-Leung, especially in terms of hand-based choreography and acrobatics. We wonder why Ching decided to be an action director instead of an action director. He must've been prophetic and guessed that there was more for him behind the camera than in front of it, considering how fickle Hong Kong cinema has always been.

Hau Chiu-Sing had a more limited career than his colleague. As an action director, his main credits are this film and *Crystal Fist*, a fan favorite starring Indonesian actor Billy Chong. Other than that, he appeared in a few other independent films like *Sun Dragon* and *Super Power*, both of which starred Billy Chong. He also played a teacher in *Snake in the Monkey's Shadow*.

Stroke of Death was a Shaw Brothers production. Comparing it with the other films that the studio produced that year, including those of The Venom Mob and Lau Kar-Leung, this film easily is just as good, if not better, than those, which is really saying something.

Encounter of the Spooky Kind (1980)

Encounter of the Spooky Kind is generally considered to be a very influential film in Hong Kong cinema, as it set the foundations for numerous other Hong Kong horror/comedy/kung fu films that would we be produced over the next few decades. Yes, you read that last sentence right: Hong Kong filmmakers were throwing monsters, gore, goofy slapstick, and high-octane martial arts battles into the proverbial cauldron long before *Scream* (1996) reduced a lot of American horror films into self-referential comedies with gore. The Yuen Clan's sorcery films (like *Miracle Warriors* and *Taoism Drunkard*) and Lam Ching-Ying's *Mr. Vampire* series all owe a lot of their existence and success to this film, which is, not surprisingly, one of the best examples of the genre.

The basic gist of the film is that Bold Cheung's (Sammo Hung) wife is fooling around with his boss, the rich Mr. Tam (Huang Ha). To get Cheung out of the picture, Mr. Tam hires an evil sorcerer (Peter Chan) to wipe Cheung out. Cheung luckily receives some help from the sorcerer's colleague (Chung Faat), all of which eventually leads to a showdown between the two magicians. In the final magic standoff, the evil magician possesses his assistant (To Siu-Ming) with the spirit of the Chinese god, Na Cha, while the good mage invokes the Monkey King to possess Bold Cheung's body. What erupts is an absolutely delight duel: monkey style vs. iron ring.

Now, this is neither the first nor the last time that Sammo Hung would depict the monkey style in his movies. The year before, he and Yuen Biao had performed some great monkey kung fu in the finale of *Knockabout*, a duel many believe is one of the best put onscreen. It is a wonderful match up, although the monkey style is a bit diluted by a bit too much posturing and acrobatics and not enough techniques. In the sequel to this film, *Encounter of the Spooky Kind 2* (1990), Sammo Hung and co-star Meng Hoi fight a monkey stylist in one of the film's later fights. This one is the best of the three, as it gives the appropriate attention to the style's unique handwork without overdoing it on the flips and somersaults.

Sammo's handwork here is quite fast and intricate, a hallmark of Sammo's old school choreography. He uses the monkey claw hand position, which appears to be less rigid than other animal techniques. Besides striking, the claw is used for grabbing an opponent's arm and weapon (the metal hoop in this case). Sammo fights in both the upright and crouching positions. He moves a lot in the crouching position, suggesting the "Lost Monkey" technique of *tai shing men*, which symbolizes the monkey moving furtively into another "tribe's" territory, foraging for food, and quickly getting out of dodge. Although he doesn't do a lot of kicking, which would be more characteristic of Northern *houquan*, he does get in a nice front kick and an awesome drop kick to his opponent's head.

To Siu-Ming, who plays the poor sap possessed by the spirit of Na Cha[44], does some really good fighting with the metal hoop here. As a weapon that doesn't always get as much attention as the more conventional Chinese arms, it's a really cinematic object and looks good onscreen, if only because it looks like a hula hoop with the "evil" switch turned on.

The Hung Ga Ban (Sammo Hung's Stuntman Association) are credited as the film's action directors, more specifically: Sammo Hung, Yuen Biao, Lam Ching-Ying, and Billy Chan. They also had put together the action direction for *Knockabout* the previous year and, as we already mentioned, they find a better balance between the flowery and the authentic. One interesting thing they do is set a large portion of the fight (well, this portion of the climax) in a wooden scaffolding, so we get to see Sammo Hung

---

[44] See chapter on the Iron Hoop.

do some monkey-like acrobatics while trading blows with To Siu-Ming. Also appreciated are the light comic touches, mainly Sammo Hung and To Siu-Ming exchanging dialogue, but with a monkey's calls dubbed in for Sammo's voice and To Siu-Ming's voice dubbed with a sped-up voice that sounds like a Chipmunk on speed.

It's a novel and entertaining fight and a great addition to an already novel and entertaining film.

Part 2: Northern Kung Fu Styles

Northern Kicking Techniques

When talking about the differences between Northern and Southern kung fu styles, the most common (and probably generic) stated difference is that Northern styles feature higher stances and more kicking while Southern styles feature lower stances and more hand-based techniques. While the Southern systems to utilize some kicks, they rarely tend to be aimed higher than the midsection in most systems. The Northern styles, however, tend to take advantage of a wide variety of kicks.

The most diverse kicks can be found in the *changquan*, or Long Fist style. The kicks used in this style range from your basic front kicks to jumping crescent kicks and whirlwind kicks. *Changquan* is taught in most *wushu* academies today as one of the principal styles. Another well-known kicking technique in Northern kung fu is *tan tui*, which means "Springing Leg". The Northern *chuojiao* style, which means "poking foot", incorporates a lot of fast and powerful kicking techniques as well. In addition to these styles, most of the Northern animal styles, such as the Eagle Claw and Black Tiger styles, feature a lot more kicking techniques than their Southern counterparts.

Now, the tricky part is distinguishing between Northern-style kicking and *tae kwon do*, which a lot of Chinese actors have studied in addition to Chinese kung fu. Sometimes there's so much of a mix that it's nearly impossible to distinguish between the two. Donnie Yen is a good example of that, as his kicks are a mixture of both Chinese and Korean martial arts. Moreover, there are a lot of films that feature a character who's a "kicker from the North", but who is played by a *tae kwon do* stylist. The difference tends to be in the execution: Northern kicks tend to be a lot more rounded and circular in their movement and presentation than *tae kwon do*, which is often more jointed or straight-legged. But even that description is rather vague and most of the time it's best to know what the performer's background is in order to really know what his/her style is.

Most films featuring Mainland *wushu* stylists will feature Northern footwork, especially the films of people like Jet Li, Vincent Zhao Wen-Zhuo, or Wu Jing. To be honest, most Mainland Chinese kung fu films made in the 80s and early 90s will feature more Northern legwork than kicking derived from Korean or Japanese martial arts. Most Peking Opera-trained actors, like Jackie Chan, The Venom Mob, Sammo Hung, Angela Mao, and many others received some training in Northern styles as much as in Southern styles. However, it is important to note that most of them studied other forms of martial arts later on, so it can be a bit difficult to know what style they're performing at any given time. Other actors like Bruce Leung Siu-Lung, Johnny Wang Lung-Wei, and Michael Chan Wai-Man were trained in Northern styles of martial arts.

Call Me Dragon (1974)

When looking at the Bruce Lee imitators, it goes without saying that all of them were inferior fighters compared to the real thing. While they each had their moments, the often low-budget films in which they starred more often than not had untalented people in the action director's chair, and whatever skills they had would not get the showcase they might've deserved. However, there was one Bruce Lee imitator who not only was an incredibly-talented fighter and choreographer in his own right, but was one of the best screen kickers for most of the 1970s. His name is Bruce Leung Siu-Lung, aka Bruce Liang.

Studying under his father, Leung Siu-Lung studied a number of Northern styles of kung fu. Leung Siu-Lung was something of a brawler, being discovered by producers who saw him fighting in the street. He would continue this sort of behavior for a big part of his early career, even taking armed opponents unarmed.

Call Me Dragon is considered a tour-de-force for Leung Siu-Lung and is easily one of the best martial arts movies, in terms of action, made in the time period bookmarked by Bruce Lee's death in 1973 and Jackie Chan's rise to stardom in 1978. Leung and his co-star, Japanese actor Yasuaki Kurata, both get ample time to demonstrate their respective skills in one of the all-time kick fests of the 1970s. All of this would peak in the climax, which is a 10-minute-long kicking contest between Leung and Kurata, broken up by a very well-choreographed weapons duel.

For a good portion of the fight, Leung and Kurata throw flurries of kicks at each other. Practically every kick in the book, including spin kicks, roundhouse kicks, flying kicks, front kicks, jumping crescent kicks, and others are showcased by the two actors. Each kick is performed with the speed and snap that many films made in that era lacked. While it may be improbable that normal human beings would not being take as many kicks to the head as our two actors do and still live, there's no denying the ability on display.

The handwork showcased in the fight is simple, but never degenerates into the powerless "flailing arms" style of choreography that Jimmy Wang Yu had made so popular. Yasuaki Kurata was a student of Japanese *kempo*, which is a Japanese style with roots in Chinese Shaolin styles. His handwork is solid in this fight. The most interesting moment for the handwork comes at part where Leung and Kurata perform the splits to scale the walls of two adjacent buildings and trading blows as they push themselves up the building. It's an excellent display of physical prowess and endurance.

Near the end of this exhausting duel, Kurata whips out a *tonfa*, or night stick, while Leung arms himself with a *nunchaku*, which Bruce Lee had made famous. Leung puts on quite a show with his weapon and Leung is able to trade blows with his opponent and integrate the *nunchaku* into the choreography with a little bit more *panache* than Bruce Lee. Where Bruce Lee was a whirlwind in showing off his skill with the *nunchaku*, he usually used it against unskilled henchmen. Here, the choreography is a lot more balanced in showing both weapons in action.

Black Sheep Affair (1998)

One of the unsung heroes of Hong Kong cinema during the 1990s is a fellow named Vincent Zhao Wen-Zhuo. Like his contemporary, Jet Li, Zhao was a Mainland-born *wushu* stylist who came to Hong Kong to make his fortune in film during the wire-fu glut of the early 1990s. He had everything that an aspiring action actor could need to be a star: good looks, solid acting ability, and very good martial arts skills. His first films were a number of high-profile movies made by successful directors. He was the main villain in *Fong Sai Yuk* (1993) and was Jet Li's replacement as Chinese folk hero Wong Fei Hung in the fourth and fifth entries in the *Once Upon a Time in China* series.

Unfortunately, audiences seemed to not be interested in another *wushu*-trained actor and several of these films that made were box-office disappointments. Then, like Jet Li, Vincent Zhao tried his hand at making a few action films set in the modern day, churning out passable fare like *The Mahjong Dragon* (1996) and *Fist Power* (2000), and less-passable fare like *Body Weapon* (1997). He ultimately was relegated to being a TV actor, making a number of successful TV series, including a number of series based on popular movies (that he didn't star in). He has since become a popular actor in Taiwan, although he never got the movie career that he really deserved.

The Black Sheep Affair was one of the modern-day action films that Vincent Zhao made in the second half of the 1990s when he was still trying to become the next Jet Li. Opinions regarding this film are decidedly mixed, although we feel it's probably his best overall film. We especially enjoy the final fight in this movie, which shows that Vincent Zhao was really one of the super kickers of the 1990s and that he did not get the recognition he so deserved.

In the final fight, Zhao, who plays a Mainland agent, Ah Dong, working in a fictitious Eastern European country, storms the Chinese embassy which is being held hostage by a maniacal Japanese terrorist, Mishima (Andrew Lin). After the requisite gunplay that leaves all of the other terrorists dead, Ah Dong and Mishima go at it in hand-to-hand combat for the final time.

The fight can be divided into three parts. In the first part of the fight, Vincent Zhao and Andrew Lin fight in the lobby of the embassy. They fight in an open space, after which they move the fight up a staircase and onto the balcony. There is no shortage of furniture destroyed in this particular scene, as our combatants become practically superhuman and start throwing each other *up the staircase* and even through the banisters.

They end up in another room upstairs, where begins the second part of the fight, in the ambassador's office. This is where Zhao Wen-Zhuo really shines as he performs almost every single fancy *wushu* kick in his repertoire. There is also a neat bit here, which looks like an homage to Gordon Liu's fight against the Judo master in *Heroes of the East*, where the sweat on Zhao's arm prevents Andrew Lin from being able to hold on to it and perform any grappling.

The final part of the fight takes place in a dark hallway and is mainly a swordfight. Zhao Wen-Zhuo gets to perform a nice *wushu/jian* routine on Andrew Lin while wielding a rapier. He also gets to throw in some nice aerial kicks, which is always welcome. Their battle is interrupted by a military helicopter, which leads to one of the film's tragic moments. However, both hero and villain survive long enough for the fight to end on a very over-the-top note.

This fight is really one big showcase for Zhao Wen-Zhuo's *wushu* skills, especially his kicking. Having trained at the Beijing Wushu Academy, Zhao had studied a number of styles, including the Northern *changquan*, or Shaolin Long Fist. Thus, Zhao was a very adept kicker, which didn't always get the appropriate showcase it deserved in a number of his films. Here we can see all of his kicks in all their fury. While fighting on the balcony, Zhao performs a nice horizontal whirlwind kick. Once he and Lin enter the office, he starts performing a number of spinning and crescent kicks, all of which get some great height and distance on them. In one great move, Zhao does a spinning double back kick to Andrew Lin. In another, Lin grabs Zhao's leg, which he turns into a spinning heel kick with the other. His kicks are a lot more rounded than what we'd see from a *tae kwon do* stylist, and they look great. Zhao Wen-Zhuo would get to show off his kicking skills to a lesser degree in his other modern films, although problems like bad editing or just relegating Zhao to a supporting role kind of hurt that.

The action duties were given to Ching Siu-Tung for this film, which is interesting considering how little Ching had worked on modern action during the 1980s and 1990s. To be honest, most of the modern movies he did were either bullet ballet films for John Woo, like *A Better Tomorrow 2* and *The Killer*, or super hero fantasies like *The Heroic Trio*. Ching Siu-Tung, who has always been better at wire-assisted fighting than modern kickboxing, does quite a good job here. Back in the 1990s, one rarely watched a film featuring action from Ching in order to see the actors fight at the peak of their abilities. Thus it comes across as rather ironic that Zhao's *tour-de-force* would be choreographed by Ching.

What comes as less of a surprise, however, is that Ching Siu-Tung evidently felt little need to curb his tendencies to exaggerate his action almost to the point of fantasy. He's does this in other films set in the modern-day, including *My Schoolmate is a Barbarian* and *Belly of the Beast*, not to mention a number of others. The scene of Andrew Lin throwing Vincent Zhao up the staircase was obviously done with wire assistance, as were a few Ryu-inspired hurricane kicks that Zhao performs during the fight. There is a bit of undercranking to be seen, allowing Zhao to punch Lin a dozen times in a few seconds, something that Ching had done a few years earlier in Jet Li's *Dr. Wei and the Scripture with No Words* (1996). It is this sort of exaggeration which has caused a bit of a division about the quality of this particular fight. Needless to say, we didn't mind it at all.

When it comes to awesome kicks from a Mainland *wushu* stylist, this is really one of the best places to go. Vincent Zhao really deserved a better career than what he ended up getting, and the final fight to this film really proves it.

Eagle Claw (Ying Jao Pai)

The Eagle Claw style (know as *ying jao pai* in Chinese) is one of the main Northern animal styles and one of the oldest styles still practiced today. The style was founded by the famous General Yue Fei during the Song dynasty. The story is that Yue Fei's martial arts teacher taught him a style known as "Elephant Boxing" and Yue Fei expanded upon the grappling techniques of that style to create the Eagle Claw style. General Yue then taught the style to his soldiers, which helped them immensely in battle. The style evolved during the Ming Dynasty when a monk named Liquan Seng met some soldiers who were practicing the Eagle Claw style and incorporated it into another style he had studied.

The Eagle Claw style is known for its extensive use of *chin na*, or joint locks. The claw is formed by keeping the four fingers curled close together and the thumb opposite the fingers. The eagle's claw is used for attacking nerves, tendons, and blood vessels, gripping them with a powerful force and breaking them. Attacking pressure points is encouraged. The Eagle Claw style is also known for its acrobatics and kicking skills, too. Today, the Eagle Claw style is taught in most Mainland Chinese *wushu* academies, although some Eagle Claw masters complain that the *wushu* version of the style is stripped of its martial applications and is more of an exhibitionist style than a practical fighting style.

The Eagle Claw style is oft seen in films, frequently as the style performed by the villains. In a lot of traditional kung fu movies made in Hong Kong and Taiwan, the heroes are trained in some sort of Southern style kung fu (hung gar, crane, wing chun, etc.) and thus the lead villain (or one of the lead villain) will use the Northern Eagle Claw as a sort of counterpoint. However, it should be noted that in most of these films, the Eagle Claw being used is *not* the Northern Eagle, but rather a Southern variation, sometimes known as the "Shaolin Eagle" style. The easiest way to identify if the Eagle Claw being used is the authentic *ying jao pai* or simply the Southern variation is by the claw itself. The Southern Eagle claw is three-fingered (thumb, index finger, and middle finger) while the Northern Eagle claw uses all the fingers. Most films featuring the Northern Eagle Claw are either Mainland Chinese films or films featuring *wushu*-trained martial artists.

The Shaolin Eagle was used extensively by Korean *tae kwon do* master Hwang Jang Lee as a hand style meant to balance out his kicking skills. Films like *Invincible Iron Armour*, *Snake in the Eagle's Shadow*, and *Hell's Wind Staff* feature some solid claw work from Hwang. Fellow Korean actor Eagle Han Ying did something similar to *South Shaolin vs. North Shaolin* and *Shaolin and Tai Chi,* although to a lesser effect. Kam Kong, who played a villain in a lot of traditional films, uses Southern Eagle techniques in Chen Kuan-Tai's independent classic *Iron Monkey*. Taiwanese director Lee Tso Nam's classic *Eagle's Claw*, focuses mainly on the Southern Eagle Claw style and features solid performances by Lee regular Don Wong Tao and Shaw Bros veteran Chi Kuan Chun

Shek Kin, best known for playing the villain Mr. Han in *Enter the Dragon*, incorporates some *Ying Jao Pai* into his fighting against Cliff Lok for the excellent and brutal finale of *Roaring Lion* (1972). There is some very good Northern Eagle Claw to be seen in Bruce Leung Siu-Hung's classic *Ten Tigers of Shaolin* (1978). Be on the lookout for some solid Eagle Claw in Billy Chong's *Crystal Fist* (1979). Sammo Hung stunt team member Chung Fat also uses the Northern Eagle Claw in *The Pedicab Driver*. There's a brief demonstration by Cynthia Rothrock of the Northern version in the final fight of *The Magic Crystal* (1986). Most Mainland kung fu films, many of which make a concentrated effort to show off as many styles as possible, feature brief (at the very least) demonstrations of Northern Eagle. *Young Hero of Shaolin* (1985), *Shaolin Assassin*, and *Disciples of Shaolin* are just a few examples of films where you can see the *Eagle's* claw in action. More recently, actor Fan Siu-Wong of *Riki-Oh* fame performs some solid Eagle Claw in his cameo appearance in the recent wuxia-fantasy *The Butterfly Lovers* (2008).

Passage of the Dragon (1981)

Passage of the Dragon, also known as *Twins of Kung Fu*, is a relatively obscure little kung fu film made in the waning days of the genre. The actors in it aren't that very well known, save a young Simon Yam in an early role as one of the supporting protagonists and genre veteran Jason Pai Piao as one of the villains. The director, Ang Saan, who was also the film`s fight choreographer, is not a very well known name in Hong Kong cinema and his credits as action director are for films that are even more obscure than this film. Nonetheless, the film offers a fair amount of solid, quality kung fu action, including a finale that runs about 18 minutes and has been considered by some to be one of the best moments in old school fighting.

The climatic showdown can be divided into two major fights: three supporting protagonists vs. Jason Pai Piao, and the main showdown, Michelle Mai and Jackie Liu against Hon Gwok-Choi. It is the latter we especially want to look at, considering that this chapter's focus on the Eagle Claw style will immediately bring our attention to Hon Gwok-Choi. He does use the Northern Eagle Claw throughout the first half of the climax, after which he and the two leads switch to more weapons-oriented combat (a spear for Mr. Hon and bullwhips for the Michelle and Jackie).

Hon really steals the show from our two leads, the two of whom really aren't that impressive in the fight. Hon uses some fairly authentic Northern Eagle, mixing a lot of joint locks with five-fingered eagle strikes and few well-thrown kicks in for good measure. He never allows his footwork to outdo his handwork, but he does it in a very crisp and powerful way. His handwork is quite fast and he believably is able to fend off attacks from Michelle Mai and Jackie Liu. He does a lot of wrist grabbing and manipulation in the fight, which is part of the style. As in most film's dealing with *ying jow pai*, Hon often goes for nerves and blood vessels around the neck and in the armpit areas with his claws.

This was far from being Hon's first appearance in Hong Kong cinema; he had been working in the genre since the late 1960s. Hon is Peking Opera trained and thus is proficient in a number of styles and acrobatics He has played major and supporting roles in dozens of feature films for both major studios like the Shaw Bros and independent studios like Seasonal Films. He's probably best known for showing up alongside Bruce Liang in a lot of his films during the 1970s.. Most recently, Hon Gwok-Choi showed up in one fight sequence of Johnnie To's acclaimed *Running on Karma* (2003), showing us that he was just as flexible at around 50 that he was a few decades earlier. While not a whole lot of films really do much to showcase the man's talent, this film more than makes up for it. He's one of the better villains we've seen in post-*Drunken Master* kung fu comedy, so he has that going for him.

Speaking of post-*Drunken Master*, the Ang Saan's choreography is very much in that same style. There are a number of a traditional styles like the dragon, snake, and phoenix eye technique (part of the Leopard style) to be seen mixed with the usual acrobatics, group fighting, and generic mix of Southern styles. Since Hon Gwok-Choi sticks to the Eagle Claw for most of the fight, before going back to the spear, his fighting sticks out a lot more in terms of being a style showcase. The action direction is fast and the moves are crisp, at least in the fight between Hon and the brother/sister team. The use of the bullwhip in the second half of the fight is pretty interesting, considering how little the weapon is used in martial arts cinema, especially in traditional films.

And obscure little film with a great fight and a showcase for one of the more prolific, but lesser-known names in the genre.

Kickboxer (1993)

Back in the early 1990s, when the historical wire-fu craze was hitting full swing, it seemed that nearly every important historical figure in martial arts would get some movie dedicated to him. It also seemed that Jet Li would play all of these people at least once. Chang Sanfeng, Fong Sai Yuk, Hong Xiguan, Wong Fei Hung, Beggar So Hat Yee, Wong Kei Ying, and the Yim Wing Chun all got films about them during this period. The most popular of these films was the *Once Upon a Time in China* franchise, which consisted seven official films and one unofficial prequel (that being Yuen Woo-Ping's *Iron Monkey*). Beyond those films, there was a spoof (Wong Jing's *Last Hero in China*) and two films that are generally counted as spin-offs. One of them was Yuen Woo-Ping's *Heroes Among Heroes* (1993), which tells the story of Beggar So, the original drunken master himself. The other is *Kickboxer*, which tells the story of Gwai Geuk Chat (translated as "Ghost Foot Seven"), known as "Clubfoot" in the *Once Upon a Time in China* series.

In the final set piece, Lau Zhai (Yuen Biao) storms the manor owned by a villainous opium dealer, played by Yuen Wah. The villain had previously captured and murdered a police constable and now Lau Zhai wants revenge. After a prolonged fight against the villain's henchmen, the two face each other in a deadly final duel. It's Lau Zhai's kicks against the bad guy's Eagle Claw style.

Yuen Biao and Yuen Wah are great martial artists and were two of the most flexible and acrobatic guys in the business at one point. Being trained in Peking Opera, they have knowledge of multiple styles, not to mention both having trained in *tae kwon do* following their training at their Peking Opera school. Both of them are accomplished action directors and stuntmen[45], too. This would be the fourth and final time that two would mix it up onscreen. In their first showdown, in the film *Eastern Condors* (1987),

---

[45] Yuen Biao had experience as a stuntman for people like Lau Kar-Wing and even Jackie Chan while Yuen Wah went as far as to be the stunt double for Bruce Lee on occasion.

Yuen Wah overpowered Yuen Biao with his Eagle Claw style. Two years later, in *The Iceman Cometh*, Yuen Biao and Yuen Wah would duke it out with swords, guns, and then some awesome kicks courtesy of Biao at the film's climax. In 1991, Yuen Biao would try his hand at directing in *A Kid from Tibet* and the two would go at with swords and fisticuffs again in a fight just as entertaining as the ones preceding it.

And finally we have this fight. Yuen Biao's kicks are quite good, despite the fact that injuries over the years and dampened his leg skills quite a bit more than his brothers Jackie Chan or Yuen Tak. Nonetheless, Yuen Biao proves to be quite acrobatic in his late 30s and is always a joy to watch. In one sequence on top of a table, Yuen Biao performs some break dancing moves that lead into a ground-based kick. His round and spinning kicks are all solid, too.

Yuen Wah makes a great villain with his deadly Eagle Claw technique. Although he uses the five-finger claw at some moments in the fight, Wah sticks with the three-finger Eagle Claw associated with the Southern, or Shaolin Eagle Claw technique. He uses the claw mainly for grabbing Yuen Biao's legs during kicks and throwing him to the ground. He does use his claws for some more complex arm locks, in addition to a bit of flesh tearing. Yuen Wah was also just as good a kicker as Biao was, and he gets to show off a few solid kicks, including some aerial ones in this fight.

A lot of these films from the 1990s are understandably attacked by martial arts purists for their excess of wire tricks and lack of actual technique. What's refreshing about this film is that action directors Yuen Biao and Yuen Miu are content to keep the wires to a minimum and focus on the actors' real abilities. Most of the wires in the final portion of the fight are used for people getting knocked back several yards. At the very end of the fight, the two combatants jump on top of a chandelier and continue their duel until the chandelier falls. While it may be considered a bit exaggerated, scenarios like that were common at the time and it really could've been worse. Nonetheless, Yuen Biao, who was a co-choreographer on most of Sammo Hung's films from the late 1970s all throughout the 1980s brings in the 1980s flavor of hard-hitting action that favors real hits and kicks to the wire stuff. Yuen Miu, who was the action director on a number of Sammo Hung movies during the 1990s, like *Slickers vs. Killers* and *Don't Give a Damn* provides solid support. Miu was one of the Seven Fortunes who studied at the same Peking Opera school as Yuen Biao, Yuen Wah, Sammo Hung, and Jackie Chan. The work he does here and in those films makes one wonder why never established more of a name for himself as an action director.

The Champions (2008)

There exists something of a 2's rule in Hollywood that two films based on the same theme may be released during the same year. For example, there was *Dante's Peak/Volcano* (1996), *Deep Impact/Armageddon* (1998), and a number of others. In 2008, in Chinese cinema, something similar occurred. Two movies emphasizing Mainland *wushu* were produced and released to theaters. One film was *Wushu: The Young Generation*, which was produced by Jackie Chan and starred Sammo Hung. The other was *The Champions*. While both films sought to showcase Chinese *wushu* and give it the attention it deserves, the main focus of each film was a bit different. The former was made in hopes of finding new talent for onscreen action, considering that most of the beloved actors for Hong Kong action cinema are getting on in age. The latter, however, was more a Nationalistic tale capitalizing on the 2008 Olympic Games being held in China.

As one can imagine, there are quite a few fights highlighting *wushu* and the many styles that are taught to *wushu* practitioners. Master On (Xu Xiangdong) is a Northern Eagle Claw master who is desperate for his sons to compete in the 1936 Olympics. Demanding tryouts, he ends up challenging a number of the athletes who are in line to go be on China's Olympic team. He challenges all of the students, who try to withstand his Eagle Claw with a variety of styles, including more kick-heavy styles and the Northern Mantis style. It isn't until Cheung Chi-kong (Yu Rongguang), the head of the martial arts delegation for the Chinese Olympic Team, steps in that the scuffle is resolved.

It's a short scuffle in question, but Xu Xiangdong, a real-life master of the *yingquan* ("Eagle Fist") style, really steals the show here. He takes on quite a number of students, including the main protagonist, played by non-martial arts master Dicky Cheung. For being a bit advanced in age (he must be in his late 40s or early 50s) and a slight bit rotund, the man can move quite well. He uses a number of high kicks, including a few well-done ax kicks. His handwork is fast and he seems to switch between the five-finger claw associated with Northern Eagle Claw and the three-fingered claw associated with the Shaolin Eagle style. He does a fair amount of *qin na*, or joint locks, which is to be expected in an Eagle Claw fight. It looks really good an is a lot more sustained than the *yingquan* seen in most Mainland *wushu* films.

Xu does get some solid support from his opponents. Dicky Cheung, who isn't really a martial artist, studied *wushu* intensively for six months prior to filming and looks pretty good, especially when he starts performing *tanglangquan*, or the Northern Praying Mantis. There's a female fighter who does some really nice multiple kicks, but is dispatched of rather quickly. Finally, Yu Rongguang, best known for his role in *Iron Monkey* and *My Father is a Hero*, shows up and performs some more Praying Mantis himself. It's really a treat to see so many animal styles on film, after so many years of wire-enhanced swordplay and modern kickboxing.

The choreography is handled by director Tsui Siu-Ming and Benz Kong. Tsui Siu-Ming, the other fat man of Hong Kong action cinema, had previously worked Yu Rongguang on films like *Holy Robe of Shaolin*[46] and *Mirage*. Benz Kong, a lesser-known action director, had collaborated with Tsui Siu-Ming just a few years earlier on *Twins Mission*, which featured the martial talents of Wu Jing, Sammo Hung, and Yuen Wah. The choreography seems very reminiscent of the anachronistic choreography that popped up in 1980s action films with the actors performing traditional kung fu or wushu in a modern setting. The pace is fast and the exchanges are quick, but the moves are based on real movements of traditional styles. There is some wirework used here, although it mainly used for enhancing falls and throws. Dicky Cheung is assisted in some of his aerial kicks by wires, but it's minimal and understandable considering his limited background in martial arts.

Whatever the shortcomings and criticisms leveled at the film itself are, we need more movies that are a return to depicting animal styles on film. *The Forbidden Kingdom* did that a little bit. Lau Kar-Leung did it to some degree in *Drunken Monkey*. Tsui Siu-

---

[46] See chapter on *Bagua Zhang*.

Ming did it with the Eagle and Mantis styles in this film. The fight mentioned here is really a neat little experience and something that martial arts fans need more of.

Praying Mantis Kung Fu

Northern Praying Mantis kung fu (*tanglang quan* in Mandarin) is one of the major Northern styles of kung fu. As one can imagine, the movements of the style are based on the movements of praying mantis. The founder of the style is generally believed to be a martial artist named Wang Lang, although the legends vary. One legend states that Wang Lang was defeated at a martial arts tournament and, as he was leaving, saw a praying mantis attacking the wheels of a cart. Impressed by the mantis's display of courage, Wang Lang sought to copy the insect's movements and thus founded the style. According to another legend, Wang Lang had gone to the Shaolin Temple to challenge the monks and was soundly defeated. While recuperating in the forest, he saw a praying mantis attacking a cicada and was inspired to mimic the animal's method of attack. Upon perfecting the technique, he returned to Shaolin and defeated the monks in combat.

The Northern Praying Mantis style is considered to be something of a "high" style, in that it foregoes hard blocking techniques in favor of parries and grasping techniques. The hand techniques of a mantis stylist mimic the "hook" at the end of mantis's claws and generally are used to attack the eyes or different pressure points. Both strikes and defensive techniques tend to be circular and whip-like in their execution. Most of the kicks found in the style were taken from the monkey style and assimilated into it.

There also exists a Southern Praying Mantis style of kung fu, often known as *chow gar*. The style has its roots in Southern China in the Hakka region around the Pearl River. It has very little, if anything, in common with Northern Praying Mantis and shares similarities with other Shaolin animal styles: deep, strong stances; short, quick strikes; few kicking techniques; and the use of the forearm as a striking surface. Southern Praying Mantis practitioners don't mimic the mantis itself like their Northern counterparts, but they do use clawing hand techniques which help them grasp and control their opponent's arms.

Like the Eagle Claw style, the Northern Mantis technique frequently pops up in Hong Kong and Taiwanese martial arts films as the style performed by the main villain. Thus, the Northern Praying Mantis technique functions as a polar opposite for the protagonist's Southern technique. One of the actors who most used the mantis style in film is probably Chang Yi, who was a Peking Opera-trained actor who played the main heavy in some of the better Taiwanese films of the traditional era, including *Eagle's Claw* (1977) and *Shaolin Iron Claws* (1978). He also used the style in the Bruce Li film *Ming Patriots* (1976), with which he stole the show. Fung Hak-On is another actor who frequently used the Mantis style, whom we'll discuss in more depth in the next section. Hwang Jang Lee gets to perform the Drunken Mantis technique in *Dance of the Drunk Mantis* (1979), the unofficial sequel to *The Drunken Master* (1978). Sammo Hung can be seen using the mantis style in *Shaolin Traitorous* (1976), although he's not the main villain here. There is some good mantis style performed by Taiwanese genre veteran Lung Fei in *Snaky Knight against Mantis* (1978).

But of course, there are some heroes that portray the Northern Mantis style in a more positive light. Taiwanese action powerhouse Don Wong Tao does some solid mantis boxing in *Death Duel of Kung Fu* (1979) and *To Catch a Ninja* (1984). Lau Kar-Leung directed David Chiang as the founder of the mantis style in the Shaw Bros film *The Deadly Mantis* (1977), although the film takes great liberties with the legend. Jackie Chan performs the mantis style briefly in the finale to *New Fist of Fury* (1976). There is a film called *Death Duel of the Mantis* (1979) which focuses on that style. Finally, veteran Taiwanese action director Tommy Lee plays a heroic mantis stylist in Lee Tso-Nam's classic *Phantom Kung Fu* (1978).

Because the Northern Mantis style is taught in most Mainland wushu schools, many Mainland-produced films or films starring wushu-trained actors will feature the style. One of the villains in *Young Hero of Shaolin 2* (1986) performs a Mantis variation. Cynthia Rothrock performs the style briefly in *The Magic Crystal* (1986). Jet Li and Yue Hoi team up to use the mantis style against Yu Chenghui in *Martial Arts of Shaolin* (1986). Yue Hoi uses that style in a lot of films, including Yuen Woo-Ping's *Tai Chi II* (1996), which features a nice demonstration from him and Wu Jing. The style is used several times in the recent martial arts blockbuster *The Champions* (2008), directed by Tsui Siu-Ming.

Warriors Two (1978)

One of the greatest onscreen Northern Mantis stylists was a fellow named Fung Hak-On. Fung was one of those unfortunate types born with a face that almost immediately labeled him as a villain, what with his high cheek bones and devilish face. He spent a good portion of his career playing villains, often as a rapist. Fung Hak-On was trained in Peking Opera under Madame Fan Fok-fa became a expert in a number of styles, in addition to being trained as a stuntman. He is best known for playing a villain, which he has done from the 1970s up until recently, appearing as one of the killer harpists in Stephen Chow's *Kung Fu Hustle*.

In 1974, Chang Cheh directed *Five Shaolin Masters*, which kicked off Chang Cheh's "Shaolin cycle". Fung plays a Manchu official trained in the Northern Mantis style, and squares off with Chi Kuan-Chun in the lengthy final fight. In *Shaolin Martial Arts*, made the same year, he can be seen performing the same style in climatic brawl as well. When Fung Hak-On left the Shaw Bros to work for Golden Harvest, he appeared as the rapist villain in Sammo Hung's directorial debut *The Iron-Fisted Monk* (1977) and used the Mantis style against Sammo's Southern animal styles in the final showdown. However, it is in this film that Fung Hak-On gave his very best Mantis demonstration in a fight some consider to be one of the best around.

In the final showdown, two *wing chun* students, Fei (Sammo Hung) and Hua (Casanova Wong), confront an evil businessman, Mo (Fung Hak-On), who was responsible for the death of their master and for trying to use treachery to take over the town. After an extended battle with Mo's henchmen, Fei and Hua wipe them all out and Mo is left to take on the two heroes by himself. Nonetheless, Mo is an expert Mantis expert and the two just may or may not make it out of the final fight alive.

Fung Hak-On is simply magnificent in this particular fight. In black garb and a hairpiece that gives his head a slightly sloping look; he looks like a vampire in this fight.

His mantis techniques are performed with great speed with little undercranking used to speed things up. He uses his fingers to grab, parry, and throw, and in a few moments, to even puncture his opponents' skin. In one great moment, he steps up onto Casanova Wong's knee and pushes off to deliver a wonderful flying knee smash to Wong's head. Fung handles to the simultaneous attacks from both Sammo Hung and Wong with great aplomb, never allowing himself to slow down amidst the obviously complex choreography.

The choreography was handled by Sammo Hung and this fight shows us how much of a genius Hung was in the choreography arena. This fight accounts for some of the fastest and most entertaining old school fighting ever caught on film, bar none. Sammo keeps the mantis sequences authentic, although he does through in a few creative touches. In one notable scene, Fung Hak-On is shown with his body slanted a near-45° angle while performing numerous hand techniques against Sammo and Casanova. It's a move that is achieved with wires, but they are obviously being used only for a compelling visual and not in any way to take the place of Fung's skills.

Despite the fact that the film is considered to be a *wing chun* showcase film, Sammo allows does not limit himself to just that style. Sammo uses *wing chun*, but also throws in a smattering of hand-based Southern styles, like the crane style, into his fighting. One of the stranger choices for the character of Moneychanger Hua, a real-life figure in the history of *wing chun*, was Casanova Wong, who was a Korean *tae kwon do* stylist. There's a sharp difference between the kick-oriented *tae kwon do* and the hand-oriented *wing chun*, especially seeing as how the latter only uses short, low kicks that rarely go above the abdomen. Nonetheless, Casanova's handwork is solid throughout and he does kick during the fight. Of special note is a magnificent jumping spin kick that Casanova performs while jumping over a table.

Warriors Two represents a high point in Fung Hak-On's career as an screen fighter that he would never quite reach again during his career, although he would do some stellar work in films like *Gold Hunters* (1980) and *Snake Deadly Act* (1979). This fight also represents the zenith of action direction that Sammo Hung would reach during the 1970s. And most of all, it is the single best sequence involving the Northern Mantis style ever committed to celluloid. It's just that great a fight.

Invincible Shaolin (1978)

When it comes to Southern Mantis boxing on screen, there's one name to keep in mind for that rather (in a cinematic sense) rare style of kung fu: Lo Meng. Lo Meng was a rather muscular fellow who trained in *chow gar* and started working for the Shaw Brothers in the late 1970s. He's something of a favorite among martial arts fans for having been a member of the famous Venom Mob troupe. While Kuo Chi, Lu Feng, and Chen Shiang were the weapons and acrobatics experts of the troupe, and Sun Chien was the kicker of the gang, Lo Meng was the hand stylist and the muscle of the group. In *The Five Deadly Venoms* (1978) he played the near-indestructible Toad venom. In *Kid with the Golden Arm* (1979), another Venom Mob favorite, he played the titular villain. Although he occasionally played the villain, he usually played the hero who'd end up dying (heroically) before the film ended, often before the final fight. He was one of the few members of the troupe who ended up having something resembling a solid career after the Shaw Brothers declined in the early 1980s.

Of all the films that Lo Meng made, *Invincible Shaolin* (1978) went to greatest lengths to accurately portray the Southern Mantis style of kung fu, although *Shaolin Rescuers* (1979) and *Killer Army* (1980) come pretty close. This film is about three students of Southern Shaolin kung fu that are tricked into thinking that their compatriots were murdered by the three Northern stylists working for the local Manchu warlord. Lo Meng is one of the Southern students, and is told by his master to study the mantis style under a retired master. Upon completing his training, he teams up with his two colleagues (played by Kuo Chi and Wei Pai). The three confront the three Northern stylists (played by Lu Feng, Chiang Sheng, and Sun Chien), with Lo Meng taking on Lu Feng, who is an expert in the Northern Iron Palm style.

The final fight is broken up into three segments, which include Wei Pai (using *wing chun*) taking on Sun Chien's northern kicks[47] and Kuo Chi (pole) taking on Chiang Shang (jointed, or thrashing pole). We want to focus on Lo Meng and Lu Feng's duel. This is one of the purist demonstrations of *chow gar* on film, as it was the purpose of the fight itself. The other Venom Mob films feature Lo Meng using *chow gar*, but it is kind of dressed up with a little bit of movie fu to become some other style, like deaf boxing (in *Crippled Avengers*) or toad kung fu (*The Five Deadly Venoms*). So here we have a less-diluted version of the style. One can see Lo Meng grabbing with all of his fingers and not just one or two, putting the Southern Mantis style more in line with Southern Shaolin kung fu rather than the Northern Mantis style. He uses his fists a lot in this fight scene, as well as deep stances. One may also note that the style's emphasis on withstanding blows is given both in Lo Meng's training sequence and in this fight.

Robert Tai was the principal choreographer of this fight and he does quite a good job here. Despite the fact that he is known for his wacky wire-fu and ninja antics from a lot of his later independent films, Tai keeps things realistic and relatively authentic here. The only time in the fight between Lo Meng and Lu Feng that things get a bit fantastic is when Lu Feng knocks a bamboo tree over and Lo Meng uses his mantis boxing to strike a path through the tree. We should also note that, being a Chang Cheh film, there is a bit of gruesome violence at the end of their fight when Lo Meng rips open the skin on Lu Feng's chest, briefly exposing his sternum. Those two bits aside, it's a fast and intricate exchange of hand techniques between the two and a very satisfying fight.

Shaolin Drunken Monk (1982)

When we talk about traditional kung fu films, we often consider those only made in Hong Kong, Taiwan, and Mainland China. Hong Kong films have generally been the most well known, considering that Hong Kong was home to the big studios like The Shaw Brothers and Golden Harvest, where most of the biggest starts got their starts. Taiwanese cinema has traditionally been considered the low-budget counterpart to Hong Kong, home to second-tier martial arts talent or first-tier actors who had suffered a decline in their popularity in Hong Kong, but had willing fans in Taiwan. Then there's Mainland China, who waited until the final days of the genre's popularity to start

---

[47] - Which is actually *tae kwon do*.

producing films, but, when they did, filled the films full of talented *wushu* practitioners and some of the most beautiful scenery you'll ever see on film. Now, what some people don't know is that South Korea participated in the traditional kung fu film as well.

South Korea started producing low budget kung fu films around the late 1970s, generally with Korean actors who had previous experience in Chinese cinema. Sometimes Chinese actors or action directors would be brought on to direct the fight scenes. Many Korean productions would try to imitate their Chinese contemporaries, setting their films in China and trying to portray Chinese kung fu or the Shaolin Temple. Korean actors who had background in Chinese cinema like Casanova Wong, Dragon Lee, Hwang Jang Lee, Elton Chong, and others were the biggest stars in these films. One name that garnered a lot of respect among the biggest fans of the genre is a fellow named Eagle Han Ying.

Like his contemporaries, Eagle Han Ying was trained in Korean martial arts, specifically *tae kwon do* and was thus a rather talented kicker. Nonetheless, he found himself being typecast as the villain in most of his films, and, like Hwang Jang Lee, was instructed by his action director to compliment his legwork with Chinese kung fu. Like Hwang, he occasionally used the Eagle Claw to compliment his kicking. However, what he most well-known is for playing a high kicking mantis stylist in his films. In *Death Duel of Kung Fu* (1979), he stole the show from such greats as John Liu and Don Wong Tao in the film's big finale. In *South Shaolin vs. North Shaolin* (1984), he used the mantis, eagle, and snake techniques against Casanova Wong. However, his best mantis fist, if not his kicking, was to be found in the Korean-Taiwanese co-production *Shaolin Drunken Monk*, opposite the legendary Gordon Liu.

The finale begins with Eagle Han Ying and a cohort of his confronting a one-armed fighter, played by Chin Yuet-Sang, the film's principal action director. Despite his good kung fu, Chin is no match for the tag-team mantis boxing that Han Ying and his colleague perform. He takes quite a beating before Gordon Liu shows up. Obviously, they divvy up their opponents and Gordon Liu takes on Han Ying's lackey with his Southern animal styles while Chin goes one-on-one with Han Ying. Although Gordon Liu is able to find an easy victory on his side, Chin is overpowered and beaten to death. Seething with anger, Gordon confronts Han Ying and finds that even his animal styles are no match for the Northern Mantis style. In the final part of the fight, Gordon switches styles to something more appropriate for a film called *Shaolin Drunken Monk.*

Han Ying performs his best mantis fist in this fight. Unlike *Death Duel in Kung Fu*, which had a more electrifying final fight, the mantis fist was treated more as a compliment to Han Ying's formidable kicking prowess. Here, Han Ying is a mantis stylist front and center. He does perform a few solid aerial kicks, but his hand techniques are definitely highlighted this around. He does a lot of striking with his fingers, going for a number of pressure points. Moreover, true to the spirit of the style, Han Ying does not block with his mantis fist as much as he simply parries and grabs his opponents' arms, opening them up for grabbing or striking techniques. His kicks are well executed and his footwork is solid.

One of the more interesting parts of the fight is in the first quarter of the duel, when Han Ying and his colleague are ganging up on Chin Yuet Sang. They attack Chin in unison and, every time they are able to strike him or knock him back, they get into a fighting pose together. At one point, Han's colleague grabs him by the waist and lifts him up, allowing him to attack only with his hands for some odd reason.

Gordon Liu is given a solid showcase here, focusing his attacks mainly on the tiger and drunken styles. His tiger style is quite solid and is as good as anything that Chen Sing did in his career. We should also look at his drunken boxing. This isn't the first time that Gordon Liu fought using drunken boxing; he used it against a Japanese karate expert in *Heroes of the East* (1978). It's faster and more brutal here; his character is definitely not holding back. Although he doesn't reach Jackie Chan heights in this fight, he looks good using it and he performs it with more power than other users have done. What's more interesting is that the drunken technique is a style belonging to the Tiger family and the short, fast strikes that Gordon performs are very similar to the Tiger style in spirit, if not execution.

Chin Yuet Sang had previously choreographed Han Ying in *Death Duel of Kung* and obviously was familiar with the man's talents. He does a great job of showing us that, like Han Ying's contemporary Hwang Jang Lee, he was more than simply his feet. This final fight of *Death Duel of Kung Fu* features some of the better handwork performed by a Korean *tae kwon do* stylist. It's fast, intricate, and reasonably true to the style. Despite the fact that the film itself may not amount to more than a low-budget independent film made at a time that the genre was fast becoming an anachronism, there is some wonderful mantis fist on display here.

Part 3:

The Internal Styles

Tai Chi Chuan (Taijiquan)

Tai Chi Chuan (generally spelled *taijiquan* nowadays) is the Chinese martial arts style that is probably most misunderstood by the common populace. When someone mentions tai chi, most people will think of elderly people who practice it in parks as a form of exercise. While the movements and breathing associated with tai chi are certainly beneficial to a person's health, it is also powerful fighting style to those who master the technique.

The origins of tai chi are long and complicated, due to the large number of conflicting stories and legends about its founders. Its founder is generally considered to be Zhang Sanfeng, a Taoist monk from the Ming Dynasty. Depending on what story you're reading, Zhang either lived in the Ming Dynasty, the Yuan Dynasty, the Song Dynasty, or, in some versions, all three(!). According to one legend, which is the basis of the 1993 film *The Tai Chi Master*, Zhang had studied at the Shaolin Temple and applied Taoist principles, including breathing techniques, to his kung fu to create tai chi. According to other legends, he didn't found tai chi as much as he established certain movements and principles that others would develop into tai chi. Others argue that Zhang Sanfeng is simply a myth and that tai chi chuan was founded by Chen Wangting (1600-1680), for whom the Chen Tai Chi style is named.

Tai Chi Chuan is one of the three main "internal" styles of Chinese kung fu. When we say "internal", we refer to the necessity of the cultivation of one's *qi*, or inner energy, as an important part of practicing the style. Thus, while practicing, movements tend to be slower and put less emphasis on speed and power (although this obviously will change when applied in a real fight). Tai Chi is also a "soft" style, meaning that it does not depend on sheer, brute force as much as it does on redirecting the force of your opponent's attacks. Tai chi stylists will strike in a variety of ways and will use a variety of body parts, including fists, palms, both sides of the hand, the back of the hand, forearms, hips, elbows, shoulders, and even their backs. Open-handed strikes and pushing are probably the most common techniques. In a fight, a tai chi practitioner will attempt to exploit his opponent's center of gravity and thus throw him off balance.

There are several schools of Tai Chi Chuan. The oldest is Chen Style Tai Chi Chuan, which was founded in the 17th century. Chen Tai chi is distinguished from the other tai chi styles by its low stances and occasional bursts of energy. The second and most-practiced style is Yang style Tai Chi Chuan. It was founded by Yang Luchan, a disciple of a Chen Tai Chi master, during the 19th century. Yang Style Tai Chi Chuan dispenses with a lot of the more erupt, powerful movements of its predecessor in favor of slower, more sweeping movements. Another style, the Wu Style of Tai Chi Chuan, is also very popular today and gives a greater emphasis on grappling, pressure point attacks, joint locks, and throwing techniques than the other two styles.

VHS cover for *Revenge of the Tai Chi Master* (1983).

Tai Chi Chuan has had limited opportunities to be shown on film. Reference to it was made as early as 1972 in the Angela Mao film, *Lady Whirlwind*, it being the style that Chang Yi learns. However, like other movies made in the 1970s, like *Tai Chi Shadow Boxing* and *Born Invincible*, the "tai chi" on display is not the real thing. The earliest example of real tai chi being used is the 1974 Shaw Brothers classic, *The Shadow Boxer*. The fights in that movie were choreographed by a young Yuen Woo-Ping, who would, over the years, become the best director and choreographer of tai chi chuan on film.

As Tai Chi Chuan is taught at most wushu academies in the People's Republic of China, a lot of the tai chi on film is performed by Mainland actors (or at least actors who studied wushu on the Mainland). Mainland films like *Tai Chi Chuan* (*Revenge of the Tai Chi Master* – 1983) and *The Magic Beggar* (1985) both prominently feature tai chi, although the choreography in the latter is very sloppy. In 1984, Yuen Woo-Ping directed an unknown Donnie Yen in *Drunken Tai Chi*. Yuen would go on to direct the 1993 Jet Li classic *The Tai Chi Master* and *Tai Chi 2* (1996), which was the debut of fan favorite Jacky Wu Jing. Jet Li has used tai chi frequently in his movies, like *Kung Fu Cult Master* (1993) and *Dr. Wei and the Scripture with No Words* (1996), in addition to other movies where the techniques are integrated with other styles.

Last year, actor-director Stephen Fung directed a pair of films that served as a steampunk retelling of Yang Luchan's life: *Tai Chi 0* and *Tai Chi Hero*. Mainland wushu newcomer Jaden Yuan plays Yang, although the film takes great liberties (and I mean "great") with the story. Sammo Hung helmed the action in both films and even received a nomination for Best Action Design for *Tai Chi 0*. Jaden's talents are wasted in the first film, with most of the tai chi being performed by non-martial arts actors Tony Leung Kar-Fei and Angelababy[48]. Jaden finally busts out in *Tai Chi Hero* after his character has sex with Angelababy[49] and results are far more satisfying, although not up to Yuen Woo-Ping's standards. Speaking of which, Woo-Ping teamed up with Keanu Reeves to make *Man of Tai Chi*, starring Tiger Chen, a member of Yuen's stunt team.

The appeal of tai chi on film is the fact that so many people think of it more as an exercise than a martial art, and thus it becomes all the more impressive to see it used as a fight. It's quite a sight to behold. You might say that cinematic tai chi chuan is kind of

---

[48] - Yes, this is a name.

[49] - I'm not lying, this is the actress's name.

like watching what Steven Seagal did at the peak of his abilities, only more graceful and beautiful.

Drunken Tai Chi (1984)

Drunken Tai Chi sticks out for a number of reasons, one of them being that it was Donnie Yen's debut film. Moreover, despite the fact that the movie is not much more than a remake of director Yuen Woo-Ping's previous *The Drunken Master* (1978), the movie contains some of the most realistically-portrayed *tai chi chuan* on film. Compare this with Yuen Woo-Ping's other tai chi epics, *The Tai Chi Master* (1993) and *Tai Chi 2* (1996). While those films both featured some great tai chi, they were a lot more exaggerated and featured moments like the hero of the latter using his queue as a weapon and Jet Li in the former flying around hitting people with his head. This movie, like *The Tai Chi Master*, doesn't have a whole lot of tai chi until the final act, but the final fight is a wonderful showcase for the style.

The last showdown is between Donnie Yen and Yuen Shun-Yi (brother of Yuen Woo-Ping), who's essentially playing the same role he had played two years earlier in *Dreadnaught*. Yuen Shun-Yi's "The Killer" character has already killed Yen's father and brother and has been contracted to kill Yen as well. Yen, obviously, is willing to take Yuen on to avenge his family's murder.

Probably more so than other movies involving *tai chi chuan*, this fight demonstrates the contrasts between "hard" and "soft" styles. Yuen Shun-Yi's fighting style, which is apparently an amalgam of Southern hand-based techniques, is the epitome of "hard" kung fu. This idea is emphasized in the moment in which Shun-Yee removes his gloves to show hands covered with calluses. His attacks are based on sheer brute force, his blocks are meant to hurt as much as defend, and his throws are intense. Shun-Yi is an underrated screen fighter and pulls of his role in this fight with appropriate menace (as an actor) and intensity (as a fighter).

Donnie Yen does some great *tai chi chuan* in this fight. Such is to be expected, as Donnie's mother, Bow Sim-Mak, was renowned *tai chi* teacher in the United States and in Southern China. Donnie performs all of the moves, handwork, throws, and strikes with near-perfect exactness. It is one of Donnie's better moments. Interestingly enough, he hasn't used more pure *tai chi* in movies, although his knowledge of the style has shown up in films like *Crystal Hunt* (1991) and the TV series *Fist of Fury* (1995), although his demonstrations of the art were mixed with other styles.

One of the more interesting aspects of Taoist philosophy is the analogy of water. Water is considered to be something of a soft and formless element, but we know that the rushing action of water can wear down rock. Thus water can be both soft and hard simultaneously. There's a literal interpretation of this principle in the fight, where Donnie Yen spits a jet of water into Yuen Shun-Yi's eye, leaving him with a black eye.

Yuen Woo-Ping shows here that he had improved a lot since 1974, when he choreographed the fight scenes for the early tai chi chuan film *The Shadow Boxer*. The choreography in this scene is something of a transition between the more modern fights that Woo-Ping would choreography later in the decade and the over-choreographed fights he had been doing since the mid-1970s. While the emphasis is on technique here, the moves are quicker, the attacks are more direct, and there is less digression into acrobatics and physical comedy than in other films in the same vein.

Tai Chi Master (1993) (a.k.a. Twin Warriors)

Despite the title, the movie in question only features two fights at the end in which Jet Li's character, the legendary Chang Sanfeng, performs any *tai chi chuan*. This is not to say that the previous fights aren't any good, because the set-pieces involving the Shaolin pole formations and an entire army are incredibly impressive. Nonetheless, the tai chi chuan in this movie only shows up for the last act. Nonetheless, in both the technical and sub-textual senses, the final fight is an important moment in Hong Kong cinema.

The context of the fight is that Chang Sanfeng, the historical founder of tai chi, is taking on his former friend and now mortal enemy, Tianbao, played by Chin Siu-Ho. The latter has become the right-hand man of the evil Ming Dynasty Eunuchs and has been responsible for the ruthless slaughter of rebels, innocent people, and even his own soldiers. With his master, a high-ranking eunuch, held hostage by Sanfeng and Qiaoxue (Michelle Yeoh), Tianbao submits to a duel with Sanfeng.

Up to this point, Chin Siu-Ho's style has been characterized as being "hard". His punches, kicks, breaks, throws, and other techniques have had the sole intent of maiming and crippling his opponents, if not killing them. The viewer will have seen him counter punches from others with punches of his own, resulting in the breaking of the other fighter's hand. Basically, sheer, brute force is the aim of Chin Siu-Ho's fighting style.

Thus, when Jet Li challenges him for the last time, he'll be using his softer tai chi chuan as a counter for Chin's harder Shaolin moves. It makes for an excellent contrast: Chin's brutal punches and kicks against Jet Li's gentler, flowing open-handed attacks and throws. While incredibly stylized due to the trends of the era, the philosophy of combat tai chi is apparent. For example, in one scene, Chin tries to execute a kick against Jet, who catches his leg with his shoulder and strikes him with it, knocking him back.

Jet's character does not use his fists very often in this fight, and when he does, he does so to great effect. Most of the time, however, he's parrying, deflecting, and striking Chin Siu-Ho with the palms or the dorsal side of his hands. Characteristic of tai chi chuan, Jet grabs Chin's arm at the wrist and at the shoulder to throw him to the ground. Most of these moves are performed in slow motion, giving the viewer a good chance to see how tai chi chuan is really applied in combat.

While the hard vs. soft side of the showdown represents an achievement in representing tai chi onscreen, it is nothing that hadn't been seen before—although only the final fight of *Drunken Tai Chi* really matched it. What really is striking about the fight is how it not only portrays the conflict between hard and soft, external and internal in the martial arts, it is a fight that practically becomes a stand-off between authentic, ground-based martial arts (ground-based in that one character practically never flies around during the fight) and over-the-top "wire-fu."

It won't take long for viewers to notice that this fight, among others, is completely over-the-top and unrealistic. However, careful viewers may notice that for the greater part of this fight, it is only Chin Siu-Ho has his martial arts skills enhanced by wires. Yes, he performs all manner of wire-fu, from flying jump kicks that cover about 20 feet in distance to ground-based kicks where he walks along the ground on his hands for several fight while unleashing numerous kicks. In one scene, he runs sideways across the bodies of his fellow soldiers, sending them flying in Jet's direction.

Jet Li, however, stays grounded for all of the fight. It is part of the tai chi philosophy that energy comes from the ground and goes into the body through the feet, which travels through the legs and is stored in the hips, which then emanates through the fingers. Therefore, the ground can become a source of the strength to the fighter. While one may feel that a person who has "mastery over the laws of physics" and thus is flying around, kicking through the air would have a definite advantage in a fight, Jet Li and Yuen Woo-Ping show us that the contrary is true: Chin's flying kicks in fact leave him vulnerable and easy to manipulate. Jet Li's character is able to find strength in the earth and exploit all of Chin's attacks, sending him sprawling to the ground throughout the whole fight. Thus, this fight shows us that as showy as a wire-fu fight can be, it is the ground-based fighting that reigns supreme.

Now, this isn't to say that Jet Li doesn't use wires at all during the entire set-piece. There is one scene where they fight atop a large cargo net and their trampoline-esque antics make it pretty clear that wires are being employed. Nonetheless, the whole sequence becomes the springboard for more moves performed by Jet that are literal interpretations of tai chi philosophy, so it's acceptable.

This is an excellent fight and represents a high point in both Jet Li's and Yuen Woo-Ping's careers. While not their very best, it is one of the pinnacles of tai chi chuan in cinema and proof that there is no better place to turn than Yuen Woo-Ping and his family when it comes to choreographing combat tai chi.

Bagua zhang (Pa Kua Chang)

Bagua Zhang (sometimes written *Pa Kua Chang*) is one of the three "internal" styles of Chinese martial arts (*tai chi chuan* and *hsing-i chuan* being the other two). The style is about 200 years old and was founded by Dong Hai Chuan around 1813. Dong was a master of a Northern kung fu style similar the Long Fist Style (which Jet Li studied) and had traveled to Southern China, where he joined a Taoist sect. One of the practices of the sect was to recite mantras while walking in circles. Dong Hai Chuan combined those circular movements with his own knowledge of martial arts to create *Bagua Zhang*.

Bagua is not defined by any particular types of strikes or kicks, although we should note here that "zhang" in this context means "palm", and thus many of the strikes are made with the palm of the hand. Rather, it is defined by the circular moments that the fighter uses in combat. The circular movements are often compared to guerilla warfare, where the guerillas will attack from all angles or will look for a weak point in the opposing army's defenses, exploit it, and quickly move to another angle of attack. Thus, the *Bagua* practitioner is always moving in circles, ducking and rising and hitting from all angles, seeking to throw his opponent off balance and catch him at a weak angle. When this occurs, the *Bagua* stylist becomes superior to his opponent, no matter how big or strong he is.

Bagua Zhang occasionally appears in kung fu movies. As it is generally taught in Mainland Wushu schools, the style is often seen in movies produced in Mainland China or movies that feature actors from the mainland. Some movies that include demonstrations, albeit really short ones, include *Martial Arts of Shaolin*, *Blade of Fury*, *The Undaunted Wudang* and *Young Hero of Shaolin part 2*. American audiences got a taste of Bagua Zhang in *The One*, starring Jet Li. Two Mainland flicks that revolve around *bagua* are *Pride's Deadly Fury* and *Eight Diagram Lotus Palm*. The action in the latter leaves a lot to be desired.

Holy Robe of Shaolin (1985)

Most kung fu movie fans warmly receive martial arts films produced in Mainland China. Why, you ask? Simple: Whereas Hong Kong movies often (and American movies) are often saddled with making a martial arts movie around a bankable star who doesn't actually have any real martial arts background, Mainland kung fu movies made in the 1980s and the early 1990s employed entire schools or troupes of Wushu practitioners. Thus, the need for wires, quick cuts, and stunt doubles was practically nonexistent, as all the actors were capable of pulling off dazzling moves themselves.

There is a small flaw in this, however. Many of the greatest action directors from Hong Kong, like Lau Kar Leung and Yuen Woo-Ping, had dozens of films and quite a few years to hone their crafts and create the masterpieces for which they are loved by fans of the genre. On the other hand, a lot of Mainland action directors didn't have that same training or experience and it showed on film. Fights often lacked power and seemed more like exhibitions rather than good kung fu fights. To improve this, Mainland filmmakers often would hire choreographers from Hong Kong to help provide a more refined quality to the action, which is the case here. *Holy Robe of Shaolin* is directed and choreographed by Tsui Siu-Ming, whom we might call the "Second Greatest Overweight Martial Arts Actor, Director, and Choreographer", after Sammo Hung.

Poster for *Pride's Deadly Fury* (1983).

The fight in question is a rather short duel near the end of the first act when the Governor comes to the Shaolin Temple to introduce its new "abbot", Wudan stylist Tian Yuan (Yu Rong Guang of *Iron Monkey* fame). The current abbot states that he cannot concede his position without first challenging Tian Yuan's kung fu, and thus the fight begins.

The duel begins with Yu Rong Guang using a lot of Northern techniques, including a number of kicks and acrobatics. You can see some traces of *bagua zhang* in his movements, but it's obvious he's going for a more direct, hard style. He uses his elbows quite a bit here, and he throws some nice spinning kicks. The abbot shows himself to be quite the fighter, using an "external" style with some good handwork and entertaining flips.

In the second half of the fight, Yu Rong Guang switches over to *Bagua Zhang*. You can see Yu fighting with his palms and using more circular movements, both in his footwork and in his hand techniques. His strikes are like pushes and he occasionally uses his shoulders as a weapon, too. It's not an incredibly long scene, but it is very well choreographed by Tsui Siu-Ming, who gives the fight more direction and power than it would've had under a Mainland action director. Sure, there are some acrobatic flourishes here and there, but the fighting is solid and this sticks out as one of the better sequences in the film itself.

There is some more *Bagua Zhang* exhibited in this movie, especially in the finale, which mixes the style with some weapons fighting. For a long time, the only fight scene that rose to the level of this fight is the final fight from *The One*, where the good Jet Li uses this style to defeat the evil Jet Li's *hsing-I* style. In recent years, however, that has changed with a series of Sammo-choreographed *bagua* fights in *Tai Chi Hero* and the one from our next film.

The Grandmaster (2013)

For years Hong Kong arthouse director Wong Kar-Wai tried to get this project off the ground, even before Donnie Yen and Wilson Yip started their own *Ip Man* franchise. During *The Grandmaster's* pre-production phase, non-martial arts actor Tong Leung Chiu-Wai studied the *wing chun* style in preparation for his role as famed teacher Ip Man, while Chang Chen, who became famous in the wake of *Crouching Tiger, Hidden Dragon*'s success, learned the *bajiquan* art. In fact, Chang took first prize in a provincial kung fu tournament on account of his growth in that style. The role of the *baguazhang* stylist and Ip Man's chief challenger, Gong Er, went to Zhang Ziyi, who had previously collaborated with Wong on *2046* and Tony Leung on *Hero*.

Following the defeat of her father, an aged *baguazhang* stylist, Gong Er challenges Ip Man to a duel inside the brothel where the previous challenge had taken place. Thus begins an artistic exchange of palm strikes and punches from both as Ip Man takes the defensive against a relentless Gong Er. The fight takes them around the large room where the duel begins, atop a table, and finally up and down a flight of wooden stairs.

Wong Kar-Wai is known for his beautifully-crafted and photographed movies, even though *The Grandmaster* is only the second martial arts movie he has made (the first being his 1994 *wuxia* film *Ashes of Time*). The flowing, circular movements of *baguazhang* especially lend themselves out to a more calculated visual aesthetic, which Wong is able to capture perfectly. Watch the camera as it moves in circles around the two combatants, the same way Gong Er tries to maneuver around Ip Man. As the footwork and side steps are as important to the style as the palm strikes, Wong Kar-Wai and cinematographer Philippe Le Sourd give us several shots of only the performers' feet moving, as if to emphasize that kung fu, and martial arts in general, is a lot more than simply throwing punches and kicks. Each style is defined by its attacks, but also by its stances, angles of attack, and foot movements, which Wong is trying to underscore here. There is a surfeit of slow motion which is in line with post-millennial flicks like *The Banquet* and *Hero*, but it makes for a neat contrast with the wire-enhanced Impressionistic swordplay of Wong's own *Ashes of Time*.

Tasked with the choreography is the legendary Yuen Woo-Ping himself. The last time Yuen had worked with the *wing chun* style, it was on the exaggerated wire-fu farce *Wing Chun*, which featured more fantasy fighting than authentic *wing chun*, despite having Donnie Yen in the cast. As usual, Yuen's tendencies toward going over-the-top in his fighting are curbed by the director, allowing Yuen to give us one of his most pure displays of authentic martial arts choreography in years. The wirework is refreshingly restrained, limiting itself to a few jumps and flips—watch for the slow-motion butterfly twist that Zhang Ziyi performs in which her lips nearly graze Leung's as she passes over him.

Zhang Ziyi has come close to being typecast in martial arts and *wuxia* movies ever since her breakout role in *Crouching Tiger, Hidden Dragon*. Indeed, her extended cameos in big-budget productions like *Legend of Zu* and *Hero* can easily be understood to be examples of Ziyi riding on the success of Ang Lee's film. From those films to this film, it's easy to see how much she's matured as an actress and a screen fighter, even if it's likely that the latter was never Zhang's intent when getting into the business. Zhang show's a dancer's poise as she performs the soft, rotating movements of her style. Her demeanor has also matured from the frequently petulant character that she played during the first half of her career. This marks her fourth collaboration with Yuen Woo-Ping[50] and also her most satisfying, not to mention one of the best depictions of *baguazhang* on film.

---

[50] - The other two being the aforementioned *Crouching Tiger, Hidden Dragon* and the equally-opulent, if not well-received *The Banquet* (aka *Legend of the Black Scorpion*, because all Asian movies with flying people have to have "Legend" in the title, otherwise we idiot westerners might complain about the film not being grounded in reality). Yuen Woo-Ping also furnished the choreography for the CGI-heavy (and entertainment-light) *The Legend of Zu*, in which the only actual martial arts was a swordfight between Zhang Ziyi and Wu Jing. Said scene could've been cut from the film without affecting the story, but that didn't keep American distributors from making Zhang Ziyi out to be the main character in its trailers.

Hsing-I Chuan (xingyiquan)

Hsing-I Chuan (*Xingyiquan* in Pinyin) is one of the older Chinese martial arts, its origin dating back to the Song Dynasty (960 – 1279 A.D.) and credited to General Yueh Fei. It is the third of China's "internal" martial arts styles, in that the cultivation of one's inner energy, or *qi*, is essential to unlocking the style's potential in combat. Nonetheless, unlike tai chi and *bagua*, *hsing-I* is a far more offensive martial art than its two colleagues.

Hsing-I is said to be the application of spear-fighting techniques to open-handed fighting. Strikes are short, quick, and straight, all of which are directed toward the opponent's "center line" (i.e. the imaginary line running down the middle of a person's face and torso). Thus, points like the throat, solar plexus, groin, and the philtrum are the targets of a hsing-I stylist. Kicks are directed toward the shins, the knees, the groin, and the belly, but rarely higher than that. Movements are linear and direct; when the practitioner has built up his *qi* energy, he then "explodes" into a series of quick and direct attacks designed to take down his opponent as quick as possible with minimum energy spent on defense.

Hsing-I is often taught at Wushu academies and schools in Mainland China. It is considered to be a fairly rare martial art, and thus is not very well represented in martial arts movies. Like *pa-kua*, if *hsing-I* is demonstrated in a movie, it will either be in a movie produced by Mainland China or be performed by an actor who studied wushu in Mainland China. The best example of hsing-I on film is arguably that demonstrated by the evil Jet Li in *The One* (2001). However, since that movie falls out of the criteria of films to be discussed in this book, we'll take a brief look at *Hsing-I* in some Mainland films.

The Undaunted Wudang (1983)

The Undaunted Wudang is a fairly obscure Mainland kung fu film that found some watchers in the West when it was it was released on VHS in the late 1990s and stocked—rather surprisingly—at a number of *Blockbuster Video* stores. When the DVD revolution hit, it was released by Xenon in a DVD pack with the name of the rap group Wu-Tang Clan slapped on it. It features all of those qualities that kung fu fans love about Mainland films: beautiful scenery, numerous fight scenes, and fight choreography that doesn't depend on wires, but on the talent of its Wushu-trained actors.

We can see *hsing-I* being used in the film's major set piece. Set in a tournament between a group of Japanese fighters and Chinese kung fu stylists, two righteous kung fu fighters, played by Zhao Changjun and Li Yu-Wen get in a big fight with the Japanese fighters. The fight spills out of the "ring" and into the streets, where our heroes dish out the kung fu justice until one of them gets killed and the Japanese fighters flee.

VHS cover for *The Undaunted Wu Dang* (1983).

The *hsing-I* seen here is not pure; Li Yu-Wen seems to mix it up with some fancy kicking characteristic of Northern wushu—as stated above, *hsing-I* favored low, direct kicks to fancier high kicks. However, if you watch closely you'll see that a lot of his handwork is made up of the short, angular, and direct strikes that define the style. Zhao Changjun does a few *hsing-I*-influenced strikes, mixed with what looks like tai chi chuan.

The choreography in this scene is relatively realistic by traditional kung fu movies standards: the actors trade a few blows and break up. The moves used, at least in this scene, aren't as ornate and flowery as in other Mainland movies. While there are a few exaggerated jump kicks, the tone of the fight is rather realistic and that really is what matters. Action directors Ma Zheng-Ban and Han Ming-Nan don't exactly reinvent the genre, but the choreography may be a breath of relief for those tired of the so-called "CGI-Fu" or the more mannered fighting from the 1970s. There isn't much to say about the Japanese fighters—they're Chinese actors doing generic judo throws and reverse punches. All in all, it's a solid fight and one opportunity to see a rather rare style in action.

Disciples of Shaolin Temple (1985)

Disciples of Shaolin is an even-more obscure Mainland film that deserved a larger audience than it does. It features a number of different styles on display, including your typical Northern *wushu*, *pa-kua*, Northern Mantis, *hsing-I*, and even some *tai chi chuan*. The choreography, as provided by Wong Chek, who plays the film's villain, and Ng Git-Keung, a Hong Kong actor who made a living as a stuntman, extra, and a hired thug in old kung fu movies. This fight features some of the best choreography in a Mainland film.

The fight begins with a rather excellent weapons duel. Our hero, a Shaolin monk, fights with a staff while Wong Chek wields a saber. The techniques are sharp, quick, and precise. You never get the feeling that the two are putting on a demonstration; they are two men who are really trying to kill each other. The highlight of this part is where the two exchange blows while running down an incredibly steep slope. How they did it without losing their balance is a testament to the talent on display.

It is after both of them are disarmed that we can see them using *hsing-i*. The choreography once again is fast, direct, and sharp. There are lots of quick and short hand-based attacks performed by both Wong Chek and Faang Dung-Yue, who plays the monk. Pay attention and you'll notice how straight and direct most of the attacks are. The exchange goes on for about a minute before Wong Chek switches over to *tai chi chuan*. This must be one of the few films in which the villain uses *tai chi* and not the hero. Faang Dung-Yue switches over to the Eagle's claw style, but is owned by Wong Chek's arm locks, palm strikes, and throws. It isn't until Faang receives some help from his monk colleagues that he's able to get the upper hand.

Yes, like *The Undaunted Wudang*, the *hsing-I* on display is mixed with other styles. But for such a fast and intense display, this film does deserve notice. Excellent talent and choreography merits a high recommendation from us.

Part 4: Non-Chinese Martial Arts

Japanese and Okinawan Open-Hand Styles

Karate is something of an umbrella term for Japanese open-handed martial arts founded on the Ryukyu Islands south of Okinawa. Like *kung fu*, if someone says that they know *karate*, it would be wise to ask them what specific style, since there are a number of styles in existence today. A number of factors influenced the development of *karate*, including the immigration of a number of Chinese families to the region (circ. 1392), who brought with them Chinese martial arts. Chinese *wushu* was combined with fighting arts that already existed among the Ryukyuans and gave rise to *karate*. Another factor that influenced the development of this fighting style was the weapons ban placed on the islands (both Okinawa and the Ryukyu Islands) by the Shimazu Clan (1609). The style was practiced predominately in Okinawa until the beginning of the 20th century, when Gichin Funakoshi, the founder of the *Shotokan* style, worked the popularize *karate* in Japan itself.

Some of the main styles of *karate* practiced today include: *Shotokan, Goju-Ryu, Shito-Ryu, Shorin-ryu, Wado-Ryu, Kyokyushinkai,* and *Budokan. Karate* uses a variety of fighting techniques, including blocks, punches, and kicks. Open-handed techniques, such as chops, hand ridge strikes, and finger jabs are also very common. *Karate* techniques tend to be straight and direct, although some styles like *Goju-ryu* utilize more circular attacks. Animal techniques aren't very common, although some styles like *shito-ryu* do have some crane and tiger movements to them. Throws, take-downs, and other grappling moves are also taught in all *karate* styles.

Karate is pretty common in world martial arts cinema. A lot of American martial arts actors have some training in different *karate* styles. Obviously, *karate* has been the focus of a lot of Japanese films, including a slew of action films made by the legendary Sonny Chiba during the 1970s and early 1980s, including the *Street Fighter* series, *Karate Warriors, The Executioner,* and *Karate Bearfighter.* Korea recently made *Fighter in the Wind*, a film about the founder of *kyukyushinkai*.

Karate has been present in Hong Kong cinema since 1970, when the first modern kung fu film, *The Chinese Boxer*, depicted the Japanese as nothing but evil villains. Such a trend would continue throughout most of the decade, and still can occasionally be seen in recent films. Despite the constant presence of Japanese characters in old school chopsockey films, they were often played by Chinese actors who did more of an approximation of Japanese martial arts and not authentic *karate.* There are a few Japanese actors who appeared in the older Chinese movies, including Yasuaki Kurata, Yasuyoshi Shikamura (*The Big Family*), Goro Kumon (*Hapkido*) and Riki Hashimoto (*Fist of Fury*). Later on, a number on non-Chinese actors who make themselves a constant presence in Chinese cinema would bring authentic *karate* to the screen, including Kurata, Aussie actor Richard Norton (*The Millionaire's Express*), Sonny Chiba-protégé Hiroyuki "Henry" Sanada (*Royal Warriors*), femme fatale Yukari Oshima (*Angel, Avenging Quartet*), Paul Rapovski (*Hitman/Contract Killer*), and a number of others.

Besides *karate*, there are a number of other Japanese styles that have got some attention in Chinese cinema, if not quite as much as *karate*. *Jiu-jitsu* is one of the oldest Japanese martial arts, its origin going back to the 16th century. Its focus is on locks, throws, and ground fighting. In the 19th century, *jiu-jitsu* practitioner Jigoru Kano developed *judo*, which is similar to wrestling and whose philosophy is to turn one's opponent's strength against him. Due to the growing popularity of mixed martial arts (MMA) and Brazilian *jiu-jitsu*, it has started making more appearances in film. Johnnie To's *Throw Down* (2004) is all about *judo*, while Donnie Yen's recent hit films *SPL* (*Kill Zone*)(2005) and *Flash Point* (2007), use a lot of *jiu-jitsu* in addition to the usual kickboxing and *tae kwon do*.

Another style that has gotten rather little attention in Chinese cinema is *aikido*. *Aikido* was founded in the beginning of the 20th century and, like *jiu-jitsu,* uses a lot of joint locks, breaks and throws. There are a lot of circular movements in the style, the idea being that a person can transform an opponent's punch or kick into a throw or lock in a single movement. There are a number of similarities between this style and the Chinese internal styles, notably *tai chi quan*, in which the stomach and legs are the source of one's strength; and *hsing-I,* in which some of the movements are based on the techniques of the spear. The most famous actor to use *aikido* on film is Steven Seagal, who is famous for such films like *Above the Law* (1987), *Hard to Kill* (1990), and *Under Siege* (1993). He worked with Hong Kong action directors Ching Siu-Tung and Lau Chi-Ho on the films *Belly of the Beast* (2003) and *Out for a Kill* (2002), respectively. Actor Yasuaki Kurata also has training in *aikido*, and it can be seen in films like *Anna in Kung Fu Land* (2005).

Finally, the Japanese open-hand style that has its roots closest to Chinese kung fu is *kempo*. There are a number of legends surrounding the style's origin, the main theme generally being that some Japanese man had studied Shaolin kung fu in China and brought it back to Japan, modifying it somewhat and incorporating some of the harder movements of *jiu-jitsu* and *karate*. The style features a lot of a fast handwork and strike combinations, which can be seen in all their beauty in a number of American martial arts films featuring kempo stylist Jeff Speakman, including the classic *The Perfect Weapon* (1991), *Deadly Outbreak* (1995) and *Street Knight* (1993). Other kempo exponents include Yasuaki Kurata, Jim Kelly (*The Tattoo Connection, Enter the Dragon)*, and Carl Scott (*Soul Brothers of Kung Fu, Sun Dragon*).

A Girl Called Tigress (1973)

Alongside Angela Mao[51], Polly Shang Kuan Ling Feng is one of the true kung fu queens of the 1970s. To be honest, she's actually one of the first divas of the genre, as she first showed up in King Hu's classic *Dragon Inn* (1967) and would continue making films up through the late 1970s. Interestingly enough, Polly did not have much martial arts training when her career started. It was while she was at the United Film Corporation that she was schooled in *karate, judo*, and *tae kwon do*. After appearing in a number of *wuxia* films in the late 1960s and early 1970s, she would move on to the "basher" subgenre and that's where she'd really start shining. Unlike her colleague Angela Mao, Polly's style of acting was a bit more tomboyish and loveable, as compared Angela's

---

[51] - See chapter on Korean Open-Handed Styles.

unbridled feminine fury and gaze that could melt a hole in solid steel. Later in her career, Polly would become one of the queens of kung fu weirdness, appearing in films like *Little Hero* (which featured a giant rubber kung fu squid) and *Zodiac Fighters* (which featured kung fu fighters dressed as lobsters).

In the early 1970s, Angela Mao made a series of chopsockey films alongside Japanese actor Yasuaki Kurata, a couple of which are considered to be her best films in terms of fight quality. They are *Seven to One*, *The Rangers*, *A Gathering of Heroes*, and *A Girl Called Tigress*. The films feature choreography that is a few notches above the sloppy, swingy-armed basher choreography that was common in early 1970s movies. In the last film, we have a great example of Japanese martial arts as Polly Kwan and Yasuaki Kurata duke it out, putting all of their skills to the test.

The final fight of *A Girl Called Tigress* stems from a conflict between Polly Kwan, Yasuaki Kurata, and Kam Kong. Polly Kwan's sister was married to Kurata, who was in reality a criminal looking for gold stolen by his wife's ex-lover. Polly Kwan, who was simply looking for her sister, got involved in the conflict. Kam Kong is a policeman who's trying to find the gold as well. Kurata eventually kills his wife and, upon finding the treasure, is confronted by Kam Kong, who wants to bring him to justice. Polly Kwan then jumps into the fight in order to avenge her sister.

VHS Cover for *A Girl Called Tigress* (1973).

The eight-minute climatic fight is divided into two parts: Kam Kong vs. Yasuaki Kurata and Polly Kwan vs. Yasuaki Kurata. The first part is a good fight and shows off both combatants' strengths quite well. Kam Kong, who was trained in *tae kwon do* by Dorian Tan Tao Liang, was a tough fellow and had some very powerful, if basic, kicks. He gets to show off some good spin kicks, although his roundhouse kicks leave a bit to be desired on the altitude front. His handwork here is pretty basic: mainly reverse punches and boxing-type punches.

In the second part, Polly Kwan takes on Kurata and ultimately kills him. Their fight is pretty straight-forward, with the exception of a pick ax that Kurata uses near the end. Polly fights quite fiercely here, one of her best fight scenes period. Her *karate* skills are quite evident: reverse punches, roundhouse kicks, front kicks, backfists, etc. She does it all with more intensity than say, Shih Szu, another female contemporary of hers. Her kicks are pretty good and she gets some good height on them. Look for her spinning kicks and crescent kicks, which are particularly impressive. Most of her fighting is pretty crisp and stands up to any other fight made in the time period outside of what Sammo Hung was doing.

Kurata, who was already something of a genre regular by this time, shines throughout the fight with his Japanese martial arts. Like the other fighters, he does a lot of reverse punches, together with some knife hand and ridge hand attacks. It's miles ahead of some of the swingy arm choreography so popular at the time. His kicks are solid, especially his side and roundhouse kicks. He does some front kicks as well. There's not a lot showy fighting her, but it's the basics done right. And sometimes, the basics done right is better than any sort of wire trick, trampoline jump, special effect, or any other nonsense that occasionally populates films of the genre.

Ninja in the Dragon's Den (1982)

By 1982, the ninja craze was really taking root, what with the success of *Enter the Ninja* (1981) the year before. While Japanese fighters weren't strangers to Chinese cinema—they had been present in the genre since its early days—*ninjitsu* had been given relatively little attention by the early 1980s. There had been *Heroes of the East* (1978) and *Five Element Ninja* (1980), but that was about it for the most part. When the ninja craze began, it was Taiwan that actually embraced the trend more than Hong Kong did, but nevertheless, Hong Kong did come to produce two classy films that are considered classic ninja movies to this day. One of them was Ching Siu-Tung's *Duel to the Death* (1983). The other was this film.

Unlike most of the ninja films produced during this period, Corey Yuen actually casted a Japanese actor to play the Japanese ninja. The actor was Hiroyuki "Henry" Sanada, a member of Sonny Chiba's action club. Sanada had already appeared in a couple of martial arts movies in Japan when the film was made, namely the cult classic *Shogun's Ninja* (1980) and *Samurai Reincarnation* (1981) and was becoming one of the hot talents of the time. When Corey Yuen brought him on the team, Sanada had his team of Japanese stuntmen go with him in order to insure that the film would do justice to Japanese martial arts.

The big fight scene between Hiroyuki Sanada and co-star Conan Lee in the pagoda is one of the best fights in the film, and easily the best fight to showcase Sanada's martial arts prowess. The set-up is rather simple: Conan Lee accuses Sanada of having his killed his adopted uncle. The two go inside the pagoda Conan trains in and start duking it out, each fighter using different tricks and strategies to gain the upper hand. They fight to a draw and end up making their peaces, which will come in handy in a few subsequent fights.

The fight begins with something of a more straight-forward fight. Conan Lee uses kung fu (no identifiable styles) and Hiroyuki Sanada uses his Japanese styles. They fight something to a standstill, at which point they go upstairs and Sanada changes tactics. In the second part of the fight, Sanada starts performing some of his ninja tricks, namely the ability to hang on to the wall a la Spider-Man. They continue fighting with Sanada performing a wide variety of kicks while hanging from the rafters, and which they proceed to the next level of the pagoda and Conan Lee adopts a new (albeit very improbable) strategy, use a white sheet to cover himself and blend in with the wall, after which he'll attack Sanada when he's off guard.

Henry Sanada looks just great throughout the fight, using a kick-heavy style of fighting. Sanada performs a variety of kicks, including roundhouse, spin, hook, and front kicks. They're all performed with great flexibility and coordination, considering the low stances he's in for a big part of the fight. He does do some hand techniques, although he does a surprisingly amount of fist hammers and downward chopping techniques. He's put on a great show of speed and power here.

Conan Lee was a newcomer at this point who was most likely brought on not because of his athletic ability, but probably be he looked frighteningly a lot like Jackie Chan at this point, who was setting himself up to be Hong Kong's top action actor. Conan Lee had little, if any, martial arts experience, but like fan favorite Leung Kar-Yan, was simply an athletic individual who had the uncanny ability to do everything the action director asked him to do. Conan Lee doesn't do anything distinctive; he performs what appears to be an amalgam of Southern styles with a few nice kicks and flashy kick-ups thrown in for good measure. Despite his lack of formal training, Conan Lee demonstrates a physicality here that could've made him a big star, had it not been for his bad attitude that nearly stopped his career in his tracks. He'd make one more important film after this: *Tiger on the Beat* (1988), which co-starred Chow Yun-Fat and was directed by Lau Kar-Leung. His other films were a bit less conspicuous, like the sequel to the aforementioned film, *Prince of the Sun* (1990), and *King of the Sea* (1994).

The choreography here is especially inventive for the early 1980s. Corey Yuen and assistant action director Mang Hoi show us that they'd be a force to be reckoned with in terms of creative action for the next few decades. The hand-to-hand combat in the first part of the fight is quite solid by old school standards, especially considering that the film was made at the twilight of the popularity of the genre in Hong Kong. Where their talent really shines is in the next portion, where Sanada does his wall-crawler routine. It's smart and inventive, a good way to integrate wire tricks into the proceedings without cheapening the skills of Sanada. The next part is a bit out there, what with Conan Lee disguising himself as a white wall; it requires a bit more suspension of disbelief. Nonetheless, the technique on display is undeniable. The action here was nominated for the Best Action Design award at the Hong Kong Film Awards in 1983, but lost to Sammo Hung's *The Prodigal Son*. However, as one of the key fights in a film that represented the last gasps for air in a dying genre, it succeeds quite well.

Twinkle, Twinkle, Lucky Stars (1985)

Sammo Hung, in addition to being one of the greatest action directors, actors, and film directors of all time, was also one of the greatest scouts for new talent in the industry. He brought a lot of people into the Hong Kong film industry, including Yukari Oshima, Billy Chow, Collin Chou, and many others. Although no novice to Hollywood, Australian martial artist Richard Norton was another name who owes a great part of the reputation today to Sammo Hung, since Norton's Hong Kong efforts are remembered far more fondly than most of his American films.

Richard Norton was originally trained in *judo* since, according to Norton himself, was the only martial art available in the city he grew up in. When the opportunity arrived, Norton began to study *karate*, more notably *goju-ryu*, in which he has become a black belt. Norton has since studied a number of other styles, including Brazilian *jiu-jitsu*, *aikido*, *muay thai*, and a number of weapons, too. He worked as a bodyguard for a number of famous rock stars before being brought on to work with Chuck Norris on the ninja classic *The Octagon* (1980). He eventually caught the eye of Sammo Hung and went on to Hong Kong to make a number of classic films, including *The Magic Crystal* (1986), *The Millionaire's Express* (1986), and *City Hunter* (1992). His first film, however, features one of his all-time best fights and that's the fight between him and Sammo Hung in this film.

Describing the context of the fight in what is practically a plotless film is a daunting task. Basically, Richard Norton plays one of three assassins who's trying to kill a woman who's due to receive a package from a murdered friend that contains incriminating evidence against some random drug lord. Jackie Chan and Yuen Biao play cops who are trying to catch the assassins, while Sammo Hung and his gang are protecting the woman (Rosamund Kwan). Eventually all parties end up in the same place and Sammo ends up in a fight with Richard[52]

Their fight is straight kickboxing, that is pure punches, kicks, and blocks. No weapons, few stunts, no BS, just pure fighting. Norton's *goju-ryu* background is quite apparent in the way he fights. He throws a lot of straight reverse punches and uses a number of chopping and ridge-hand techniques, too. He even does some *nukite*, or knife-hand strikes, too. His kicks aren't that flashy, but are powerful. He does a few spinning front kicks and regular front kicks, in addition to some low roundhouse kicks. You can tell he's still trying to get into the Hong Kong rhythm of fighting, but acquits himself quite nicely.

Sammo Hung is, unsurprisingly, spectacular in this part of the fight. He does his usual 1980s kickboxing style with a lot of speed and panache. He gets in the fight's best money moves, including a drop kick to Norton's face and a somersault off a table. He moves quite well for a man of his girth and his moves are just as powerful as Norton's are, especially his kicks.

Philip Ko plays a "Japanese" karate master in *Duel of the Seven Tigers* (1979).

The choreography for this film was provided by the Hung Ga Ban, more specifically Sammo Hung, Yuen Biao, Yuen Wah, Lam Ching-Ying, and Chin Kar-Lok. They did a spectacular job with this fight, as with all of the other fights in this film, especially those dealing with Jackie Chan and Yuen Biao, who get some of their best showcases in this film. Ironically, this film didn't even get nominated for the Best Action Design Award in 1986, although its predecessor, *My Lucky Stars*, did. We think that the action in this film, including the climax that features this fight, surpasses *My Lucky Stars* and that's it's a shame this film wasn't nominated. But then, Awards Ceremonies have not always been the fairest choosers of the best, have they?

Book of Heroes (1986)

---

[52] - There are three other fights in this sequence: Jackie Chan vs. Yasuaki Kurata (who uses the sai); Sammo Hung (armed with tennis rackets) vs. Yasuaki Kurata; and Yuen Biao vs. Chung Faat. All of them are superb pieces of action.

One of the more infamous names in Hong Kong and Taiwanese cinema is Kevin Chu Yin-Ping. Kevin Chu is a director of mainly Taiwanese films, best known for being a hack on the level of Wong Jing. Chu has worked on a number of films that can be described as memorable, if not actually any good. One of his earliest films was *Fantasy Mission Force* (1980), the film that Jackie Chan worked on simply because he owed his life to actor Jimmy Wang Yu. That wacky film mixed WW2 action with Chinese Nazis, ghosts, and amazons and is generally considered to be one of Jackie's all-time worst films. Chu would revisit the Chinese Nazi sub-genre in the female action films *Golden Queen Commando* (1982) and *Pink Force Commando* (1982), both of which starred a pre-stardom Brigitte Lin. During the 1980s and early 1990s, Kevin Chu would be one of the driving forces of the butt-kicking children sub-genre, being director and producer of a number of films in the *Young Dragons: Kung Fu Kids* and *Shaolin Popey* franchises. More recently, Chu directed the film *Kung Fu Dunk* (2008), which tried to copy the success of Stephen Chow's *Shaolin Soccer* (2001), but with less success.

Despite his very spotty track record, Kevin Chu has one unmistakable classic on his filmography: *Book of Heroes*. The film is obviously an attempt to ride the success of films like *Police Story* and *Yes Madam!*, both of which had set the standard for stunt-fueled action the year before. Drawing from latter in terms of making the main protagonists a trio of beautiful, high-kicking women and the former in having stuntmen break unprecedented quantities of glass and furniture, the film is one of the best action films of the 1980s and an unsung hero of liberated female action.

The plot of the film deals with some stolen gold and the attempts of several parties to find it, namely a criminal mastermind, Yamashita (Yasuaki Kurata); a wannabe cop (Lin Xiao Mei) and her cop friend; and the sister of one the original thieves (Elsa Yeung), plus her two male friends. After a number of double-crosses and twists, all of our characters end up at Yamashita's mansion. A fight eventually breaks out (they always do) between the good guys (Lin Xiaomei, Elsa Yeung, their friends) and the bad guys (Kurata, his bodyguard played by Eugene Thomas). Kurata's other bodyguard, Yukari Oshima, eventually reveals herself to be a Japanese interpol agent and joins the cause of our heroes.

To talk effectively about this fight, you'd to have to talk about the various little fights going on simultaneously. For one, we have Elsa Yeung taking on a contingent of thugs. She uses everything from her (admittedly) nice legs to some golf clubs that just happen to be lying around. Elsa Yeung is a regular of Taiwanese cinema and had appeared in a number of director Kevin Chu's films before, most notably *Golden Queen Commando* as a bible-toting, gun-packing gambler. Her most famous role is as the titular character in Lee Tso-Nam's *Challenge of the Lady Ninja*. She fights well her and is choreographed a lot better here than in some of her other movies. There's a running gag in Yeung's fight in which she often has to stop to make sure her hair is okay.

Lin Xiaomei and her partner spend most of the set piece fighting African-American actor Eugene Thomas. Lin is a lesser-known Taiwanese actress who doesn't have much of a filmography beyond this film. Her skills are nonetheless apparent in this fight, as she performs a number of great looking kicks, including one where performs a crescent kick over Thomas' head and then kicks him with her other foot. Thomas also performs quite well, as he has to fend off the attacks from two opponents while dishing out punishment of his own.

Thomas is a well-known (well, at least by genre fans) African-American *karate* stylist who appeared a lot in these Taiwanese films during the 1980s. He's best known for starring alongside Alexander Lo Rei in a number of ninja films made that decade, most notably as "The Black Monk of Harlem" in Robert Tai's *Ninja: The Final Duel* (1987). In addition to the quality fighting, the scene is notable for a bit of racist humor and a bit where the two protagonists try to cuss Thomas out in English[53].

Finally, we have Yukari Oshima and Yasuaki Kurata, two of the greatest Japanese actors to grace the Jade Screen. The two duke it out with fisticuffs, using a style of fighting that could be described as kickboxing with a strong *karate* influence. Oshima does it all in this fight: acrobatics (not really a *karate* trait), punches, kicks, and some nice jump kicks as well. Kurata, does some more conventional *karate*, after which he switches to the *katana* blade for the duration of the fight. Oshima is eventually joined by colleagues Lin Xiaomei and Elsa Yeung.

While Japanese actors were often hired to play villains in Hong Kong films, one of the most prolific of all of them was not only a female, but actually got to play the heroine quite often: the beautiful Yukari Oshima. Yukari Oshima is the femme fatale fighting female that most deserves to be called the successor to Angela Mao, as she possesses not only the physical talent, but the sheer fighting intensity that Angela possessed at her prime. Yukari Oshima was trained in *goju-ryu* as a teenager, as well as in several different types of weapons, including the *sai*, *bo* staff, and *katana*. Her action career began in Taiwan with films like *Kung Fu Wonder Child* and this film, but also took her to Hong Kong, where she appeared in a number of classic modern actioners, like the Jackie Chan-produced *Outlaw Brothers* and the landmark Girls n' Guns film *Angel* (1987). She would make quite a few films in Hong Kong, and then later in the Philippines and China, when the "Girls n' Guns" genre lost its popularity with general audiences.

The action director credits go to an individual named Lam Man-Cheung, who we don't hesitate to say is the best action director to work in Taiwanese cinema from the 1980s onward. One of Lam's earliest films was *Fantasy Mission Force*, which actually featured some decent fights from Jackie Chan in the midst of the madness. Lam basically spearheaded the action direction on the myriad of *Kung Fu Kids* films that came out during the 1980s, culminating in *Kung Fu Kids 6* (1989), whose finale is one of the greatest fights we've ever seen. On the subject of fighting kids, we must also note that Lam Man-Cheung also was the action director for *The Three Ninjas Knuckle up*. Lam Man-Cheung would also perform choreographer chores in Terry "Riki-Oh" Fan Siu-Wong's *The Death Games* (1997), a highly-underrated B-movie, and *City of Darkness* (1998), which featured Donnie Yen. Both of these films feature some of the best martial arts action of the late 1990s.

Lam Man Cheung really gets the best out of everybody in this fight, most especially the three female combatants. It's a shame that Lin Xiaolan didn't do more

---

[53] - I guess we can't be *too* surprised at that, considering that we're talking about a film directed by a man who made *three* films featuring Chinese Nazis and another film where a kid walks around with an elephant mask on his penis. We'll note parenthetically here that there is quite bit more humor here, including a goofy animal fight between Lin Xiaolan's partner and a guy who does a goofy snake style imitation, and any scene dealing with Elsa Yeung's companions and a gang of knife-wielding goons.

films, because she would've been a great addition to the Girls n' Guns lineup of the 1980s. We haven't seen Elsa Yeung perform better than this, and she's at her most beautiful here, too. Yukari Oshima, who at this stage was in the beginning of her career, really gives us a great sample of the mad fighting skills she'd bring to the genre for the next decade. Lam's action direction is just as assured as that of Corey Yuen and Sammo Hung at the same time, and the influences of Jackie Chan, in the sheer quantity of stuff being broken and use of found objects (including those golf clubs that just seem to pop out of nowhere). It's Taiwanese action at its best.

Fist of Legend (1994)

By the time the readers finish the book, they will have noticed how much we hold Yasuaki Kurata to a high esteem, considering how many chapters will have featured fights that he's been a part of. We hold Kurata in almost as high esteem as we hold legendary super kicker Hwang Jang Lee. He is truly one of the great "outsiders" of Hong Kong cinema, and has honestly been a part of such a great tradition of onscreen fighting since the 1971. That's more than three decades of high quality Japanese fighting we've gotten from him. Yasuaki Kurata is practically the epitome of Japanese martial arts on film, even more than Sonny Chiba, simply because Kurata got to work with better action directors for most of his career than Chiba did.

Yasuaki Kurata was trained in a number of styles, including *karate*, *kempo*, *aikido*, and *judo*. His first appearance was in the Shaw Bros film *The Angry Guest*, where he fought opposite Ti Lung and David Chiang. From there on out, he would be typecast as a villain for the next decade in dozens of cheap chopsockey films, although he occasionally starred in stuff of greater quality. It wasn't until 1978 that Lau Kar-Leung cast Kurata as Sanzo, the honorable Japanese ninja, in his masterpiece film *Heroes of the East*. That was one of the first Chinese films to ever show any respect to Japanese martial arts. In the 1980s, Kurata was able to continue his career appearing in some films set in the modern day, like *To Catch a Ninja* and *Twinkle, Twinkle Lucky Stars*. His best showcase films are: *Call Me Dragon*, *Heroes of the East*, *Legend of a Fighter*, *Book of Heroes*, and this film. His career began to slow down a bit in the 1990s, but it was in 1994 that he made another one of his crowning achievements in cinema: *Fist of Legend*.

As most people are already aware, *Fist of Legend* is a remake of Bruce Lee's all-time classic *Fist of Fury*[54] (1972), which tells the story of the murder of real-life kung fu master Huo Yuanjia by the Japanese and how one of his students, Chen Zhen, sought vengeance. This film tells much the same story, but with a more politically correct story and themes of racism and prejudice. Jet Li plays Chen Zhen in this film, whose character is in love with a Japanese girl, Mitsuko (Shinobu Nakayama). Her uncle, Fumio Funakoshi (Yasuaki Kurata) is considered one of Japan's greatest martial artists and decides to challenge Chen Zhen to a duel.

This fight is divided into two sections. In the first part, the two fighters go at pretty much out in the open without any weapons or environment to fight off of. Kurata begins the fight by performing a few wire-assisted jump kicks, notably a flying side kick and a jumping ax kick. They then get to down to business with a flurry of roundhouse kicks and punches. Kurata unloads his skills and *karate* techniques, fighting with a

---

[54] - Also known as *The Chinese Connection* in the U.S.

number punches (mainly reverse), chops, and ridge hand attacks. Most of them are straight in their execution (as opposed to the more circular moves in Chinese martial arts), but they are performed with obvious speed and precision. There are few moments when it looks like Kurata is dipping into *muay thai*, with him grabbing Jet Li's head and trying to perform some knee smashes.

The next part of the fight is what most viewers most remember from it. A sandstorm comes, which starts obscuring Kurata's vision. Jet Li asks if he's okay, but it's obvious Kurata's character is handicapped by the weather. Wanting a fair fight, Jet Li whips out a handkerchief, which he uses to blindfold himself. Kurata does likewise and thus we have a fight between two blindfolded men. There are some nice moves here, and we get to see Kurata dip into his *judo* and *aikido* training in using a number of hand locks and throws. Jet Li, obviously, responds with the *chin na* training which is basic to most Chinese martial arts. There is a bit more strategy in this fight, including red herrings in the form of rocks and dry grass, which they both use to fool each other. It's very clever fight and most people will marvel at what both fighters are capable of doing.

Yasuaki Kurata was 48 years old when he appeared in this film. He doesn't show it, though, and fights as good as he did a decade earlier. This is such a special role for him, as he had spent a good part of his career playing the villain. Here he plays the honorable Japanese master who has some important lessons for his opponent, lessons that Jet Li will end up using in the final fight. We get to see the full range of Kurata's training in the span of five minutes, which is impressive.

Jet Li, whom we've talked little about so far, does an excellent of job of fighting in this fight. Between this fight and all of the other set pieces in the film, there's a reason why 1994 became a point of comparison for practically all of Jet Li's movies made since. After *Romeo Must Die*, when fans sent e-mails to Li about the movie, most of them said that they wanted a movie with *Fist of Legend*-style fights, which eventually came in the form of *Kiss of the Dragon* (2001). Jet Li does a more economical brand of fighting here, although he has some great kicks here, especially a Pelé-bicycle kick during the blindfold sequence. His punches are strong, his kicks are high and fast, and he does do some *chin na* to keep things varied. It is one of his better moments.

The action direction here is provided by Yuen Woo-Ping, who really outdoes himself here. Yuen Woo-Ping had become something of the hottest thing during the early 1990s after he won the Best Action Design award for his work on *Once Upon a Time in China II*, and from 1992 to 1994 hit a peak of creative output that he hadn't enjoyed since the end of the 1977-1982 period. *Fist of Legend* is considered to be one of his best overall films, one of the reasons being that he used wires a lot more sparingly here than he did in a lot of other films he made from 1992 onward. We mentioned the wire-assisted jump kicks that Kurata performs early on. There are a few other wire tricks here, including a spinning jump punch that Jet Li does in the first part[55]. However, none of it takes away from the high quality of fighting on display, for which Jet Li, Yasuaki Kurata, and Yuen Woo-Ping deserve quite a bit of praise. The film was nominated for the Best Action Design Award in 1994, but ultimately lost out to Jackie Chan's *Drunken Master 2*.

---

[55] - Jet Li must have really liked that move, since he does it in *Black Mask* (1996), which was choreographed by Yuen Woo-Ping; and *Romeo Must Die* (2000), which was choreographed by Corey Yuen.

Ninjitsu

One of the most popular martial arts icons in popular culture is the ninja. Deadly, mysterious, elusive, and (if we're dealing with female ninja) sexy are the words we associate with this class of Japanese assassins. The style of martial arts they study, *ninjitsu*, is often called "the art of stealth" and "the art of invisibility", furthering that romantic image of the ninja in the West. However, like the ninja themselves, things are not quite what they same and there's more to *ninjitsu* than people in black robes armed with swords and killing people *en masse*, as we see in video games and film.

The original ninja were the members of the Iga Clan, who resided in the Iga and Koga regions in Japan. Despite their reputations as super cool assassins, they were essentially the Japanese equivalent to so-called "country folk." According to film critic and journalist Keith Allison, the mountain clans from which the ninja would originate "developed into legendary famers, healers, and weather forecasters with a profound respect for the land that lent them their livelihood." Moreover, the influence of the *Shugenja*, a sect of people that sought enlightenment through physical suffering, including exposing one's body to the elements like rain, snow, and blistering heat, contributed to the creation of *ninjitsu*. Add that to the adoption of Chinese martial arts introduced to the clans by T'ang dynasty exiles and you have what would become known as *ninjitsu*.

Ninjitsu in its original form was more than simply learning how to fight with one's hands or weapons. Yes, they were taught in personal combat; weapons techniques, including the spear, staff, the *kusari-kama* (sickle-and-chain), and the sword; *shuriken* throwing, and other methods of combat. However, their training went beyond just learning how to fight. After all, as spies, it was not their duty to take on an entire castle or manor full of trained samurai. Thus, they were trained in areas like meteorology, geography, pyrotechnics and explosives, escaping, concealment, horsemanship, and disguise. Modern *ninjitsu* generally focuses on the weapons techniques and hand-to-hand combat, as the other disciplines studied in *ninjitsu* don't have any practical value to someone that isn't a spy or assassin.

While most Westerners are familiar with the term "ninja", Japanese people don't use that term to describe a person trained in *ninjitsu*. The correct term is *shinobi*, which many readers will recognize from a number of video games and films. The term for a female ninja is *kunoichi*. Their services were contracted by members of the *samurai* warrior class. Their specialty: sabotage, espionage, assassination, and so forth. They were essentially outsiders hired to do the dirty work of the *samurai*, who were bound by codes of honor to not engage in such acts.

American poster for *Super Ninjas* aka *Five Element Ninja* (Shaw Brothers, 1980)

In their country of origin, ninja have gotten ample cinematic exposure ever since the 60s. The *Shinobi no Mono* series is one of the most realistic portrayals of the ninja in world cinema. Nonetheless, cinematic depictions in Japanese cinema range from fairly realistic to over-the-top in movies like *Ninja Wars* (1981) and *Shogun's Ninja* (1980). Movies dealing with *kunoichi* often deal with the erotic side of ninja mythology, and movies like *Kunoichi Lady Ninja* (1996) are fairly exploitive films.

The ninja made their first appearance in Western cinema in the 1967 007 film *You Only Live Twice*. However, it wasn't until the beginning of the 1980s that the ninja would become a pop culture phenomenon in the United States with the success of films like Chuck Norris' *The Octagon* (1980) and *Enter the Ninja* (1981). During that decade, Americans saw people like Sho Kosugi and Michael Dudikoff taking on evil ninja in movies like *Revenge of the Ninja* (1983) and the *American Ninja* franchise. For kids, there were the *Teenage Mutant Ninja Turtles*, who had three movies, a cartoon series, comic books, and a number of popular video games. Hollywood depictions of the ninja have always been a little bit more down to Earth—although often just as silly as their Asian counterparts—as American filmgoers generally seem to expect their movies to be rooted in some sort of reality and adherence to the laws of physics.

The ninja has been popular in Hong Kong cinema since the early 80s as well. However, very few Chinese movies have portrayed ninja in a realistic way and thus Chinese movies tend to be even more fantastic, if less exploitive, than their Japanese contemporaries. Robert Tai was one of the first action directors to heavily use ninja in his movies. Working on classics such as the gore-fest *Five Element Ninja* (1980) and *Ninja: The Final Duel* (1985), Tai gave audiences ninja dressed as trees, ninja in shiny gold outfits, and, best of all, ninja riding on the backs of giant water spiders(!). Ching Siu-Tung is another director who has used ninja extensively in his films, such as *Duel to the Death* (1983), *Swordsman II* (1992), and *Dr. Wei and the Scripture with No Words* (1996). Ching's ninja fly through the air, ride on top of giant *shurikens*, and can merge with one another to form one *giant ninja*(!). Infamous fans of B-movies are the Godfrey Ho/Thomas Tang ninja movies from the 1980s, in which they would take a movie that had not been finished, splice in footage of Caucasian guys in ninja outfits fighting, and change the dubbing so as to create a connection between the two films. It never worked, and those films are generally recommended to fans of so-bad-they're-good films.

Heroes of the East (*aka* Shaolin Challenges Ninja *aka* Challenge of the Ninja) (1978)

As we've stated in earlier chapters, 1978 was an excellent year for kung fu cinema. Not only did Jackie Chan and Sammo Hung make their first masterpieces; nor only did the Venom Mob rise to fame; but Lau Kar-Leung entered his personal masterpiece period. From the late 1960s until 1975, Lau Kar-Leung had worked almost exclusively with Shaw Brothers director Chang Cheh. In 1975, Lau Kar-Leung struck out on his own and started directing, as well as choreographing, his own movies. In 1978, he directed three movies: *Heroes of the East*, *The Deadly Mantis*, and *The 36th Chamber of Shaolin*. Two of those titles have become all-time favorites among fans and from here on out, practically every film that Lau Kar-Leung did would become a classic. This film in particular is an excellent film and not only is it one of the earliest Chinese movies to feature *ninjitsu* in it, it is probably the most realistic depiction of the art in Chinese cinema.

The big showdown between kung fu master Ho (Gordon Liu) and Japanese ninja Sanzo (Yasuaki Kurata) begins at Ho's house a few minutes before midnight. Ho, knowing that Sanzo will try to sneak up on him, starts throwing walnut shells all over the ground outside his house. A figure appears dressed in a *kimono*. Ho thinks it's his wife, Kuda. Going out to meet her, Ho discovers that Kuda is actually Sanzo in disguise. Sanzo slashes him across the stomach with his sword, only to discover that Ho is two steps ahead of him and had put padding in his shirt. Soon they are throwing daggers and *shurikens* at each other with reckless abandon. All this happens over the course of a couple minutes and best yet: it is only the appetizer to the main course, which is their showdown at the lake.

Much like the beginning of the earlier skirmish, the fight at the lake begins with both of our fighters in disguise. This really captures the true spirit of *ninjitsu*, as opposed to the colored outfits that the ninja would wear in other movies. What's funny is that for all the hidden weapons and *shuriken* that Yasuaki Kurata has come armed with, Gordon Liu has some sort of Chinese kung fu equivalent to it. Especially nice are tube arrows that Liu has hidden in his back and sleeves. Kurata shows quite a bit of surprise at his discovery of Liu's hidden arsenal. Keeping up the illusion of disguise and concealment, Yasuaki Kurata has a number of hidden weapons, including a spear disguised as a pole for carrying water.

Following the spear duel, Kurata whips out his next surprise: a field full of straw dummies. The hook is that the straw dummies are connected via a series of cords and are full of spikes. One false move and the cords will pull the dummy toward Gordon Liu and impale him on the spikes. Not only that, Kurata leaves some explosive *testu bishi* (spiked balls) on the ground as well. But luckily, Gordon Liu has come equipped with his trusty rope-dart to get through those traps.

In the next portion of their fight, Lau Kar-Leung shows us subtly how he was trying for something authentic, logical, and yet didn't want to repeat the same fights from earlier in the film. Following the whole straw dummies sequence, the two have a sword fight. Prior to this, there had already been a sword fight between Gordon Liu and *kendo* expert Harada Riki. So, Lau has Gordon Liu fight with a saber, whose techniques are different from a sword. Kurata's sword stance is also visibly different from Riki's; it involves lower positions and more strategy than the earlier sword fight. As we said, it's subtle, but it helps the fight not become redundant.

For the final part of the battle, Lau Kar-Leung gives us an empty-hands duel between the two. Gordon Liu uses the crane technique, whereas Kurata uses a seemingly made-up style that is impressive, considering his speed, agility, and low positions and movements the style has him using. We won't spoil it what it is for readers who haven't seen the film, but it is a very interesting twist on the whole animal styles notion. What is neat about this scene—and this would be recurring theme in Lau Kar-Leung's traditional kung fu movies—is how it shows the practical application of kung fu philosophy. The "secret" style that Kurata uses is very dependent on close-up attacks and strikes, including elbows. Thus, the logical way to beat that style is to keep the person at bay. What better style to use than the crane style, whose long hits and kicks are designed for defensive fighting and for keeping the enemy at a safe distance? We also applaud Lau

Kar-Leung for not having Gordon Liu use the drunken style again, as he had done against the karate master; that would've made the style lose its novelty within the film.

As mentioned earlier, this fight stands as the most realistic fight involving ninja on the Jade Screen. For a genre that would eventually get so wrapped in the fantastical aspects and legends of *ninjitsu*, to the point of having ninja fly through the air while throwing dozens of *shuriken* in a matter of seconds, this fight keeps everything grounded and authentic. Here we have a real Japanese martial artist doing things that a real ninja would do. No brightly colored ninja here. No Caucasians wearing headbands with "Ninja" written on it. No female ninja firing shockwaves out of her genitalia. Like a real ninja would, Kurata uses a number of disguises, hiding places, and even the good ol' hide in the water routine. Yes, we recognize that the choreography does have that intricate, style-based quality that was par for the course in that time, but there's nothing wrong with that.

It is widely recognized that this is the first movie that would really take Japanese martial arts seriously. While Yasuaki Kurata had starred in dozens of Chinese movies since the beginning of the decade; and some Chinese vs. Japanese actually employed a Japanese actor to play the main heavy; the great majority of the kung fu films that featured Japanese villains—and they were many—had Chinese actors doing generic "karate" fighting instead of the real deal. Not only in this fight, but in the previous fights as well, we get to see real Japanese masters doing real Japanese martial arts.

The reason for this stems from the Chinese resentment of the Japanese occupation during the Second World War and the atrocities such as Rape of Nanjing, which had continued for several decades following the war. It was for this reason that the Japanese were an easy target as villains in kung fu movies. As a result, the portrayal of the Japanese in these movies was almost always racist and one-sided; they were always portrayed as lecherous, murderous thugs with no redeeming aspect whatsoever about them. Although there is an obvious bias towards kung fu, the Japanese in this movie are men of honor. Even in the final series of twists, Kurata and the other Japanese masters don't show any arrogance, but show a lot of respect for their opponent. Like many of Lau Kar-Leung's masterpieces, the movie ends without anyone getting killed. The resolution of the fight shows that all of the people involved have reached a certain level of enlightenment and can become friends—something extremely rare in a genre like this.

On the whole, there are a myriad of reasons to recommend not only this fight, but the film on the whole. It's an excellent comparison of Japanese and Chinese martial arts styles. Nobody dies in this film, and so it's a perfect movie for younger audiences without having the dumbed-down fighting of movies like *3 Ninjas*. The authentic *ninjitsu* on display is simply a wonder to watch. It's the first movie to show the Japanese in a positive light. The final fight is a classic finale to an all-time classic kung fu movie.

Korean Open-Hand Styles

Of all the Korean martial arts, the most famous is undoubtedly *tae kwon do* (the "foot fist way"). *Tae kwon do* is a style of fighting that has become very popular as an exhibition sport because of its emphasis on flashing kicking, including a wide variety of aerial kicks. There are over 21 different types of kicks in *tae kwon do*, the philosophy being that the leg is the longest and strongest part of the body. There are a number of strikes, blocks, locks, and pressure points, although it's the legwork that really gets the most attention in this style.

The style itself can trace its roots all the way back to the Koguryu Dynasty, one of the three kingdoms that ruled the Korean peninsula during the first century B.C. Paintings on Koguryu tombs show that a fighting style resembling modern *tae kwon do* was practiced as far back as 50 B.C. The fighting style, known as *taek kyon*, was developed and promoted by the neighboring Silla kingdom, which was constantly under attack from Japanese pirates.

Nonetheless, it was mainly practiced as a sport until the Koryu Dynasty (935 – 1392 A.D.), when it became an important fighting art. The fighting art, whose name had been changed to *subak*, lost its popularity in the second half of the following Yi Dynasty (1397 – 1907) and even then was practiced mainly for recreation. It was only when the Japanese began occupying the Korean peninsula that some Korean people began practicing the art in secret once again. An influx of influences from Japanese and Chinese martial arts in the 1940s led to the creation of a number of styles and variations of *subak*. Korean martial arts gained popularity in the 1950s and were eventually unified by the government in the early 1960s, who formed the Korean Tae Kwon Do Association (KTA).

Another important Korean style is *hapkido*. The style was founded by a Korean national, Choi Yong Sul, who had studied martial arts in Japan during the Japanese occupation of Korea. He returned to Korea and taught the style to his students. The style originally consisted of throws, joint locks, elbow locks, and ground fighting techniques, much like Japanese *Jiu jitsu*. It was later on that a wide number of kicks were added to the style to make it distinctly Korean. Double kicks, which consist of one type of kick being thrown and then moving the leg and body to perform another type of kick without lowering the leg, are very common in the style.

Poster for *Hap Ki Do* (Golden Harvest, 1972).

Korean martial arts have been popular in world cinema ever since the early 1970s. In American cinema, martial arts films have often favored actors who could perform fancy kicking. Chuck Norris was trained primarily in the Korean martial art of *tang soo do*, although he has additional black belts in other styles. B-movie favorites like Billy Blanks and Loren Avedon have very impressive kicking skills that come from their *tae kwon do* training, which can be seen in films like *No Retreat, No Surrender II* and *King of the Kickboxers*. Other popular actors who are masters of *tae kwon do* include the Ernie Reyes Jr. (*Teenage Mutant Ninja Turtles 2* and *Surf Ninjas*) and Philip Rhee (*Best of the Best* series).

Chinese films have featured *tae kwon do* in them ever since the early 1970s. In Jimmy Wang Yu's classic *The One-Armed Boxer* (1971), one of the villains is a Korean *tae kwon do* expert. In 1972, actor Jason Pai Piao starred in a couple of films highlighting Korean martial arts, specifically *Crush* and *Action Tae Kwon Do*. In 1973, real life *tae kwon do* master Jhoon Rhee appeared alongside Angela Mao in *Sting of the Dragon Master* (*When Tae Kwon Do Strikes*), but ended up being outshined by his female co-star.

From the mid-1970s forward, there would be a number of talented Korean *tae kwon do* stylists that would appear regularly in Chinese kung fu movies Most famous was legendary super kicker Hwang Jang Lee, who was one of the few actors who could get top billing in a movie, even though he was a) the villain and b) had limited fights. Tan Tao Liang, also known as Dorian "Flashlegs" Tan, was one of the earliest screen super kickers and was also the teacher of a number of actors like Yuen Biao, John Liu, and Shannon Lee (daughter of Bruce). Casanova Wong, the "Human Tornado", would make a solid career appearing in Hong Kong, Taiwanese, and South Korean productions up through the mid-1980s. Kwan Yung Moon, affectionately referred to by fans as "The Mad Korean", was one of the more versatile of the Korean actors, and would showcase his excellent kicking skills in films like *Inheritor of Kung Fu* (1980), *Rebellious Reign* (1981), and *The Loot* (1979). In 1992, audiences were introduced to the stylish kicking skills of Kim Wong-Jin (Yuen Jeung) in the film *Operation: Scorpio* and Kim would go on to appear in films like *No Problem 2* (2002) and *China Strike Force* (2001).

There are also quite a few Chinese actors who have studied *tae kwon do* and assimilated it into their fighting style. Polly Shang Kuan Ling Feng, one of the queens of Chinese action cinema, had training in both Japanese martial arts and *tae kwon do*. Kam Kong, a large fellow best known for playing the titular character in *Master of the Flying Guillotine*, was also a *tae kwon do* stylist, which was often trumpeted in the trailers to his earlier films. Alexander Lo Rei and Chen Shan were two Taiwanese actors known for their powerful kicking skills. Yuen Biao, one of the greatest kickers of the genre, mixed *tae kwon do* with a number of Chinese kung fu styles in his films. Donnie Yen, another one of the great genre bootmasters, trained in *tae kwon do*, in addition to *wushu*, tai chi chuan, and *wing chun;* his best films include *In the Line of Duty IV*, *Tiger Cage 2*, and *Legend of the Wolf*. Sun Chien, a Taiwanese actor best known for being a member of the Venom Mob, got his famous kicking skills from *tae kwon do* as well, his best showcase films being *Invincible Shaolin* and *Kid with the Golden Arm*. The list could go on forever if we wanted it to.

Hapkido isn't so well known in American cinema, although it has shown up in some popular cult films. One of its masters was Bong Soo-Han, who taught his skills to Tom Laughlin, who would go on to use *hapkido* in the well known Billy Jack films. Bong Soo-Han himself would appear in the famous *Enter the Dragon* parody, "A Fistful of Yen", in the classic 1980s comedy *A Kentucky Fried Movie*.

In Chinese cinema, *hapkido* has gotten a lot more attention. Ji Han Jae, one of the most popular masters and promoters of the style, fought Bruce Lee in the final sequence of fights of his *Game of Death* film. Ji also appeared in the film *Hapkido*, which starred Whang In-Sik and Angela Mao, both of whom were also masters of the style. Whang In-Sik, in particular, is probably the most well-known cinematic *hapkido* fighter, having fought Bruce Lee in *Way of the Dragon*, Jackie Chan in *The Young Master* and *Dragon Lord*, and Angela Mao in quite a few of her films. One of Whang's students was muscular fellow named Keo Ryong, who took upon himself the moniker Dragon Lee and became one of the most beloved (and hammy) Bruce Lee imitators. Unfortunately, Dragon Lee often worked in low-budget productions with some very untalented action directors, so few of his films really feature any interesting fighting. If you want to see Dragon Lee perform moderately well, which was about as good as you could expect from him, check out *Enter the Invincible Hero* (1978) and *Emperor of the Underworld* (1994).

The Tournament (1974)

One of the great super booters of the early 1970s (and then the early 1980s) was a (Surprise! Surprise!) Korean man named Whang In-Sik. Whang was a *hapkido* expert, and had studied under Ji Han Jae, the same man who went toe to toe with Bruce Lee in *Game of Death*[56] (1978). It was while Whang was doing an exhibition of the style in Hong Kong that he met Sammo Hung and Angela Mao and started training them, especially Angela. It was due to their efforts that they were able to make the film *Hapkido* (1972), which starred Angela, Sammo, Whang, *and* Whang's master Ji Han Jae. *Hapkido* is considered to be a classic film, showing us that Bruce Lee wasn't the only person capable of filming some classic fight scenes in 1972.

Although Whang admittedly didn't enjoy doing films, he appeared in a number of films at the request of Sammo Hung and Angela Mao from 1972 until 1975. Those films include *When Tae Kwon Do Strikes, Stoner, The Skyhawk,* and *The Association.* He re-entered the scene briefly in the 1980s, fighting Jackie Chan in *Young Master* and *Dragon Lord,* and then Indonesian star Billy Chong in *Fistful of Talons* (1983). Most people believe his 20-minute fight with Jackie Chan in *Young Master* is his greatest fight ever. We tend to disagree. Whang does give a masterful performance, showing us practically every facet of *hapkido* and its application in a fight. However, the fight goes on for far too long and Jackie Chan spends *way* too much time playing the human punching bag. In essence, the fight is far too one-sided to really be interesting.

Better than *The Young Master* are Whang's dust ups with Angela Mao. In their first movie together, *Hapkido,* the two are on the same side and thus don't actually fight. However, in subsequent films, the two would square off a number of times. In *When Tae Kwon Do Strikes,* the two hit it off fairly well…until Angela bows out and lets Jhoon Rhee take over, at which point the fight becomes less interesting. In *Stoner,* Angela and Whang have a memorable final duel while one-time 007 actor George Lazenby beats up Sammo Hung and some other stuntmen. However, our favorite onscreen depiction of *hapkido* has to be a sequence of *The Tournament,* where Angela must take on Whang In Sik, Sammo Hung, and Wilson Tong, among others.

The fight begins with a group of young kung fu fighters insulting Chinese kung fu, much to the chagrin of Feng (Angela Mao) and her brother, played by Carter Wong. Carter reacts by beating up all of the students, incurring thus the ire of their master, played by Whang In-Sik. Whang enters the fracas and kicks Carter into an oblivion, at which point Angela steps in to help. After a prolonged fight, Angela bests him in front of a number of Chinese onlookers. Following the fight, Angela gets into an argument with a young Chinese fighter, played by Sammo Hung, who subsequently challenges her. She accepts the challenge and beats him. As he leaves, a number of fighters, including Sammo Hung regular Billy Chan and Wilson Tong challenge Angela.

This is Angela Mao's fight all the way, even though everyone involved looks quite impressive. Angela does a combination of Chinese kung fu and *hapkido,* which she performs with a speed and intensity that no other female fighter of that era, not even Judy Lee or Polly Shang Kuan Ling Feng, could duplicate. Her kicks are just something else and every time she does a round kick or an inside crescent kick, it just fills a person full

---

[56] - See chapter on Jeet Kune Do.

of joy. As stated in the introduction, there are a lot of double kicks in *hapkido*, which Angela performs admirably. She does roundhouse kicks that become front kicks, side kicks that become crescent kicks, and inside crescent kicks that become outside crescent kicks. Her handwork is quite fast and intricate, and in her duel against Whang In-Sik, she does a lot of throwing, which is characteristic of *hapkido* as well.

Speaking of Whang In-Sik, he does get a pretty good showcase here, though mainly for his kicks. He's known as one of the original super kickers, and gets to perform quite a bit in his fights against Carter Wong and Angela Mao. He mainly does side and roundhouse kicks, although he does a few flying side kicks as well. There's no doubting his skill in this fight, even if he does end up losing. However, it's much more satisfying to see him using his skills against someone who's fighting back with all they've got than his longer duels with Jackie Chan, who's obviously holding back (for comic purposes).

The players are quite impressive. Sammo Hung, who was 22 at the time, fights using Southern Chinese styles, most notably the tiger style. Surprisingly, his use of Southern styles is about concurrent with the adoption of the same styles by Chang Cheh and Lau Kar-Leung, but much more animated and interesting to see. Billy Chan and his cohort use no definitive styles, but look great and move very fast. Wilson Tong and Angela Mao fight on top of a series of poles and both show pretty good balance, although Tong is shown up when Mao starts performing an amazing series of kicks while trying to keep balance.

The choreography here is provided by Sammo Hung, who proves that he is one of the true geniuses of the genre. Just the fact that Sammo was able to provide action this authentic, this fast, and this crisp as far back as 1974 (or even 1972, when we consider the work he did on *Hapkido*) is a testament to the man's talent. Moreover, consider the fact that he and Carter Wong are using *hung gar* variations in their fighting, and yet they pull it off quite a bit more intensely than the films that Lau Kar Leung was choreographing at the time (and Lau Kar-Leung had far more experience as an action director at this point). Sammo brings out the best in everyone he works with and this fight is no exception. Compare this fight to some of the other "basher" films being starring people like Shih Szu, Jimmy Wang Yu, David Chiang, and others. The choreography and quality of the martial arts is light years ahead of its time.

This sequence in *The Tournament* is a miracle. It is ten minutes of pure martial genius.

Secret Rivals (1976)

One of the most influential films in the history of the genre is *The Secret Rivals*. The film can be considered important for a number of reasons. First, it launches the careers of three important names in traditional kung fu cinema: Don Wong Tao, John Liu, and legendary super kicker Hwang Jang Lee. Don Wong Tao would go to become one of the best actors in Taiwanese cinema, which is saying a lot when you consider how cheap and sloppy a lot of their films were. John Liu was one of the great super-kicking heroes of Chinese cinema in the late 1970s and early 1980s. And legendary super kicker Hwang Jang Lee? Well, his title says it all. He would become one of the most sought-after actors to play movie villains for the next several years.

Moreover, this film made kicking popular again. Around the time that Bruce Lee was making movies, and shortly after his passing, kicking was somewhat popular, but limited to a few talented people like Bruce Leung Siu-Lung, Angela Mao, and *hapkido* specialist Whang In-Sik. Nonetheless, the success of Chang Cheh's *Five Shaolin Masters* in 1974 put Southern Shaolin martial arts on the map, which featured very limited kicking. All of a sudden, *hung gar* and the five animal styles became the vogue and high-impact kicking was kind of left behind. Not even the likes of Dorian Tan Tao Liang and the continuing efforts of Bruce Leung could really influence the genre. Then, this film came along and its director, Ng See-Yuen, was able to cast some new faces with some genuine kicking ability and that fabulous footwork became hugely popular once again.

What *The Secret Rivals* also did for the genre was push the bar for choreography standards quite a bit higher than it was. As popular as Southern Shaolin martial arts was at the time, it was often quite stiff and often slow in its presentation. Moreover, a lot of the "basher" films that were made in the first half of the 1970s featured some rather sloppy choreography to boot. Thus, the pitch-perfect choreography of Tommy Lee, who would become one of Taiwan's all-time greatest action directors, showed viewers once again that technique, crispness, speed, and power were not all mutually exclusive.

The set-up for the fight is quite simple. John Liu and Don Wong Tao are in Korea looking for a legendary fighter named Silver Fox (Hwang Jang Lee). They eventually become romantic rivals, as both of them like the same Korean lady. This eventually culminates in a fight between the two of them, which John Liu wins. John Liu is congratulated by the Silver Fox, who has been watching the entire fight. John Liu offers to have a duel with Silver Fox, whom we learn is responsible for Liu's parents' murder. The two begin to fight and then Don Wong shows up and joins Liu, as the two of them had planned this strategy from the beginning.

In this fight we basically get the combined talents of three different *tae kwon do* stylists. John Liu studied *tae kwon do* under the tutelage of Dorian Tan. As the story goes, he became something of Tan's servant, cleaning his house and cooking his meals in exchange for lessons. Thus, one will notice a lot of similarities between the onscreen fighting styles of the two actors, although Liu's talent was better exploited throughout his career. John Liu eventually adapted his *tae kwon do* training into his own style, which he called *zen kwun do*. Following the end of his movie career in the early 1980s, John Liu moved to Paris, France where he opened up a school.

In this fight, John Liu gives us everything we love about his fighting, but much faster and direct than some of the more intricately-choreographed fights that he would perform in his other films. His specialty here is the spin kick, which he does with great speed and accuracy. Nonetheless, we can see the immediate influence of his master's teachings, as he does do some of Tan's patented hop kicks here, too. His flying dragon kicks are nothing to scorn, either.

Don Wong Tao also performs some interesting kicks in this fight. Don Wong Tao was trained in a number of styles, including *tae kwon do*, *hung gar*, and the Northern Mantis style. Oddly enough, Wong Tao does quite a bit of kicking here, even though the film title of *Northern Kicks, Southern Fists* suggests that Wong Tao should be doing more *hung gar* than *tae kwon do*. All of his moves are solid, though. His hand techniques are the best of the three actors here and his kicking is solid. Following this film, Don Wong Tao and action director Tommy Lee would go to Taiwan, where they would work with each other on quite a few classic films, including *Along Comes a Tiger* (1977) and *Eagle's Claw* (1977).

Last, but certainly not least, is legendary super kicker Hwang Jang Lee. Hwang's portrayal of *Silver Fox* as an old, but highly formidable fighter is classic and Silver Fox would eventually become of one Hwang's nicknames by his fans for years to come. Hwang is best known for his arsenal of aerial kicks, although he doesn't use as much of those here. Hwang sticks to the more basic spinning and roundhouse kicks for the greater part of the fight. He does do a few jumping spin kicks, including one that covers a wide enough range that he's able to hit both Wong Tao and John Liu in a single blow. Also impressive is a leg lock that Hwang performs by catching John Liu's leg in mid-kick with his own leg, twisting it, and bringing John to the ground, following it up with another spin kick to the back of John's head.

Kudos goes especially to action director Tommy Lee. Tommy Lee had an ability to choreograph a traditional kung fu fight in a way that you would believe that people actually fought that way centuries ago in China. He avoids undercranking (speeding up) and, despite his Peking Opera background, doesn't over-choreograph his fights or throw in too many acrobatics. Oh sure, there are some nice flips and somersaults on display, courtesy of stunt doubles Yuen Biao and Corey Yuen, but nothing that reaches the level that the Venom Mob and the 7 Fortunes reached in the late 1970s. There's a level of speed and power on display that would make this film one of the true successors to Bruce Lee's filmography, more so than most of the Brucesploitation films of that era. John Liu and Hwang Jang Lee would perform more impressively in other films, but never this brutal.

It's really a triumph for everyone involved. The genre today really needs people like producer/director Ng See-Yuen, who was one of the best guys out there for finding new talent. Tommy Lee is one of the unsung heroes of old school action direction, often left in the shadow of Sammo Hung, Lau Kar-Leung, and the Yuen Clan. John Liu and Hwang Jang Lee are two of the best kickers the genre has ever known and Don Wong Tao is one of the most talented and well-rounded fighters of the late 1970s.

Showdown at Cotton Mill (1978)

Dorian Tan (aka Tan Tao Liang) was one of the first super kickers to come on the scene in Hong Kong cinema after the death of Bruce Lee. He first made his impression with *Tornado of Pearl River*, and would go on to appear in a few important films before becoming a Taiwanese mainstay. Dorian Tan has something of a tragic career, despite the number of films he made and his talent, in that his talent was often not used the way it should've been in far too many films he made. To be perfectly honest, though, Tan's talents were limited to his legs, mainly his left leg. He was capable of kicking with great flexibility and could often use his legs as if they were his own arms. His trademark kick was his "hop kick", in which he could throw multiple high side kicks with his left leg while hopping forward on his right. In action, it's very impressive.

Unfortunately, "Flashlegs" Tan was never more than his legs. As an actor, his range never went past that of a stoic hero. Sure, he appeared in some kung fu comedies and even appeared as a villain a few times, but he was most convincing as one of those righteous heroes that we love so much. Not only was his acting range limited, but his fighting was, too. His hand techniques were never that great, nor were his ability to wield weapons. Talented choreographers like Sammo Hung or Tommy Lee could milk his kicking for all it was worth. However, Tan often worked with a number of less-talented action directors in the Taiwanese films he did, so he often didn't get the full showcase his talents deserved. Compare this with his student, John Liu, who had some of the same limitations, but managed to always work with choreographers who knew how to use his kicking to the hilt.

Tan Tao Liang has a few very memorable films on his résumé. There's *The Himalayan* (1976), which features some of his best kicking ever, courtesy of action director Sammo Hung. With director Lee Tso-Nam, he appeared in the independent classics *The Hot, the Cool, and the Vicious* (1976) and *Challenge of Death* (1977), two high points of Taiwanese kung fu cinema. *Revenge of the Shaolin Master* (1979), while not his best film, does feature one of his best moments where he fights off a gang of spearmen with his legs, with action direction by Yuen Woo-Ping. One of the best showcases for his kicking comes from this independent Taiwanese feature.

In *Showdown at Cotton Mill*, Shaw Bros veteran Chi Kuan Chun plays Chinese folk hero Wu Wai-Kin (Hu Hui Chien), a contemporary of Fong Sai-Yuk and Hong Xiguan. The general gist of the character is that his father is murdered and thus he goes to the Shaolin Temple to learn kung fu to order to avenge his father. There are a number of films that depict his character of being good, but never quite good enough, at least never quite the match for his colleagues. In this film, he avenges his father on the Wudan clan, who then seek revenge of their own, going as far as to hire a Northern Leg Fighter (Tan Tao Liang), who duels with Wu in the film's final showdown.

This is one of the few times that Tan Tao Liang played a villain, something he was never quite suited for. Nonetheless, as an opportunity to demonstrate his legwork, the final fight more satisfies. Action director Cheung Pang opts to make Tan a nearly unbeatable villain, and thus he gets to dominate for a large portion of the final fight. He shows off a number of kicking skills, including his "hop kicks", with which he gets some good height. He also does a few jump kicks off tables and a few solid flying dragon kicks. The thing about Tan Tao Liang is that his aerial kicks aren't as impressive as his regular kicks, which he does with an astounding amount of height and flexibility, especially with his left leg. So when you come into a Tan Tao Liang film, check out his double or triple side and roundhouse kicks, and the height to which is able to reach in his legwork.

Chi Kuan Chun, the film's main protagonist, is known for using Southern styles, mainly *hung gar* in his films. Here he sticks to the Five Animals technique of *hung gar*, which he used in other films like *Five Shaolin Masters* and *Shaolin Temple*. Actually, this isn't the first time he played Wu Wai Kin, he had played the same character about two years earlier in Chang Cheh's *Shaolin Avengers*[57]. His animal techniques are solid, although his character gets kicked around for most of the fight and thus his final triumph, which stems from his tiger style, ends up coming across as kind of unconvincing.

Nonetheless, this fight ends up being Tan Tao Liang's show and he steals the film out from under Chi Kuan Chun through his superior kicking and remarkable left leg.

---

[57] - This film was produced by an independent studio founded by director Chang Cheh, and directed by Wu Ma, who was one of Chang's assistant directors back in the 1970s.

Tiger Over Wall (1980)

After his breakout performance in *Secret Rivals*, legendary super kicker Hwang Jang Lee became one of the most popular martial arts movie villains in the history of the genre, beating out the likes of Bolo Yeung and Shaw Bros perennial villain Johnny Wang Lung-Wei. Following Hwang's decision to leave cinema in the 1980s, few actors would come to close to reaching his level of popularity as a villain. Billy Chow, Dick Wei, and Collin Chou (Ngai Sing) would come close, but even they would rarely get the kind of billing in films, trailers, and VHS boxes that Hwang Jang Lee would get over the next few decades. Hwang could appear in a film as a villain, get two or three fights tops, and still get his picture on the VHS box and often have only his name printed on the front cover.

Hwang's history is about as interesting as his career. He's Korean, but was born in Japan in 1945, at the end of the Second World War. He would study *tae kwon do* during a large part of his youth, eventually becoming a master of the style and joining the Korean army. One of the most popular tales of his military experience was that he was in Vietnam training Korean troops when he was challenged by Vietnamese knife fighter. With a single kick to the head, Hwang Jang Lee killed his opponent. Hwang was eventually discovered by Ng See-Yuen and cast in *The Secret Rivals*. The rest is history.

Tiger Over Wall is one of those films whose reputation rests on one scene, in this case it's the movie's final fight between Hwang Jang Lee and protagonist Philip Ko. That's not to say that there aren't other things to recommend the film with, since Ko and Hwang both have some really good fight scenes before the finale. But when all is said and done, it's this last fight that most people will always remember. The movie itself deals with a team of corrupt cops who come under pressure when a dog belonging to a foreigner disappears. Unable to find the dog, the cops start bribing confessions out of some of the townspeople. However, things quickly get out of hand and Philip Ko finds himself fighting against an increasingly oppressive police force. Hwang plays the captain of the force who Ko has to fight at the film's climax.

Their fight is divided into two parts: the beginning weapons duel and then the fisticuffs portion. In the former, Philip Ko is armed with a pole while Hwang Jang Lee is armed with a *kwan do*[58]. One of the things that we love about Hwang Jang Lee is that, unlike John Liu or Tan Tao Liang, Hwang was just as efficient and brutal with his hands or with a weapon as he was with his legs. Hwang puts on quite a show with the *kwan do*, one of the best displays of the weapon that we've ever seen. Hwang Jang Lee would make Lu Feng proud in this segment. He's matched move for move by Ko, who's a very talented martial artist in his own right, despite the crappy modern action films he made in the late 1980s. This portion of the fight is well choreographed and gives you the impression that the performers aren't just showing off their skills, their really trying to hack each other to pieces.

When both of them are disarmed, things really pick up, especially for Hwang. The last three minutes of the fight are a sublime demonstration of nearly all of the kicks Hwang was capable of doing at his prime. While he shows off the same kicks in

---

[58] - See chapter on Assault Blades.

numerous other films, he's never had a fight where he shows them *all* off, especially in such a relatively short running time. Let's take a look at what he does:

1. "No-Shadow" Kick – This is a triple side kick performed in mid-air, where Hwang is able to kick the person three times before touching the ground. It takes its name from the technique performed by Wong Fei-Hung, which in the *Once Upon a Time in China* series, was a wire stunt that looked similar to what Hwang did. The only difference is that Hwang didn't need wires. Other actors that have performed this particular kick were Alexander Lo Rei, Chen Shan, and Donnie Yen.
2. Bicycle Kick – This is a triple front kick that Hwang performs by jumping straight up and kicking the person three times before touching the ground. Gets its name from the special move done by Liu Kang in the video game *Mortal Kombat II*. Other people who have performed this kick include Benny Lai, Donnie Yen, and Bradley James Allan.
3. Jumping Kicks – Hwang does a few of these in the fight. In one impressive bit, Hwang jumps over a table to kick Ko. In another, Hwang does a long jump, kicking Ko as he passes him by.
4. Leg Lock Kick #1 – Hwang secures Ko's neck with one foot, and then jumps up kicks him in the upper back with his other.
5. Stepping Stone Jump Kick – Hwang steps up onto Ko's knee, jumps off of it and performs a back kick to Ko's chest.

Beyond that, Hwang does his usual strong and precise roundhouse and spin kicks, which are nothing to scoff at. Most of the kicks that he doesn't perform in this particular fight are kicks that involve multiple opponents, and can be seen in the superlative end fights of the films *Hitman in the Hand of Buddha* and *Hell's Wind Staff*, which we also highly recommend.

Hwang Jang Lee performs a flying double side kick in *The Drunken Master* (Seasonal Films, 1978).

Philip Ko compliments Hwang pretty well in this fight, although it's pretty clear that his character is no match for legendary super kicker Hwang Jang Lee. Ko uses mainly the Northern Mantis style for the fisticuff portion of the fight. He looks good doing it, although the film never tries to pretend that Philip Ko is capable of beating Hwang out of sheer skill. Hwang himself does use some hand techniques in this fight, notably *ying jow pai*, or the Northern Eagle Claw (Hwang often used the Southern Eagle Claw to compliment his *tae kwon do* in this films).

One of the more interesting things to look for in a Hwang Jang Lee movie is how the hero ends up beating him. Hwang Jang Lee was such a talented fighter that it usually was rather difficult to believe that any of his films' protagonists could actually beat him.

Sometimes, they'd have to use a trick or a weapon or simply gang up on him. A few of them could win out of sheer skill, like Jackie Chan or John Liu, but not without some difficulty. However, sometimes an action director would ask you to believe that someone who's been getting beaten for the past five minutes could suddenly be better than Hwang, and it wouldn't be believable for a second. It'd actually be pretty infuriating, to be honest. Thankfully, the brutal way in which Philip Ko wins the fight is fitting enough to be believable, without compromising Hwang's ability.

The choreographer of this fight is an unfortunately little known guy named Dang Tak Cheung. Dang was a stuntman and extra in quite a few kung fu movies, both independent and big studio. He was also a rather talented action director. This is easily his best work, no doubt about it. One of his other notable films is *The Sword*, which he assisted Ching Siu-Tung on. He also got some good tiger style and *tae kwon do* kicking out of *Mantis Boxer*, a little known independent film. Here, Dang does what any choreographer should do with Hwang Jang Lee, just let him and his opponent beat the living crud out of each other. Hwang has a reputation for not holding back and here it looks like Dang told him to indulge himself. The hand techniques are handled well without detracting from the kicking. The weapons choreography is as good as anything from Lau Kar Leung or the Venom Mob. The kicking is just beautiful, about as good as anything Hwang did with the Yuens (Yuen Woo-Ping, Corey Yuen, etc.). This is simply a beautiful piece of Hong Kong brutality, one of the best old school fights in existence.

Promising Young Boy (1987)

Taiwanese cinema has always been considered to be the non-Union Mexican counterpart to Hong Kong films, at least in the martial arts genre. They were generally cheaper films, often spending a big part of their budget on bringing in stars from Hong Kong to appear in their films. Garish costumes, cheap sets, washed-up Hong Kong stars, and the occasional cheesy special effect defined Taiwanese martial arts cinema for more than a decade. Nonetheless, for the most part, they seemed to match Hong Kong cinema in terms of quantity, if not quality.

However, by the time that the old school kung fu film had given way to modern, stunt-filled action, Taiwanese cinema fell way behind. Hack director Chu Yen-Ping and his associates were able to keep up to a small degree, making some modern action films like the *Kung Fu Kids* series and the superlative *Book of Heroes* (1986). Nonetheless, Taiwan's output in this area paled in comparison with the Hong Kong industry, which was churning out some of the greatest action films of all time. Nonetheless, there were a few marks of pure genius on the action front that unfortunately don't get much attention today. One of them is this film, *Promising Young Boy*, which plays like a Taiwanese version of *Best of the Best*.

The fight in question is a tournament fight between Taiwanese regular Alexander Lo Rei and (then) newcomer Ngai Sing (who'd later change his stage name to Collin Chou). Alexander Lo Rei plays a Korean *tae kwon do* champ who challenges a team of Taiwanese *tae kwon do* fighters. He bests several of them in a series of brutal fights, and is beginning to get *too* brutal when Chopin (Ngai Sing) shows up and challenges him.

What follows is one of the most fantastic displays of athletic *tae kwon do* kicking ever committed to celluloid.

Alexander Lo Rei was one of the great stars of Taiwanese martial arts cinema. He was principally a *tae kwon do* exponent, although he had training in kung fu and quite versatile, being able to use weapons and his fists as much as his legs. He first appeared in films like *Incredible Kung Fu Mission* (1979) and the classic *Shaolin vs. Lama* (1982). He would later seize hold upon the 1980s ninja craze and become the Taiwanese equivalent to Michael Dudikoff (but with better fighting skills), taking on ninjas at every turn. He would deal with ninja in films like *Ninja Hunter* (1982), *Shaolin vs. Ninja* (1983), *Super Ninja* (1984), *Ninja in the USA* (1985), *Mafia vs Ninja* (1985), and his most famous, *Ninja: the Final Duel* (1986). His output represents some of the highest quality action to be found in a Taiwanese production and some of the few modern day action films to be made in Taiwan.

This fight represents his best work of his later films. There is none of the excessive undercranking or awkward wire stunts that plagued a lot of his earlier, ninja-themed films. His kicking is the on the level of legendary super kicker Hwang Jang Lee, and seems to do it all: multiple continuous kicks, jumping front kicks, a variety of jumping spin kicks, and your usual roundhouse and spin kicks. His punches and blocks are fast and crisp, too. It's a shame that he didn't continue making films throughout the 1990s, as he surely would've been more of a legend than he is now, as he's mainly a cult favorite today.

While Alexander Lo Rei was in the latter part of his acting career, Ngai Sing was at the beginning. Ngai Sing was also a *tae kwon do* exponent who also had some *kung fu* background to round off his skills with. Ngai was discovered by Sammo Hung, who put him on his Hung Ga Ban (Sammo Hung's Stuntman Association), and would appear in films like *Blade of Fury* (1993), *Slickers vs. Killers* (1991), and the underrated *License to Steal* (1990). Ngai is now generally known as a super kicker and a career movie villain, playing bad guys in classic films like *Bodyguard from Beijing* (1994) and more recent films like *Flash Point* (2007) and *Forbidden Kingdom* (2008). In the past decade, he became (slightly) known by American audiences for playing Seraph, a role that was supposed to go to Jet Li, in *The Matrix* sequels.

Ngai Sing gives one of his best career performances here, showing off a diverse collection of kicks that didn't always get the attention they deserved (like Jet Li, Ngai Sing was unfortunate to have his career take off when wirework was becoming popular). He does a lot of double and multiple kicks, which are his specialty. However, he does some really awesome aerial kicks here, including a vertical whirlwind kick off a balcony, a spinning drop kick, and a hurricane kick that looks similar to what Ken and Ryu did in the *Street Fighter* video games. He also does a falling bicycle kick, Pelé style, which is always impressive, too. His basic kicks, punches, and blocks are all very solid, but it's the more fancy stuff that ends being more memorable.

This film represents a victory to action directors Don Wong Tao and Lee Hoi Hing. We discussed the former earlier and how he was one of the more talented Taiwanese actors and screen fighters, with solid kung fu and *tae kwon do* experience. Lee Hoi Hing has shown himself to be a solid action choreographer and is known for doing a lot of over-the-top fights for his films. Some of his films have included *Iron Monkey II* (1996), the *Ninja Death* series (1982), and *Kung Fu Wonder Child* (1986). Those films have often been bashed for their low production values, and the wire stunts are often awkward and undercranking a bit too much, but there's a lot of good kung fu on display in these films and a lot of creativity to be seen, for sure. This is easily one of Lee Hoi Hing's more accessible films as an action director, and quite good compared to the other films cited.

Muay Thai

The fighting style known as *muay thai*, Thai boxing, or sometimes even simply just kickboxing, has always been a fairly popular style in films. There's something about the style's no-nonsense, direct approach to fighting that has made it endearing to fans of martial arts cinema over the years. *Muay Thai* is particularly brutal style of fighting, using their elbows as much as their fists, their knees and shins as much as their feet. Blocking low and mid-level kicks is often done with the shin instead of the forearm. *Muay thai* is most often a tournament sport and has been integrated by many fighters to MMA (Mixed Martial Art) forms, being combined with *jiu-jitsu* and other fighting forms.

Poster for *Duel of Fists* (Shaw Brothers, 1971).

Muay Thai has a fairly rich history in cinema. It has gotten a lot of attention in American cinema, most notably thanks to the efforts of Jean-Claude Van Damme in his *Kickboxer* and *The Quest* films. Moreover, a lot of martial arts tournament films from the 1980s and 1990s, like *Bloodsport*, almost always feature a *muay thai* fighter as well. The style has gained new popularity as the result of a spate of new Thai films starring the likes of Tony Jaa and Dan Chupong, which portray *muay thai* is a very brutal manner, often accompanied by stuntwork that would make Jackie Chan proud. The most popular of those movies are *Ong Bak* (2003), *Born to Fight* (2004), and *Tom Yum Goong* (2006).

Muay Thai has been portrayed in Hong Kong cinema since the early 1970s. One of the earliest films to show the style performed correctly is the 1971 Shaw Bros film *Duel of Fists*, which features scenes of Chinese actor Ti Lung taking on Thai boxers in the ring. The 1972 film *King Boxer*, starring Meng Fei, also features a Thai boxing match early in the film. Thai boxers were also used fairly often by kung fu legend Jimmy Wang Yu, most notably in both *One-Armed Boxer* films. The fight between Jimmy and the Thai boxer in *Master of the Flying Guillotine* (1976) is one of the most blackly funny fights in the history of the genre. Kung fu queen Angela Mao also went into the ring to face a Thai boxer in *The Tournament* (1974), which is considered one of her best films.

Muay Thai made more appearances in Hong Kong cinema in the late 1980s, when Thailand became a cheap locale to shoot movies. The girls n' guns film *Dreaming the Reality* (1989) features a number of scenes of actor Ben Lam fighting Thai boxers in the ring. There were two actors trained in Thai boxing that would go on to become two of the most popular villain actors in Hong Kong cinema from the late 1980s until the late 1990s, those being Billy Chow and Ken Low. The two would bless Hong Kong cinema with their superior fighting skills and brutal demeanors in a number of films. Heck, they even appeared together in *Kickboxer's Tears* (1992), which features some of the most realistic (*too* realistic even) Thai boxing sequences in Hong Kong cinema.

Blonde Fury (1989)

Following the success of the films like *Yes Madam!* (1985) and *Righting Wrongs* (1986), Cynthia Rothrock became something of a mainstay in 1980s Hong Kong action cinema. More importantly, she was one of the few Caucasian performers to be cast more often as a protagonist than as a villain. Most of the films she worked on in Hong Kong are considered genre classics to one degree or another, with the exception to a few more obscure films like *City Cops* and *Prince of the Sun*, which Rothrock made during her final days in Hong Kong before focusing her energies on the Hollywood B-movie circuit. The author had the opportunity to briefly talk to Ms. Rothrock in the late 1990s, and it was asked what her favorite film was that she made in Hong Kong. Ms. Rothrock told him that her favorite effort was this 1989 tour-de-force, which exists mainly to show us the many ways that Cynthia Rothrock was capable of beating people up (and Hong Kong cinema is slightly richer for it).

One of our favorite fight sequences in this movie is one near the middle where Interpol agent Cindy (Rothrock, of course) goes into a chemical factory looking for clues that might incriminate a number of people in the counterfeiting industry. Accompanied by a press photographer (Mang Hoi) and an insurance agent (Chin Siu-Ho), she discovers that their presence is not wanted, in the form of two Thai boxing enforcers, played by Billy Chow and Sai Bar. A fight breaks out between Mang Hoi and Billy Chow; and then Billy Chow and Chin Siu-Ho; and then Chin Siu Ho and Sai Bar and finally Cynthia Rothrock and Sai Bar.

The first fight, between Billy Chow and Mang Hoi isn't so much a fight as it's a brief introduction to how strong Chow's character is. Mang Hoi tries to kick chow a few times, but each kick is stopped by a kick from Chow before it can even reach belt level. A well-placed front kick from Chow leaves Mang Hoi on the ground. Cue Chin Siu-Ho's appearance.

This fight is quite a bit meatier, to be sure. The two start trading blows in true 1980s fashion: little attention is given to technique, but more on economical hits, blocks, and kicks. Chow uses his *muay thai* in a fairly restrained way, doing some clinches and knee smashes, in addition to some basic punches and kicks. It's filmed quite well and does look fairly brutal. Chin, on the other hand, is a little bit more flexible, using some nifty kicks and a bit of acrobatics, reflecting the actor's Peking Opera training. In one nice scene, Chin Siu-Ho does front flip and ends it with an axe kick to Billy's head.

Upon defeating Billy Chow, Chin Siu-Ho is attacked by Sai Bar, who comes into the fight by kicking through the window on a door and hitting Chin in the head. He then unleashes a barrage of knee smashes and punches on Chin and finally leaves Chin nearly unconscious. Cynthia then shows up to show Mr. Sai what she's made of.

What's remarkable about this next portion of the fight is how little Sai Bar seems to care that Cynthia Rothrock is a woman. Sai just goes with his basic *muay thai* kicks, mainly roundhouse kicks with some spin kicks thrown in, punches and knee strikes. His power is exemplified when Rothrock picks up a large pillow from a sofa to block his kick and even the blunted impact of the kick knocks her back quite a bit. Keep watch for a nice kick that Sai Bar performs after jumping off a wall.

Nonetheless, Cynthia Rothrock is ready for conflict and handles herself quite well. Her moves are a bit more economical and practical than in films like *Inspector Wears Skirts* and *Magic Crystal*, which drew more from wushu background. Her punches and kicks seem a lot better suited for a more knock-down, drag-out fight here. In one of her most famous screen moments, Rothrock, who's wearing heels, runs up and down a wall, *Matrix*-style, with what appears to be no wire assistance whatsoever. It lasts about a second, but it looks awesome.

The choreography here is provided by Mang Hoi and Corey Yuen. Corey had directed *Yes Madam!* and *Righting Wrongs*, two of Rothrock's most popular films. In an interview, she commented that Corey Yuen not only saw her potential, but always pushed her to go farther than she had gone before, and thus it is unsurprising that her best fights were choreographed by him. Mang Hoi, who was Peking Opera trained like Corey Yuen, was a talented action director, whose credits included *Kung Fu vs. Yoga*, *Royal Warriors*, and Tsui Hark's masterpiece *The Blade*. Both Corey and Mang worked together on a number of a films and thus knew each other's style quite well.

Muay Thai here is pretty authentic and brutal, being an appropriate style for this type of movie. There are no wires, computer FX, trampolines, or anything of the sort. It's just pure intensity, which all of the performers (except Mang Hoi) give it there all with.

The Pedicab Driver (1989)

We consider legendary super kicker Hwang Jang Lee to be one of the greatest onscreen villains of all time. Nonetheless, his output greatly decreased in the mid-1980s, leaving space for other talented fighters to become great movie villains. For a big part of the 1980s, if you needed a good villain, especially a henchman, you could get *tae kwon do* expert Dick Wei. By the late 1980s though, if you wanted someone to play right-hand man to your bad guy, you had to look no further than Billy Chow. This would continue up to the late 1990s.

Billy Chow was a Canadian-born Chinese who trained in Thai kickboxing at an early age. He went to Hong Kong in the early 1980s, where he became a champion kickboxer in the ring from 1981 to 1984. It was while he was fighting in Hong Kong that he was discovered by Sammo Hung. Sammo Hung placed him on his stuntman team, where he played bit villain roles in a number of Sammo Hung films, including *Dragons Forever, Eastern Condors*, and *Paper Marriage*. This would eventually open other opportunities for Chow, although he would play the villain in nearly every film he appeared in for his entire career. There are two roles for which Chow will always be remembered: the evil Japanese General Fujita in Jet Li's *Fist of Legend* (1994) and this film, where he plays the silent bodyguard to John Sham's lecherous pimp.

Earlier in the film, Billy Chow and a number of other killers stormed the house of Rice Pudding (Mang Hoi) and killed Malted Candy (Max Mok) and his new bride, played by Fennie Yuen. Rice Pudding and Fatty Tung (Sammo Hung) swear revenge and storm the mansion of Yu #5 (John Sham), the psychotic pimp who ordered the hit. After dispatching with most of Yu's lackeys, Fatty Tung must face Yu's main bodyguard (Billy Chow), who was responsible for his friends' deaths.

Most people will agree that Billy Chow puts on his absolute best performance in this brief fight between him and Sammo Hung. He keeps his moves relatively simple, but you can't argue with the brutality and speed of it all. He does a lot of knee smashes and push kicks, often faking Sammo with an intended knee, only to kick him in the stomach and knock him back. Chow gets to show off some other kicks, including some roundhouse kicks that'd make Chuck Norris proud and an axe kick that'd probably break a regular person in half. His fists are particularly brutal here and he does a bit of head locks, too. Chow is pretty relentless in his fighting here, which makes his role particularly memorable.

Sammo Hung delivers one of his last great martial performances in this fight. He fights on the defensive for a good part of the fight, being overwhelmed by Chow's onslaught. Nonetheless, he gets in some very good moves, turning Chow's kicks into body slams and performing some good leg scissor techniques. There's some nice *chin na*, or joint locks, by Sammo in the middle of the fight, although it only ends up earning him a front kick to the mouth. Nonetheless, Sammo does get the last laugh, in the form of an awe-inspiring Pelé-esque bicycle kick to Billy Chow's face at the end of the fight. Only his films *Skinny Tiger and Fatty Dragon* and *Pantyhose Hero* would feature fight action from Sammo reaching the level of this film.

The choreography in this fight is top-notch. The action directors were Sammo Hung, Brandy Yuen (brother of Yuen Woo-Ping) and Mang Hoi. There work here got nominated for the Best Action Design award at the 1990 Hong Kong Film Awards, but ended up losing to Jackie Chan's *Miracles* (which, incidentally, also featured Billy Chow in the final fight). We feel that this film should've won, out of the three that were nominated[59]. The fighting looks great, and the camera lets us see the action the entire time. Close-ups are used to emphasize the impact of certain key blows, but it never detracts from the skill itself. Sammo, who is known for overdoing it on the slow motion later on in his career, keeps it to a minimum, mainly in the final moves. As it stands, the final fight of *The Pedicab Driver* is one of the ultimate examples of Sammo's 1980s action direction and a hallmark in Billy Chow's distinguished career as a martial arts movie villain.

Mahjong Dragon (1996)

One of the greatest onscreen kickers of all time is a fellow named Kenneth Low, or Lo Wai-Kwong. Ken Low has an interesting story. He was born in Cambodia and fled to Thailand about the time that the country was falling to Khmer Rouge. While in Thailand, he took up *muay thai*, of which he would eventually become quite proficient in. He took up competing in tournaments and ended up retiring at an early age due to lack of

---

[59] - The third film that was nominated that year was Yuen Biao's *The Iceman Cometh*.

competition. After retiring from the ring, Ken started working at a bouncer at a bar, where he was approached by HK actor Danny Lee and invited to appear in a film.

While filming another film, *Naughty Boys* (1986), he was approached by producer Jackie Chan, who invited him to be his bodyguard. So Ken Low not only became Chan's bodyguard, but also a member of the Sing Ga Ban (Jackie Chan Stuntman Association). He also worked on a number of other films, including several low budget action films starring Donnie Yen, like *Cheetah on Fire* on *Holy Virgin vs. the Evil Dead* and *Future Cops*, where he plays an analogue for the Street Fighter II character M. Bison. It was while Jackie Chan was filming his epic *Drunken Master II* (1994) that the intended villain, Korean *tae kwon do* expert Ho Sung Park, proved unable to keep up with Jackie's style of screen fighting. Ken Low ended up becoming the main villain and practically stole the entire climatic fight from Jackie with his awesome legwork.

Ken Low would occasionally appear in films after that that would capitalize on his wondrous kicking skills, although few of them would really push his skills to the limit. *Thunderbolt* (1995) came pretty close, as did *Circus Kids* (1994), which featured Ken Low fighting Jackie Chan's best friend Yuen Biao. However the best film after *Drunken Master II* to show the world how good Ken Low was at his prime was *Mahjong Dragon* (1996).

We hold *Mahjong Dragon* in special esteem in our hearts, as it features some of the best fights in a Hong Kong film made after 1994. Hong Kong films in the late 1990s became a lot glossier and more geared toward international distribution, thus good-looking actors, special effects, wires, and other nonsense became more important than good ol' fashioned dangerous stunts and actual martial talent. Moreover, our favorite actors like Sammo Hung, Yuen Biao, and Jackie Chan suffered either severe injuries, popularity loss, or a combination of the two and thus started making less films or films that featured action that was watered down considerably from the stuff they made a decade before. Hong Kong cinema has since become almost a shadow of what it was from the 1980s until the mid-1990s. Whatever one may say about the film surrounding it, the final fight of *Mahjong Dragon* is a reminder of why we all love Hong Kong cinema to begin with.

The set-up of the final fight is a classic. All of the good guys, except Quick Hands (Vincent Zhao Wen-Zhuo) have been rounded up by a group of bloodthirsty triads, led by Southern Hand Tin Lone (Ken Low). Tin Lone makes Quick Hands an offer: if he can knock him off a pile of fruit boxes, he will win and his friends can go free. If his leg touches the ground, the triads will break the legs of one of the hostages. If his hand touches the ground, they will break of one of the hostage's arms. If his body touches the ground, they'll kill one of the hostages. Seeing that he doesn't have much of a choice, Quick Hands accepts and a brutal showdown commences.

The final fight really belongs to Ken Low, not unlike the final fight of *Drunken Master II*. He unleashes the same barrage of kicks that he did in that film. He is able to throw a quite a number of kicks at varying heights without ever letting his leg touch the ground. But more impressive, his legwork is very flexible and one almost gets the impression that his legs are made of rubber. He is able to swing his legs in from one height to another, hitting Vincent Zhao on one side of the body and then lowering it to hit the other without much effort. Unlike *Drunken Master II*, Low does a lot more work with his knees here, which is a bit more characteristic of *muay thai*.

To be perfectly honest, Ken Low's style of fighting is more applied *muay thai* than pure *muay thai*. Ken Low has done some cinematic ring fighting before, in films like *Kickboxer's Tears* and *China Strike Force* (2001). The truth is that choreographing a ring fight is not always the most entertaining way to go, especially in the case of the former film. Here there are a number of flourishes to his fighting style that look great on film, but probably wouldn't fly in a real fight. Since the two action directors, Yuen Tak and Corey Yuen, are Peking Opera trained and not actual *muay thai* specialists, their job is to translate his fighting into something entertaining and memorable, but in a way, distinctly Chinese.

There are a number of people out there who feel the need to compare this film to *Drunken Master II,* often criticizing the former and praising the latter. Fans of *Drunken Master II,* especially those who like it more than this film, generally remain silent on the subject. However, *Mahjong Dragon* has its supporters who lash out against Jackie Chan's *obra prima*, pointing out that Vincent Zhao holds his own throughout the fight while Jackie Chan got whooped for the first part of his duel with Ken. It's really an unnecessary comparison when you get right down to it. After all, getting beat and then coming back has been a part of Jackie Chan's films ever since *Young Master* (1980), so it wasn't like Jackie Chan was doing anything out of character. The truth is, Hong Kong cinema is blessed to have *two* fights from two films where Ken Low gets to show off his "crazy" kicking skills in the way he does. There's really no need for any comparison.

In terms of flashy fighting, Vincent Zhao Wen-Zhuo doesn't get to do a whole lot in this fight until the end. That's not to say that he doesn't fight, because he does, and does it darn well. His usual flashy *wushu* kicks are toned down in favor of more economical hits and kicks. Nonetheless, he wouldn't be able to react and play against his environment the way he does if he weren't a skilled martial artist, which is evident here. Sometimes we fans of martial arts cinema tend to judge a screen fighter by the flashy moves that he or she can do, when a person's martial skill may be perfectly manifested by being able to do everything the choreographer asks of him without any problem.

The action direction by Corey Yuen and Yuen Tak is simply superb. There's a bit of wire-work and quick cutting here, but it seems to all blend seamlessly into a perfect whole. The use of the surroundings, in this case, the fruit boxes, is simply awesome. Our fighters have to keep their balance as they kick the boxes out from under each other. The presence of "rules" in this fight make it more suspenseful. There's a bit of object-fu here, including fruit boxes, machetes, lights, and even hollowed-out coconuts. The final bit, where Zhao puts his hands into the green coconuts and beats Low into submission was eventually reused by Corey Yuen in *Transporter 2*, who had Jason Statham do the same thing in one of that film's fights. Wires, kicking, *wushu*, objects, use of one's environment, fruit boxes…this is truly a Hong Kong movie fight and one of the last great examples of the creativity that existed in the genre before CGI and Hollywood influences showed up to dry up the well.

Yoga

When most westerners hear the word "Yoga", they think about the hundreds of exercise videos and classes available for it. However, that is simply "the tip of the iceberg", as the cliché states. Yoga can be understood to be physical and mental disciplines originating in India. The word *yoga* means "unity", and thus it can refer to not only mental and physical disciplines, but the goal of these disciplines: unity with the Universe. Moreover, there are a number of schools of thought in Hinduism, each of which is called a *yoga*.

The *Yoga* associated with exercise that most Westerners are at least vaguely familiar with is the *Hatha* school. Followers of *Hatha Yoga* believe that the physical perfection can lead to spiritual perfection. Thus, disciples of *Hatha Yoga* will practice breath control exercises and hand gestures, called *mudras*, to try to improve their health and thus become more spiritually tuned. Not surprisingly, a lot of spiritual and philosophical aspects of the *Hatha* school have been watered down, if not left out altogether, in the *yoga* that Westerners practice. Thus, many people practice *yoga* for their health, but with little spiritual significance attached to it.

Taiwanese actor Wong Wing-Sang plays an Indian yoga master in *Master of the Flying Guiolltine* (1976).

Interestingly enough, *yoga* has appeared in Chinese martial arts films as a type of Indian martial art, usually related to contortionism. While principles of *yoga* may be applied to Indian martial arts, it is not a fighting art in and of itself. Nonetheless, sometimes fantasy makes for better entertainment than fact and thus we get the rare appearance of "combat *yoga*" in Chinese cinema. Jimmy Wang Yu put some Chinese actors in brown make-up to play Indian *yoga* masters in his classics, *One-Armed Boxer* (1971) and *Master of the Flying Guillotine* (1976). The latter is notable for the Indian character being the inspiration for Dhalsim in the *Street Fighter* video game series. *Yoga and the Kung Fu Girl* (1979) features a super-flexible female martial artist in the title role. More recently, Andy Lau took on an Indian contortionist villain in Johnnie To's *Running on Karma* (2003). Although not having anything to do with *yoga*, Jackie Chan's showdowns with Indian martial artists were the most entertaining parts of his epic *The Myth* (2005).

Kung Fu vs. Yoga (1979)

This movie is notable for a number of reasons. First, the two main actors in this movie, Chin Yuet-Sang and Alan Chui, had worked more as supporting actors and action directors than as leading men. Second, according to internet movie critic Keith Allison, the film's protagonists are some of the most "ugly, mean, and unlikeable" jerks ever seen in a kung fu movie. And finally, the final fights between Chin and Chui and Indian actor Dunpar Singh are some of the most bizarre and creative fights ever seen in a kung fu movie.

In order for Chin Yuet-Sang's character to marry a beautiful woman, he has to find and bring her a number of treasures, including a jewel worn at the hat of Dunpar Singh's head. Singh is introduced as not only a *yoga* master, but as an aphrodisiac seller as well. The first showdown does not go well for our protagonists. As good as their kung fu is, our heroes are not ready to fight against a man who can contort his body in several different angles simultaneously, or who can attack them in positions that most normal people couldn't imagine. In one part, Singh rests one foot on the opposite shoulder and then proceeds to kick one of them in the head. He also seemingly dislocates his arms at one moment and continues to fight as if that were normal to him.

Having been beaten and humiliated, our heroes return to fight him again, this time with a plan. They come to Singh's abode armed with poles with nooses at the end, ready to tie him up and steal his jewel. Now, the choreography gets even more complex than the fight before it. They almost tie him up, but he is able to maneuver himself in such a way that he not only escapes from being tied up, but he ties them up as well.

Tired of losing to Singh, Chin and Chui resort to treachery—well, more so than attacking an unarmed man with poles—in order to win this fight. For their third attempt to steal the jewel, they pour glue on his body. It slows him down, especially when he has to exert extra strength in order to pull his arms off his side or one leg off the other. They also come to the fight armed with poles, which they not only use to hit the poor sap, but to help force his body into a permanent position that he won't be get himself out of once the glue dries.

In the fights in question, Chin Yuet-Sang and Alan Chui get decent showcases; they've done better work in other movies. The real star of the fight is obviously Dunpar Singh. The guy is simply phenomenal. Sure, the movie itself has nothing to do with *real* yoga. But the man's flexibility is unreal and is a joy to watch. He looks like Yuen Biao at his peak times five—he's that good. The way that he gets out of the literal bind in the second fight between him and the film's protagonists is just jaw-dropping.

Dunpar Singh is helped in large part by the creative choreography of Mang Hoi and Tsui Fat. Mang and Tsui are experienced and talented choreographers, although Mang Hoi, who worked on the choreography to classic 80s films like *Righting Wrongs* (1986), *Yes Madam!* (1985), and *Royal Warriors* (1986), is probably more talented than Tsui Fat, who is known for his low-budget action movies in the early 1990s, notably a few starring Donnie Yen that were filmed in Thailand. The action directors play a super-important part in the development of a fight and the showcase of the actor's skills; an untalented action director can make even the best fighter look uninteresting or even incompetent. Thus, Mang and Tsui are tasked with taking Singh's flexibility and not only milking the gimmick for all it's worth, but for making it look like more than a simple gimmick. It works.

Not only are Mang and Tsui to be commended for their making these fights a tour-de-force for Dunpar Singh, but they avoid making each fight a repetition of the previous one. The first fight is a simple hand-to-hand combat situation, the difference being that the hand is often hitting from under the legs or from an arm that has been flung around the neck. The second fight introduces weapons, which are the ropes and poles. And finally, the last fight has our heroes using a creative, although almost Loony Tune-ish way of winning: the glue.

We mentioned that these fights don't represent the best work of Alan Chui and Chin Yuet-Sang in front of the camera. There's no problem with that—our focus is on the *yoga* aspects of this scene. Nonetheless, we recognize how much of a treat it is for these two guys to have the lead roles in a film. This represents the best work I've seen from Tsui Fat, whose work in the 1990s ranges from competent to pretty good. Mang Hoi by this time was establishing himself to be a very good fight choreographer and these fights are no different. Finally, Dunpar Singh is a revelation and although *Kung Fu vs. Yoga* was his only movie in Hong Kong, it left one heck of a mark on the genre.

Part 5: Weapons

Pole

One of the most popular and widely-used weapons in all martial arts is the *gun*, otherwise known in English as the staff, pole, stick, or cudgel. In Japanese it is known as the *bo*. To the Chinese, it is the "Father of all Weapons", as all weapons evolved in one way or another from the pole. In prehistory, the first cudgels could be made from femurs of animals or from sturdy tree branches. It would develop over time into the weapon it is now. In Okinawan martial arts, the *bo* became a prominent weapon in *karate* following the Tokugawa Shogunate's ban on weapons because it could easily be disguised as a walking stick.

Obviously, the pole is simply a long, thin stick made out of wood, usually one that is both tough and flexible. It tends to be a bit tapered at one end for piercing and jabbing techniques. The range of techniques for this weapon is staggering. The pole has been adapted for swinging, sweeping, blocking, parrying, among others. It is one of the most oft-showcased weapons in martial arts cinema and is a rather easy weapon to improvise in films with a more modern setting. For example, in *Excessive Force* (1994), Thomas Ian Griffith is squaring off against some mobsters in a barn and grabs a broom, kicks off the bristles, and uses it as a staff. In *Shanghai 13* (1984), Ti Lung improvises a staff using a metal pipe. The simplicity of the weapon allows a skilled user to use a number of objects in place of the weapon itself, should there be any necessity.

Needless to say, there are dozens, if not hundreds, of martial arts films out there where you can see the pole in action. Some of the more notable ones may include the following: In *The Pedicab Driver* (1989), there's an excellent staff duel between Sammo Hung and Lau Kar-Leung. In *The Tai Chi Master* (1993), one of the more memorable set pieces is one where Jet Li and Chin Siu-Ho take on the "Lo Han Pole Formation", which includes about 20 monks armed with poles standing on top of each other in a pyramid formation. In *Hell's Wind Staff* (1978), there is some pretty good pole fighting courtesy of legendary super kicker Hwang Jang Lee. Any movie about the Shaolin Temple is almost guaranteed to feature some fight scenes, or at least some training sequences, involving the pole. In the recent comedy *Kung Fu Hustle* (2004), one of the characters has a pole technique that he developed from working with rolling pins as a baker.

In this chapter we shall take a look at a couple more notable films and fights using the pole than normal, since there are so many great and important examples of the weapon out there.

Opium and the Kung Fu Master (1984)

This chapter would be incomplete if we neglected to dedicate a section to the inimitable Ti Lung, one of the great Shaw Brothers actors. Ti Lung began his career appearing alongside David Chiang in a number of violent swordplay, or *wuxia*, films directed by Chang Cheh. In the mid-70s, Ti Lung hooked up with director Chor Yuen and appeared in a number of complex *wuxia* films based on Chinese literature. By the late 1970s, Ti Lung's popularity had faded somewhat and he split his time between Shaw Brothers films and low-budget Taiwanese chopsockeys. As his career went on a downward slide in the 1980s, he found himself turning to alcohol. *Opium and the Kung Fu Master* directed by Tong Gaai, who had choreographed most of Ti Lung's films at the Shaw Brothers studio. The story of a martial artist who gets hooked on opium and then kicks the habit via martial arts training has some parallels to the drinking problems that Ti Lung had had. This movie has since been deemed as one of Ti Lung's greatest starring features.

As a martial artist, Ti Lung's primary training had been in the *wing chun* style. The two primary weapons used in *wing chun* are the pole and the *bot jam do*, or butterfly swords. In a number of his classic films, Ti Lung opted to use the pole and has given many a great demonstration with this weapon. A number of his films demonstrate his prowess with the pole. In *Five Shaolin Masters* (1974), *Inheritor of Kung Fu* (1979), and *Kung Fu Instructor* (1979), Ti Lung gets to show off some decent staff techniques. Better than that were the films *Shanghai 13* (1984) and *Shaolin Prince* (1983), which featured in more impressive fighting from Ti Lung. *Opium and the Kung Fu Master*, however, stands out as his best work and his last great martial arts performance. The rest of career would be spent in "Heroic Bloodshed", or "Bullet Ballet", films and more dramatic roles.

In the finale of *Opium and the Kung Fu Master*, "Iron Bridge" Sam[60] (Ti Lung) must take on the villainous Rong Feng (Chen Kuan Tai), who had previous bested Sam in a duel. At the time, Sam was suffering from the effects of opium and thus his martial skills had been diminished. Having kicked the habit with his training, Sam is ready to win back the respect of his peers and rid the town of Rong Feng, not to mention avenge some his friends.

Ti Lung does some very awesome pole work in this fight, showing off not only his prowess, but showing that he was quite agile with the weapon as well. Some of his earlier pole fights were rather static or too technique-heavy and thus lost a bit of their energy. Here Ti Lung shows off his noble charisma as he fends off Chen Kuan-Tai's attacks and constantly knocks him to the ground, humiliating him with each hit. Anyone can throw a punch onscreen; Ti Lung does it with character.

Chen Kuan-Tai fights with a pair of medium-sized spears with spearheads at each end. He is also a lot faster and more agile than in a lot of his earlier films. In lesser hands, fighting with two-fisted spears would be quite awkward. However, under Tong Gaai's superior direction, Chen Kuan-Tai shows off a level of coordination and ability that hadn't been seen in a lot of his earlier films. Thus this fight becomes not only one of Ti Lung's best films, but Chen Kuan-Tai's as well.

---

[60] The Iron Bridge Sam character was apparently a real-life martial artist, whose life was also portrayed in a trilogy of films during the 1990s: *White Lotus Cult, Sam the Iron Bridge,* and *One-Armed Hero.*

Tong Gaai had a very long and varied career of more than 20 years as an action director. At his best, Tong Gaai possessed a knack for creative choreography and experimental wirework that put him as one of the predecessors of modern "wire-fu" masters like Yuen Woo-Ping and Ching Siu-Tung. His style was best suited for *wuxia* films, which often had fantasy overtones to them. Nonetheless, he worked on a number of films in other sub-genres, such as modern-day actioners like *Duel of Fists* (1971); traditional kung fu films like *Heroes Two* (1975); and everybody's favorite super-hero movie, *Super Inframan* (1974).

Tong Gaai is one of the great weapon choreographers and this fight stands as a testament to his ability. He gets the best out of Ti Lung and Chen Kuan-Tai. Compare this fight with the final fight of *Kung Fu Instructor*, also choreographed by Tong. Ti Lung does a lot of accurate and authentic pole work in his fight against Ku Feng, but the choreography is a bit slow and almost seems more like a demonstration rather than a fight. Here, the choreography is a lot more natural and faster, giving the fight a lot more real suspense.

Cheng Shiang wields the "Sweeper" pole in *Invincible Shaolin* (Shaw Brothers, 1978).

Also, the climatic fights to both movies feature henchmen armed with rattan shields and butterfly swords. Here, the fight direction of Ti Lung taking on the sword-and-shield baddies is a lot better and less stiff than in *The Kung Fu Instructor*, which came across as being too planned out in its execution and too "bound" by its authenticity. Thus, this film becomes more alive and more suspenseful than its predecessor. These things considered, the final fight of *Opium and the Kung Fu Master* becomes not only one of Tong Gaai's finest moments, but a symbol of his growth and evolution as an action director, even in his later years.

Whereas Tong Gaai showed that his later years were among his best as an action director, his young co-action directors, Yuen Bun and Yuen Wah, both of whom studied at the same Peking Opera school as Jackie Chan, showed promising work from the beginning. Yuen Wah would later go on to find fame as a villain in films like *Eastern Condors* (1987), *The Iceman Cometh* (1989), and *The Kid from Tibet* (1991). He played a villain throughout most of the 1990s, and recently benefitted from a career rejuvenation in Stephen Chow's *Kung Fu Hustle* (2004). Yuen Bun has become a talented action director, working in a variety of genres (bullet ballet, wire-fu, horror, girls n' guns, Triad film, etc.) and has be nominated a number of times for his work on films like *The Blade* (1995) and several films that made under celebrated director Johnnie To's direction, like *Throw Down* (2004) and *Running on Karma* (2003). Besides these three, Shaw Brothers stuntmen/choreographers Kong Chuen and Wong Pau-Gei are on hand to assist in the fight scenes.

It is said that too many cooks spoil the broth, but these men have cooked up a classic weapons duel.

Eight Diagram Pole Figther (1984)

By 1984, the once-illustrious Shaw Brothers studio was only a mere shadow of it had once been in previous decades. For whatever the reason, it had not made the transition from the classic kung fu film to the modern-day action film that their rival, Golden Harvest, was conquering the box office with. Moreover, one of their biggest stars, Alexander Fu Sheng, died in a car accident during the filming of *Eight Diagram Pole Fighter*, making that shadow loom even larger above the studio. Finally, director Lau Kar-Leung was going through a number of personal problems during the making of this movie. All of these contributed to the rather dire tone of this film, which is the bleakest and most graphically-violent movie that Lau Kar-Leung ever directed.

There are two fights in this movie that will forever be remembered by viewers. The first is the ultra-fast duel between Gordon Liu and Philip Ko, who plays a Shaolin abbot, near the end of the movie. Said fight is a staff duel, and it features some wonderfully intricate choreography and is actually considered by some viewers to be the best fight of the film. As one-on-one staff duels go, it certainly has few rivals. However, it is the final duel that most left its mark on us.

At the end of *Eight Diagram Pole Fighter*, Gordon Liu, who has become a monk and has learned to control his rage, discovers that his sister (played by Kara Hui Ying-Hung) has been kidnapped by the Mongol army and the corrupt Sung officials that had murdered his family. His rage flares up once again, and he abandons the Shaolin Temple to rescue his sister and avenge his family once and for all. Dressed as monk and pushing a cart full of sharpened bamboo poles, he arrives at the abandoned inn where the villains are holding his sister. After slaughtering the first wave of soldiers with the poles, he enters the inn and sees a large mountain of coffins. He's soon surrounded by a small army of Mongol soldiers…and the carnage begins.

As you will have noticed while reading the earlier chapters of this book, Lau Kar-Leung as a director tended to make his movies less violent than the Chang Cheh movies he had worked on as choreographer. Conflicts were resolved with the minimum of killing and, in a number of his movies, without any deaths whatsoever. That is not the case in this film, or this fight for that matter, which contains a number of images that one will not easily forget.

Throughout the duration of the fight, Gordon Liu fights off his many attackers using a pole, which he had learned to wield while at the Shaolin Temple. His techniques have improved quite a bit since *Challenge of the Masters* (1976), one of his first starring roles that also featured some extensive staff work. Here it is obvious that Gordon Liu is being choreographed not just to show off his staff techniques, as far too many old school films do in their weapon duels, but he's really trying to hit and kill the bad guys. Gordon does receive a little bit of wire assistance, but it mainly to help jump from coffin to coffin during the fight and not to take the place of his actual martial talent.

The Mongol Soldiers, with the exception of the main villains, use an interesting variation of the lashing staff, or *shaozi*. The lashing staff is a variation of the pole that is a long pole and a shorter pole connected together with a chain. The lashing staff that the Mongol soldiers use is designed to wrap around and lock their opponent's weapon, rendering it useless. It is shown to be very deadly weapon in the context of the film and does a lot of damage here. This variation is seen so little on film, so it's a refreshing change-of-pace from your usual spears and sabers.

The most memorable scenes of this set piece come in the second half of the fight, when the Shaolin monks arrive to assist Gordon Liu's character. They too are armed with poles, although their fighting style is notably different from Liu's. Whereas Gordon Liu is fighting with the intent to kill, they simply want to incapacitate the soldiers without killing them. Their strategy thus is to "defang the wolves." Thus they direct their strikes to the soldiers' mouths, literally knocking out all of their teeth. The most chilling images in this scene are those of the Mongol soldiers screaming in agony at their having lost their teeth, their mouths bleeding profusely.

Kara Hui Ying-Hung eventually gets her chops in and does some pretty good weapons work in this fight. The main villains, who are armed with the *kwan do*, or long-handled broadsword, also get in some good moves and look great under Lau Kar-Leung's direction.

The setting of the fight is an inn, which has been the site for many a kung fu brawl over the years. However, Lau Kar-Leung and his choreography team throw in that mountain of coffins to make things interesting. Not only does Gordon Liu have to fight numerous foes while jumping on and around coffins, he has to watch out, as there are armed soldiers hidden in a number of the other coffins. Both the setting and the lashing staves are neat little flourishes to an already stellar fight.

Eight Diagram Pole Fighter would get nominated for best action design in 1985 at the Hong Kong Film Awards. It marked Lau Kar-Leung's second nomination—he had been nominated for the same award for *Legendary Weapons of China* two years earlier. Unfortunately, Hong Kong filmgoers are a fickle people and there was just no room at that time for the brutal action that took traditional choreography to a new level. Thus, the award went to Jackie Chan's *Project A*, which itself had been a revolutionary film in terms of modernizing martial arts action. So that's at least a partial consolation; after all, if you're going to lose, you might as well lose to the best. Unfortunately, as obvious as that might sound, there have been a number of years in which films boasting excellent fight choreography failed to win or even get nominated for the Best Action Design award, losing to films were more gimmicky than anything else.

At the end of this fight, whoever isn't dead is horribly maimed. Gordon Liu walks off into the horizon, leaving behind his family and his Shaolin brothers forever. It is an unforgettably bleak ending preceded by an unforgettable and graphic climax. Despite the pessimism engendered by the film, it is truly one of the greatest moments in classical kung fu history.

Once Upon a Time in China II (1992)

One question that we have pondered while reflecting on this film is how much did the audiences in Hong Kong audiences in 1992 consider the pairing of Lei Lin-Git (i.e. Jet Li) and Yen Ji-Dan (Donnie Yen) a special treat? After all, the two of them are favorites in most circles of martial arts movie fandom today and are understandably considered to be among the most talented Chinese action actors of the post-Bruce Lee era. Granted, when the movie was made, Jet Li had only become a huge star the year before and Donnie Yen was still trying his darndest to make a name for himself. So we may believe that the stir caused by seeing the names of these two men in the credits to this film was not as big as it would be when it was announced on the internet that Donnie Yen would be appearing in *Hero* (2002) to fight against Jet.

Nonetheless, it is their showdowns in this film that have garnered endless praise among fans of martial arts films, among both the "purists" and those whose tastes aren't so grounded in reality and accuracy. A number of websites and online reviewers have referred to the final duel between Jet and Donnie as one of the greatest fight scenes committed to film. We have never quite agreed with so strong an affirmation, but as you can tell, we *do* feel that their showdowns represent the best of pole fighting on the Jade Screen.

The first fight between Jet Li and Donnie Yen occurs some 45 minutes into the film. Jet Li, playing Chinese folk hero Wong Fei-Hung, has come to Qing Commander Lan (Donnie Yen) seeking protection for those who have been threatened by the anti-Foreigner White Lotus Sect. Lan, who has finished his evening training, sees Wong enter the premises and without warning, throws a pole over to Wong and starts attacking with his own. What begins is a wild pole fight between the two as they make their way in, on, and around a bamboo scaffold. Jet Li fights mainly on the defensive here, kind of bewildered at Commander Lan's sudden attack. Donnie Yen is on the offensive, testing Jet Li's skills to the fullest extent possible.

In the second showdown between Jet and Donnie, at the climax of the film, Commander Lan is trying to get a list of rebel names (a popular McGuffin in these films) and Wong Fei-Hung must hold him off while his student Foon (played by Max Mok) burns the list. The fight starts off with what appears to be a vertical staff duel. The setting is a storage area for a market, which is full of bamboo scaffolds. Jet Li jumps onto one of the higher levels of the scaffold and starts attacking Donnie Yen with a large bamboo pole. Donnie, now in the defensive, fights back with a shorter, conventional staff, but at a lower level. Soon, both are on the ground and are armed with two poles apiece. In a wonderful display of choreography, precision, and timing, Donnie Yen and Jet Li fight each other: four poles in motion simultaneously. For the grand finale, which everyone seems to love except us, Donnie attacks Jet with a wet cloth acting as a lash.

So why did we choose this film? Well, for one, it is an astonishingly fast fight scene—fast in a way that *doesn't* depend on under-cranking. You see, Donnie Yen made a lot of low-budget films during the 1990s that for one reason or another, were excessively under-cranked (i.e. sped up) and often ended up looking silly. Here, we see Donnie Yen and Jet Li fighting at *über*-fast speeds, showing us why Mr. Li is called "Jet" and why HK film historian Bey Logan called Donnie Yen "the fastest man in Hong Kong."

Moreover, far too many films made during the 1990s sacrificed technique for wire-tricks and special effects. A lot of movies claimed to be about swordsmen and the "Martial World", but featured very little actual martial arts. Here we get some good old fashioned weapons combat the way we like it best: few wires and all skill. Both Donnie and Jet had trained in *wushu* in Mainland China and acquired skills in a number of weapons, including the pole. Here we can see just how good their pole skills really are. No camera tricks, few wires, no CGI.

One thing we appreciate is that Yuen Woo-Ping doesn't try to make Jet Li the better martial artist in the fights. Donnie Yen is shown to be just as quick, coordinated, and crisp in his techniques as Jet Li. Taking into account that the *Once Upon a Time in China* series had practically turned Chinese folk hero Wong Fei-Hung into Steven Seagal in terms of being untouchable in a fight, Donnie Yen's Commander Lan is shown as being able to match Wong Fei-Hung move for move. We are disappointed that Yuen Woo-Ping and director Tsui Hark chose not to have the two go at it in hand-to-hand combat, but what they do is certainly impressive, and stands as some of the finest martial arts on display in a 1990s "New Wave" film.

Saber (Broadsword)

The *dao* is one of the most common weapons to appear in Chinese cinema and is considered to be one of the four major weapons—it's nickname being "The General of Weapons." Depending on the dubbing or subtitles of the film one watches, the *dao* has been translated as "saber", "broadsword", "knife", or simply "blade." A slightly curved, single-edged blade and a short hilt characterize the weapon, often leading people to confuse it with a sword, which it is not. The tip of the weapon is generally sharpened, so that it can be used for stabbing, although slashing and chopping are the weapons main functions.

There are various variations of the saber used in different styles of martial arts. The Southern Broadsword, or *nandao*, consists of a straight, heavy blade and a metal hand guard used for hooking the opponent's weapon. The Nine-Ring Broadsword (*jiu huan dao*) is characterized by the nine metal rings on the flat edge of the blade, used for lessening the impact of the opponent's weapon. The Ghost-Head Broadsword (*gui tao dao*) has a deeply-serrated back edge, which is used for cutting and inflicting terrible wounds in one's opponent. The Horse-Cutting Broadsword, or *zhan ma dao*, had a large handle; a thin, curved blade measuring more than a yard; and was used for chopping off a horse's legs during battle. The Big Broadsword, *da dao*, is heavy, curved blade about two to three feet in length with considerable chopping power, used by civilians or revolutionaries, as seen in the classic *Blade of Fury* (1993).

The weapon has been used by foot soldiers in the Chinese army for thousands of years, and thus any movie dealing with military battles, soldiers, armies, etc. are bound to feature the saber in action. It is for this reason that the weapon is one of the most common weapons in martial arts films. Moreover, if we take *dao* to mean any single-edged weapon, then the so-called "choppers" that are so common in movies dealing with Triads would also count and raise that number any further. The weapon is very common, although finding films that show off its full martial applications require a little bit more discernment. After all, any stuntman can put on period military garb and run at the hero with a saber, only to get cut down without actually doing anything. It takes a talented martial artist to perform well with the saber.

The New One-Armed Swordsman (1971)

The concept of the one-armed martial artist goes back to 1967 with Chang Cheh's landmark film *The One-Armed Swordsman*, starring Jimmy Wang Yu. The movie set the mold for the modern male martial arts protagonist, as the *wuxia* genre at the time was dominated by powerful sword-brandishing women. The movie was successful enough that it launched Jimmy Wang Yu's career and inspired a sequel, *Return of the One-Armed*

Swordsman (1969); a remake, being this film; a cross-over with the popular Japanese *Zatoichi* series, *Zatoichi meets the One-Armed Swordsman*; a few knock-offs; and a fairly recent remake, Tsui Hark's masterpiece *The Blade* (1995). The idea behind these movies is that a talented fighter, having lost an arm, can train well enough that his skills can overcome a seemingly insurmountable handicap in order to get revenge on his enemies.

 The New One-Armed Swordsman was another entry in this "series" of films by director Chang Cheh, although by 1971 Jimmy Wang Yu had already had a falling out with Chang, leaving the director to cast David Chiang, a popular actor at the time, in the title role. The film deals with a talented swordsman (Chiang) who is framed for murder by villain Ku Feng, who then cuts off his arm in penitence. After being pulled out of a funk by another swordsman, played by Ti Lung, Chiang finds himself back in the world of swordplay in order to exact revenge on his adversary. The finale is a large battle scene as Chiang must take on an entire army of men by himself, followed by a duel with Ku Feng himself.

 The finale of *The New One-Armed Swordsman* is about spectacle. The first part of the fight takes place on a large bridge and features Chiang taking on dozens of extras armed with sabers and spears. The outdoor photography gives the fight something of an epic feel. After wiping out the army on the bridge, Chiang enters a large pagoda where Ku Feng's men continue to assault him, trying to use some tricks like ropes and grappling hooks to subdue our hero. It doesn't work, and soon the entire building is littered with the bodies of dead soldiers. Chiang then returns to the bridge for his final showdown with Ku Feng, who is armed with a three-section staff.

We should note that in most of these movies involving one-armed swordsman, the protagonist does not technically wield a sword. He actually wields the *dao*[61], the saber or broadsword. In several versions of the story, the protagonist not only fights with a *dao*, but with a broken one at that. That is the case with this film; David Chiang starts the film fighting with the *shuangdao* and then switches over to one saber after losing his arm. And as far as one-armed sword fighting is concerned, this film is the place to go.

Poster for *The New One-Armed Swordsman (Shaw Brothers, 1971)*

 The choreography is provided by Tong Gaai and Lau Kar-Leung, who were the top choreographers at the Shaw Brothers studio for most of the studio's existence. At the time, *wuxia* films were still rather popular and the choreography drew a lot of its inspiration from Western swashbucklers and Japanese *chambara* films. That isn't to say that Chinese martial arts wasn't a part of the fights, but the style of fighting was a lot faster and less drawn-out than it would become later in the decade. The moves performed by David Chiang with the saber are less ornate and more practical than a lot of the

---

[61] The Chinese title for Tsui Hark's *The Blade* was simply *Dao*.

swordplay we see in Hong Kong and Chinese films. With the exception of the final duel with Ku Feng, David Chiang rarely requires more than a few strokes to kill an enemy— and he often kills several enemies with just one swing. As a result, the fight is an excellent example of well-mounted set piece where the main weapon involved just happens to be a saber, rather than a martial analysis of the weapon.

David Chiang has never that great of an onscreen martial artist, despite his training. A good actor? Yes. A convincing fighter? Not quite. Yes, there have been a few occasions in which the choreographer has been able to make Chiang quite stunning, namely *The Loot* and *The Challenger*. Nonetheless, Chiang has frequently paled in comparison with more talented actors like Bruce Lee, Sammo Hung, the Venom Mob, and even frequent co-star Ti Lung. Thus, it is a breath of fresh air to see a one-armed Chiang doing a convincing job of leveling a whole army. His saber techniques are not particularly sophisticated; most of techniques are swinging and chopping movements filmed with style. Nonetheless, Chiang is at his physical peak at this point and does a solid job of convincing us that he's a one-man killing machine.

The Odd Couple (1979)

There have been a number of martial arts actors that seem to have a special chemistry with each when it comes to screen fighting. Legendary Super kicker Hwang Jang Lee and fellow kicker John Liu are two good examples. Jackie Chan and Ken Low are two others. For several years, anything that Donnie Yen and Michael Woods made one classic fight after another. However, one of the greatest onscreen pairs in Hong Kong action cinema was that of Sammo Hung and Lau Kar-Wing.

The two appeared opposite one another in four films, all of which have garnered extensive praise for, if nothing else, the scenes they have together. In *Dirty Tiger, Crazy Frog* (1978) the two team up against Lee Hoi-Sang in the finale, after which they have a duel with the three-section staff that Mark Pollard of Kung Fu Cinema called "one of the best fights ever filmed using [the] weapon." *Knockabout*, which features Lau as the main villain and Sammo as one of the supporting protagonists, is considered by many to be one of the greatest traditional kung fu films ever made. In *Skinny Tiger, Fatty Dragon* (1990), the final two-fisted machete duel between Sammo and Lau is easily one of the coolest knife fights ever seen. In short, the two work magic when they work together.

The Odd Couple has been declared by many to be one of the greatest weapons movies ever made. About 15 minutes into the film, there's a fight between Sammo Hung and Lau Kar-Leung that sets up the events for the rest of the film. Sammo plays the King of Sabers, while Lau plays the King of Spears. Every year, they have a martial arts duel to determine who's the greater fighter. The duel always ends in a tie, as does this fight in particular.

Sammo Hung does some wonderful work with the saber in this fight, and (as usual) shows that he's more agile that his girth would indicate. As seen in a lot of saber forms, he swings the saber around his back in a few scenes, which actually helps block a few moves during the battle. Sammo does most of his own acrobatics in this fight, and looks very impressive. He shows that there's more to the saber than simply chopping and swinging motions. Hung does a bit of a juggling act with his saber during the duel, which is a nice touch.

At the end of the film, there's another duel between Sammo and Lau, who this time are playing the students of the character the other played in the first duel. Thus, we have Lau Kar-Wing wielding the saber while Sammo fights with the spear. Once again we have an excellent showcase to a weapon that too often was relegating to simply artless chopping in so many movies. Lau Kar-Wing puts a nice spin on his attacks, often holding the flat end the saber in some of his close-quarters attacks. Lau does a bit of acrobatics, although he's doubled by Yuen Wah for most of the more physically-demanding flips and somersaults.

So what we have here are two excellent, but short (two minutes for each fight), duels between one of the greatest kung fu pairs. Both Sammo and Lau do some excellent saber work and compliment each other perfectly with their spear prowess in each duel. The choreography here is provided by the usual suspects in a Sammo Hung production: Billy Chan, Yuen Biao, and Lam Ching-Ying. These three worked on the choreography of most Sammo Hung movies from the mid 70s up until the late 80s and are very talented men. They know how to find the perfect blend of weapon technique, Peking Opera style acrobatics, and a bit of humor to keep things entertaining. The choreography is intricate without ever becoming slow, and each movement is performed with perfect precision. Yes, it's excellent weapons work all around.

Blade of Fury (1993)

One of the lesser-known names in kung fu history is "Big Blade" Wang Wu. Not much is known about him in the West. Most of what we may know about him comes the three movies made about his "life", those being *The Iron Bodyguard* (1973), *Kung Fu Hero Wang Wu* (1985), and *Blade of Fury*. The two details about his life that seem to match up among the films are that he was a master of the *da dao*, or big broadsword; and that he was involved in an attempt to reform the government by forcibly removing the Empress Dowager from power and consolidating that of the young emperor. Beyond that, details of his life are rather hard to come by.

When the "New Wave" wire-fu films took center stage in Hong Kong cinema during the first half of the 1990s, most of the films were either *wuxia* movies, many of which were based on Chinese literature; or kung fu movies, most of which were the fictitious exploits of real life Chinese folk heroes such as Wong Fei-Hung, Fong Sai-Yuk, and Hong Xiguan. It was only a matter of time before Wang Wu, whose story had gotten the cinematic treatment twice since the 1970s, would show up on film again. *Blade of Fury* ended up being one of Sammo Hung's few forays into the "New Wave" films, as by then his popularity had declined considerably.

The film deals with Wang Wu (Yeung Fan), who gets involved with Tan Si Tung (played by Ti Lung), an official wanting to reform the government by ousting the Empress Dowager from power. After Tan is betrayed by Yuen Shi-Kai (Zhao Changjun), Wang Wu seeks revenge, aided by several others. A big battle royale erupts between Wang, his friends, Yuen, and his cohorts. In classic Sammo Hung style, the climatic duel is a collection of several individual duels, with the camera jumping back and forth between each one. There are some parts of this set piece that are of little use for us in this chapter, notably the fight between Cynthia Khan and another fighter armed with a meteor hammer and a short duel involving Collin Chou.

The first scene of note is a one dealing with a young pupil of Wang Wu's. Although surrounded by soldiers, he is actually ignored by them, as they figure that a young boy would be rather harmless. Finally getting tired of everybody else getting in on the action, the pupil attacks of a couple of guards and steals their sabers. From there on out, it's total carnage as the young man cuts a swath through the attacking soldiers, who finally start taking him seriously. At one point, the soldiers actually become afraid of him, backing up whenever he looks in their direction. The scene is notable for, among other things, portraying a young kid killing so many people.

The second scene is a duel between Yeung Fan and Lau Shun, who plays an evil Eagle Claw master. Yeung Fan is armed with the *da dao* and the two put on a rather hectic display of *wushu* hand and weapons techniques. There are some wires used to exaggerate the jumps and some of the techniques being performed, but it doesn't replace the skills of the actors, as other films of the time period did.

Finally, Yeung Fan takes on Zhao Changjun. Yeung continues to brandish his *da dao*, while Zhao performs the drunken sword technique. There is some excellent technique on display here, although some of it is wire-assisted. Nonetheless, the *wushu* abilities of both are put to good use, as is expected in a Sammo Hung film. Pay attention to the camerawork, as there's a bit of slow motion and blur effects on display. These sorts of stylistic touches would be something of the norm for Sammo during the 1990s, notably in movies like *Ashes of Time* (1994) and *Thunderbolt* (1995).

The strength of this fight lies in Sammo Hung's ability to make his cast look like experts onscreen, in spite of all the wire-assisted jumping going on. Moreover, far too many films during the 1990s had the word "sword" or "swordsman" in the title, but relied on wires and optical effects instead of actually swordplay. Here we get some excellent sword and saber work, notably the young actor with the *shuangdao* (i.e. double saber) and Yeung Fan with the *da dao*. Their wushu training is obvious: agile movements, solid kicking, excellent speed, and precise technique. Everyone else in involved in the fight provides solid support, but are ultimately outshone by these two.

The wires used in this fight are rather awkward, although Sammo Hung has never been particularly talented in staging wire stunts beyond the basic stunts and falls. Thankfully, the quality of the wire-fu is really immaterial in this fight, so there's no reason to really complain about it. This is really 1990s swordplay at its best.

House of Flying Daggers (2004)

Following the international success of Ang Lee's *Crouching Tiger, Hidden Dragon*, filmmakers, including a number of high-profile Chinese directors who had no previous experience with the genre, decided that they wanted to make their own big-budget historical martial arts films. Studios were motivated by the promise of profit on the international market while many of the directors were motivated by more artistic reasons. The most successful director after Ang Lee was Mainland director Zhang Yimou. Yimou had previously received quite a bit of international acclaim for his films, especially those starring Gong Li. His first *wuxia* film, *Hero* (2002), was an international success and even got nominated for an Academy Award. His second film, *House of*

Flying Daggers, was not as successful, although it's a far more beautiful film than its predecessor and features even better set pieces from action director Ching Siu-Tung.

The final fight of *House of Flying Daggers*, that pits Andy Lau against Takeshi Kaneshiro in the middle of a huge field as a dying Zhang Ziyi watches nearby. The motives for the fight are personal: Andy Lau had originally been Zhang's lover, so when she decided that she wanted Takeshi, Lau took it to heart and tries to kill her. When Kaneshiro comes looking for her, Lau is ready for him and a violent fight erupts between the two.

Action director Ching Siu-Tung has always been known for his over-the-top style of action direction. From the early 1980s up through the 1990s and even now, Ching has been responsible for some of the craziest wire-fu set pieces in the history of the genre. Even in films set in the modern day, Ching has rarely been able to resist the wires and thus films that seem otherwise realistic are filled with jarringly-unrealistic fights. Thus it comes as a surprise that this period piece—bear in mind that his craziest work has been in period pieces—features the most realistic set piece that Ching Siu-Tung has done outside of the two John Woo movies he worked on in the 1980s[62].

There is some ruthlessly brutal saber action in this particular fight. There are a few ornate spins and overhead attacks, but the techniques are otherwise direct and economical. There is some grappling thrown in, as is some neat kicking. Late in the fight, you can see the damage that Lau and Takeshi have done to each other's blades. The realistic touches come near the end, where for once in a martial arts film, the combatants start to display outward signs of exhaustion and fatigue. The moves become sloppier and less precise, going from beautifully-realized attacks to formless hacking and slashing. It's a nice touch that shows the desperation of the two soldiers.

One thing that stands out about this fight is the art direction. When the fight first begins, the setting appeared to be in the fall. As the fight continues, it starts to snow, changing the background dramatically. It makes the fight quite beautiful to look at, creating a dramatic contrast between the beauty of the scenery and the brutality of the fighting.

Takeshi Kaneshiro and Andy Lau handle themselves well in the fight, despite their limited martial arts training. But as usual, the main star of a Ching Siu-Tung fight is Ching Siu-Tung's action direction, rather than the performers themselves. After so many over-the-top fights, flying people, exploding mannequins, and esoteric attacks, this fight (and several others in the movie) comes off as something refreshing. From an artistic and technical point of view, this fight is a winner.

---

[62] Those would be *A Better Tomorrow 2* (1987) and *The Killer* (1989), although they are admittedly "bullet ballet" films and not actually martial arts films.

Spear

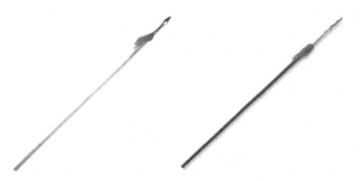

The spear is one of the oldest weapons in existence, its use going back to the Stone Age (some 400,000 years ago). Moreover, it is one of the weapons whose creation can be found in another species other than man; chimpanzees have been recording taking tree branches, stripping off the bark, sharpening one end with their teeth, and hunting small primates with them. As far as humans go, the spear started off as a sharpened stick, after which stone spearheads were invented, followed by fire-hardened tips, and so forth. All cultures have used the spear over the centuries and it has been a popular battle weapon since the time of the first Mesopotamian cultures.

In Chinese martial arts, the spear is considered to be one of the four major weapons, garnering the nickname "The King of Weapons." The Chinese spear, called in *qiang* in Mandarin Chinese, is usually made out of wax wood, which gives it certain flexibility and allows the user to hold the weapon on end and twirl it, confusing the enemy. Chinese spears are also known for having a red tassel near the spearhead, which serves the function of disguising the spear's movements and trapping the opponent's weapon. The spear is used in pricking, thrusting, blocking, poking, and wringing techniques, among others. In modern Chinese *wushu*, there is a lot of agile footwork and somersaults involved in the spear forms. There are also several variations of the spear, including the two-pointed spear, the lance (*mao*), and the snake spear, whose spearhead is very curvy.

American poster for *Flag of Iron* (Shaw Brothers, 1980).

Outside of China, spears can be easily found in any movie about cave men, historical battles, and Native Americans. Likewise, in Chinese cinema, this weapon can be found in any battle sequence, considering its popularity among infantry and cavalry. So basically, any movie that features soldiers is bound to have spear-wielding going on. But that's not all. There are lots of notable spear fights to be seen in Hong Kong cinema. In *Blood of the Dragon* (1971), the spear of Jimmy Wang Yu's preferred weapon. Jackie

Chan's old school classic *Snake and Crane Arts of Shaolin* (1977) features a very complex fight between Jackie and three spearmen. There are two fights in *Heroes of the East* (1978) that analyze the differences between Chinese and Japanese spears. Most Mainland Chinese films will feature the spear, as the screenwriters usually make it a point to include as many of the traditional weapons of *wushu* as possible in each film. In *New Legend of Shaolin* (1994), Jet Li wields a metal spear that has the ability to extend, retract, and even bend at the joints. Ronnie Yu's *Fearless* (2006) features a nifty fight that shows the differences between Chinese spear fighting and Western spear techniques.

Blood of the Dragon (1973)

In the late 60s and early 70s, a lot of *wuxia* films ended with the film's protagonist(s) taking on a virtual army of bad guys with a simple weapon like a sword or saber. These sorts of fights were a staple of a lot of Chang Cheh's earlier films, like *The New One-Armed Swordsman* (1971) and *Trail of the Broken Blade* (1968). These bloodbath endings are generally the highlight of the movie and are fairly similar to the action sequences often seen in Japanese swordplay films made in the same era. *Blood of the Dragon*, which was made when open-fisted fighting was on the rise and people like Bruce Lee and Angela Mao were at their peaks, comes across as a throwback to the *wuxia* films of the previous decade.

The final fight is fought outside of an inn where White Dragon (Jimmy Wang Yu), is in possession of a list of rebel names. The prime minister and the Mongol army—the film is set during the Yuan Dynasty when the Mongols ruled China—have surrounded the inn and demand that Dragon turn over the name list. White Dragon refuses and hands the list over to Prince Ma Tung, promising to keep the soldiers at bay while Ma Tung escapes with the list. What follows is a large-scale massacre in which White Dragon takes on the all the soldiers and General Tai (Yee Yuen), an evil general armed with a whip sword. Dozens of soldiers are killed by White Dragon, who had been wounded in a previous duel.

Jimmy Wang Yu was never a martial artist and that would become evident in the kung fu films he made after 1970. His style of screen fighting has often been described as the "flailing arms" style and he rarely rose above that in most of his films. Under most circumstances, that would kill a screen fighter's career dead in a matter of a few films, especially considering the talent Wang was up against during the 1970s. Jimmy was a resourceful chap, however, and usually had a few ways of overcoming this obvious and otherwise career-crippling shortcoming. First of all, Wang Yu would occasionally pair himself up with a talented choreographer like Sammo Hung or one of the Lau Clan. Thus, they could choreography him well enough to get around his weaknesses and accentuate his actual talents. *Blood of the Dragon*, however, doesn't have any name choreographers. In this film, we have action direction from Cheung Yee-Kwai, who worked as action director on a number of obscure Taiwanese films during the 1970s and spent most of his career as a stuntman and supporting actor in independent kung fu films.

Another thing that Wang Yu did was cast himself in films where his character fought exclusively with a weapon. Wang Yu was after all an athlete (a swimming champion to be exact) was coordinated enough that he could swing a weapon with a decent amount of aptitude. This worked in his favor especially in the earlier *wuxia* films, where the action was closer in spirit to Japanese *chambara* films and Western swashbucklers than the complex *wushu*/Peking Opera routines that would become more commonplace later on. A good actor would swing his sword with gusto and take down dozens of extras with little effort. At that sort of choreography Jimmy Wang Yu excelled. This was the case here, as Jimmy fights exclusively with a metal spear instead of his hands and feet.

Jimmy Wang Yu looks quite good, if a little rough around the edges, as he takes on a small army with his spear. He keeps his techniques simple, but effective. There are the usual parries and blocks with his offensive techniques being mostly made up of pokes. Wang Yu occasionally holds the spear by one end and swings it in a circle in an attempt to hit multiple guys that are surrounding him, or simply increase the space between him and them. Yes, his spear-wielding is as physically complex as the spear fighting we'd see in Venom Mob films or in Mainland Chinese kung fu cinema, but it works in its context. Furthermore, Jimmy Wang Yu was fairly good at playing the noble and macho hero, and thus was able to sell himself as being tough enough to take out an entire army single-handed, which he does here.

A final thing that Jimmy Wang Yu did, and it's for this that many people have so many fond memories of his films, was to throw in some rather surrealistic elements into his movies. If Jimmy Wang Yu couldn't out-fight his competition, he'd out-wierd them. Zombie fighters, yogi with stretchy arms, characters that walk on walls and ceilings, and inflatable Tibetan lamas are among some of the more bizarre elements that you'll see in Jimmy's films. *Blood of the Dragon* does feature one creative touch, although it may seem tame compared to some of the aforementioned quirks in Jimmy's filmography. In this film, villain Yee Yuen, a veteran of dozens of Taiwanese martial arts films from the 1960s to the 1990s, wields what is essentially a chain sword. The weapon is a sword with a three-edged blade with a number of joints that allow the blade to separate into smaller pieces and be swung at one's opponent just like a whip. The weapon is rather unique and video game fans will recognize the weapon as the one used by Ivy in the *Soul Caliber* video game series.

This final blowout lasts more than 18 minutes and is one of Jimmy Wang Yu's best moments in terms of gritty, violent action. Yes, it's low budget. Yes, it's quite obvious that the soldiers are taking Wang Yu's spear to the armpits and faking death. Yes, Wang Yu is not the most agile spear fighter ever. And yes, it is not one of Wang Yu's quirkier fights. But few people have his intensity and its this that sells like long, epic fight.

The Killer Army (1980)

It will become apparent throughout the course of the book that the Venom Mob, that troupe of five talented screen fighters that made about a dozen films with Chang Cheh during the late 70s and early 80s, will dominate in large part the weapons chapters of this book. All things considered, they are consistently the best onscreen martial artists to use weapons in the history of the genre. Of course, this isn't to say that there haven't been individual performers or action directors that have done a film or two that was better than a Venom Mob film, but the truth is that the Venom Mob made a concentrated effort to fill most of their films with high-quality weapons choreography and include weapons that otherwise received little attention in other martial arts films. Swords, sabers, staves, spears, tridents, halberds, hooks, horse blades, rings, axes, fans, and other weapons were all given showcases in numerous Venom Mob films of the course of just five years.

In *The Killer Army*, the film ends with a large fight scene involving spears, including a somewhat large one wielded by Venom Lu Feng, that master of long weapons. The main conflict of the film deals with a refugee city dominated by several factions of warlords. When three kung fu expert refugees (Philip Kwok, Chiang Sheng, and Lo Meng) get involved in some intrigue between the factions and the Generals they serve, they decide that they must flee the city. The best place for them to get out of dodge would be the dock. Lo Meng arrives there first and is met by Lu Feng and his four spear-wielding flunkies (not to mention another fighter who's a good kicker, but doesn't last long in the fight itself). Unfortunately, the five talented fighters prove to be too much for Lo Meng and ends up biting it. Philip Kwok and Chiang Sheng arrive on the scene and almost fall into a trap, if not for Lo Meng who warns them of the villains' presence with his dying breaths. Another big fight breaks out between our two surviving heroes and the spearmen.

Some have criticized this fight for being too gimmicky, which we feel is something of an exaggeration. The gimmick in question would be the so-called "rubber spears" that Lu Feng's goons fight with. Let's remember that spears are made of wax wood, which is naturally flexible and that the flexibility of the spear is necessary to confuse an opponent. Thus, a very flexible spear would not be too far away from the truth. Moreover, the Venoms don't let the users go overboard with the spear-bending until the last part of the fight, so the gimmick never feels over used. The actors playing the spear fighters are obviously talented and know what they're doing. Furthermore, we're talking about a fight that features one person taking on multiple spearmen simultaneously; the actors playing the spear fighters need to be just as coordinated and exact in their movements as the fighter dodging their attacks.

It won't come as a surprise (it never does) that the spear fighting brought to us courtesy of Lu Feng make that of his compatriots pale in comparison. Lu Feng doesn't really get into the fight until Chiang Sheng and Philip Kwok show up, and he spends most of the climax fighting against Chiang Sheng. There's something about the way he wields these long weapons that makes so many other fighters look almost lethargic. Lu Feng doesn't content himself with simply trying to poke Chiang Sheng with his weapon; he twirls it, performs jumping swings, performs bludgeoning attacks, and tries to cut Chiang with the side of the spearhead and not just pierce him with the tip. His performance is quite animated and he brings character to a weapon that, like the saber, is too often used by extras in mass battle scenes.

The other Venoms provide excellent support in a way that only a Venom could. Lo Meng gets to show off his Southern Mantis for a few minutes before being brutally killed. Nonetheless, he handles the complex choreography of taking on *four* spear-wielding baddies *and* a high-kicking fighter at the same time with great aplomb. There's no doubt as to the talents of Chiang Sheng and Philip Kwok, who not only are the main fighters here, but also were the film's action directors. Philip Kwok fights with the three-section staff and does a solid job here. Chiang Sheng uses a saber and a *rattan* shield against the spearmen, and then against Lu Feng. The choreography here is quite complex and certain scenes are somewhat reminiscent of previous Jackie Chan efforts like *The Fearless Hyena* (1979) and *Snake and Crane Arts of Shaolin* (1977), which featured similar fights. It's really a group effort here, as you need talented action directors to come up with the perfect combination of moves for five people to perform; a talented fighter to be able to dodge, block, and contort his body through so many strokes; and finally good performers that can execute the weapons techniques without injuring the performer.

This is not the Venom Mob's only foray into high-octane spear fighting. Let me bring your attention to the film *Flag of Iron* (1980), which features some a great climatic duel with Philip Kuo and Lu Feng duking it spear-tipped flags. There's also Lu Feng's appearance as Silver Spear in *Kid with the Golden Arm*, which we'll talk about later on in the book. Lu Feng also does some excellent work with the weapon in the independent Chang Cheh film *Nine Demons (1984)*, which deserves mention. To be perfectly honest, these films come close to being interchangeable when you get right down to it. So we give a hearty recommendation to all of these films for classic spear fighting goodness!

Yao's Young Warriors (1983)

Yao's Young Warriors is a Mainland Chinese production that was made in the wake of the huge success of Jet Li's *The Shaolin Temple*. Like most of the best Mainland films, this film benefits from a cast made up of talented wushu stylists and an epic storyline that allows for a number of authentic (if not entirely accurate) set pieces. Of note are the weapons sequences, which the website *The Martial Artist's Guide to Hong Kong Films* referred to as "some of the best weapons work you'll ever see." The movie was originally released in the United States under the title *Yao's Young Warriors*. Later, it was released on VHS by Xenon Entertainment as *Wu Tang Death Squad*, in order to take advantage of the popularity of the rap group Wu Tang Clan. When it was released on DVD, it was released under its original title again.

The film deals with the conflict between the Ching family and General Yao's (aka General Yueh Fei) forces. In the end, the Chings bring in four mercenaries to take on the General Yao's children. The four mercenaries consist of an Eagle's claw expert, a fighter with an "iron head", a pole fighter, and an assassin skilled in the meteor hammer. After getting in a fight with two members of the Yao family, the others show up and a big brawl breaks out. The Yao family are armed with spears and show off their spear formation techniques against the four killers.

In this fight, we get an excellent example of *wushu* spear techniques without the help of wires, quick-cut editing, doubles, or gimmicks. The moves are occasionally flowery, but not so much as to make the fight look like a bunch of people performing forms on each other, as in other Mainland films. Nonetheless, for a weapon that people may imagine is simple enough to use—you'd think that you just need to poke a person with a spear and nothing else—there are a lot of techniques on display, including moments where the spear is used much like a cudgel, for lateral bludgeoning strikes. Moreover, a lot of the techniques require a bit of contorting and agile body movements, something that only a trained martial artist would be able to perform.

The spear formation sequences are, compared to other films with weapons formations, realistic. In the formation that the Yao family performs, they simply form a circle and start twirling their spears around, creating something of an impenetrable barrier. A lot of "formations" require wires and trick editing for something large and impressive, but with otherwise little practical value.

The fight is greatly enhanced by the talent of the actors playing the villains. The two that stick out are the actor that plays the Eagle's Claw stylist and the one who wields the meteor hammer. Let's point out here that the Eagle's Claw supposedly has its origins in General Yueh Fei, so to have a villain use the style against the General's children is a bit unlikely. However, the actor is flexible and gives the style a better showcase than in other Mainland films. Nonetheless, the actor who fights with the meteor hammer practically steals the show from the film's heroes. It is one of the best showcases for that weapon that we've seen in a martial arts film.

The choreography here is provided by Wang Jin-Bao. This appears to be his only credit as action director, which he does a commendable job. His only other credit is as the writer of *Betrayal and Revenge* (1985), a very good Mainland film about the Taiping rebellion. Wang pulls off the often difficult feat of walking that line between exhibitionist choreography and believable screen fighting. There are acrobatics here, but it really looks like the people are trying to hit and hurt each other, rather than the players trying to use each other to showcase their skills. It's a pity that he didn't work on more films, because his action direction some of the best that we've seen in a Mainland film that didn't feature a Hong Kong choreographer. And that is saying a lot.

Hero (2002)

The great success of *Crouching Tiger, Hidden Dragon* (2000) was the catalyst for a whole slew of historical martial arts films with international distribution in mind. At this point, a lot of filmmakers, including a few high-profile ones with no experience in the genre, decided to take a stab (no pun intended) at the swordplay, or *wuxia*, genre. The most prolific and successful of these directors was Zhang Yimou, an acclaimed Mainland director known for his dramas starring Gong Li. His first film was *Hero*, a very loose retelling of the legend of Jin Ke, the man who tried to assassinate the king of Qin, who became the first emperor of China. The film is full of over-the-top fighting, beautiful costumes, philosophy, and Chinese propaganda. The movie was highly successful, getting an Oscar nomination for Best Foreign Film and winning the 2002 Hong Kong Film Award for, among other things, best Action Direction.

The three main members of the cast are Jet Li, Tony Leung Chiu-Wai and Maggie Cheung. Tony and Maggie are not martial artists, so it was decided that a real martial artist was needed for one of Jet Li's fights. After all, the duel between Michelle Yeoh and Zhang Ziyi in *Crouching Tiger, Hidden Dragon* had won quite a bit of acclaim. It would be disappointing to fans if Yimou didn't try to one-up it in some way. Jet Li had previously worked with Donnie Yen on *Once Upon a Time in China II*, which very impressive results. Jet Li told the filmmakers that if they wanted the best fight, they had to hire Yen. So Yen was brought in for the film's first major set-piece, one that is now considered to be a classic by many.

Nameless (Jet Li) is a prefect/swordsman who takes it upon himself to rid the Kingdom of Qin of three feared assassins, including the mysterious Sky (Donnie Yen).

One day, Sky is at a teahouse playing chess when he is confronted by some of the king's guards. They challenge him to a duel and quickly lose. Before he can leave the establishment, Sky is confronted by Nameless, who declares him under arrest. At first, Sky doesn't take him seriously, mistaking him for a lowly official. Nonetheless, Nameless unsheathes his sword and the two fight to a standstill. It is then that they close their eyes and continue their fight in their minds.

Analyzing the fight, we first look at Donnie Yen's initial showdown with the guards. Yen's character, Sky, wields a silver spear with a white tassel at the base of the spear head. At the beginning of the fight, the spear is sheathed. First the head guard attacks, followed by two more, and then by four more. He fends them off with his spear, twirling it around and parrying their saber strokes, never trying to actually hurt them. Being a Donnie Yen fight, he can't resist throwing in some of his trademark kicks, including his famous jumping back kick and a triple bicycle kick. Admitting defeat, the guards bow to him and let him leave. There's a lot of character in this particular scene, as we see that Sky does not needless kill or even injure people. Sky does not even unsheathe his spear while tangling with the guards.

During the 1990s, Ching Siu-Tung's style of swordplay choreography could be described as being very balletic. There was lots of twisting, twirling, running, and moving from the performers (and their stunt doubles). His work was very kinetic, the camera following the performing as they twirled and swung their swords and other weapons with great grace. However, purists will note that his fights often are devoid of actual martial arts, being pretty to look at but with little real impact. There is a great sense of ballet to this fight, although the emphasis of technique is clear.

Things get even more kinetic, but nonetheless technically correct, once Jet Li appears to challenge Yen. Both are *wushu*-trained martial artists, and thus their weapons work is decidedly *wushu*-oriented. Jet Li wields a sword and provides an excellent example of *jian* techniques. It is not his finest moment, but he does the weapon great justice and both he and Yen show themselves to be each other's equal, without a doubt.

Nonetheless, although they match each other move for move, Donnie Yen's spear handling comes out winner in the end. He does everything you can imagine with his spear. He uses the tassel to trap Jet Li's sword and to obscure Jet's vision. In one imaginative segment, he swings the spear with one arm under one of his legs. In another segment, he hangs upside down from some rafters and swings the spear with precision. Although the spear is metallic, it's flexible enough for Donnie to bend over Jet's head in an attempt to hit him from above.

Assisting action director Ching Siu-Tung is Stephen Tung Wei, another distinguished choreographer from Hong Kong. Both men are talented individuals with solid experience in different genres of action. As stated before, Ching Siu-Tung's talent has always been with over-the-top wire-fu swordplay. Tung Wei, on the other, hand is pretty apt at just about all types of fighting, although we point to his slick modern-day kickboxing and "gun-fu" as his specialty. Here, they go for something more traditional, downplaying the use of wires (although they are present) and opting for a style of fighting that the two hadn't done since the early 1980s. The result is a fight that is easily one of the best fights that either of the two choreographers ever worked on. This is especially true for Ching Siu-Tung, whose fights tend to be so creative and wire-assisted that they're rarely a showcase for the actors themselves, but for Ching's boundless imagination. We can thank director Zhang Yimou, who wanted the fights to be more grounded than airborne.

From an aesthetic point of view, the fight is quite beautiful. The costumes are all well-made. When the fight in the characters' minds begins, the screen switches to black and white, in order to distinguish the fight from reality. There's a nice contrast between the Donnie Yen and Jet Li fighting in black and white, while the two in color are standing still, letting water fall all over their bodies and weapons. The photography by Peter Doyle is quite beautiful. He gets some nice angles and thankfully lets the camera soak in the talent of the two men, rather than breaking it up with too many quick cuts like a lot of Ching Siu-Tung's earlier work.

The fight is an absolute work of art from all involved. Donnie Yen's spear fighting is some of the best spear fighting ever seen, ranking of there with Lu Feng's best work from the early 1980s. Jet Li also fights quite well and should be commended. The cinematography is excellent and Zhang Yimou's artistic vision makes this fight quite memorable. The action direction by Ching Siu-Tung and Stephen Tung-Wei is impeccable and they deserve praises for letting two talented screen fighters do what they do best. It's a triumph.

Sword (Jian)

The sword is one of the universal weapons and can be recognized by just about every culture in existence. The design is simple: a long blade, single or double edged, with a hilt and one end for the user to hold on to. The sword is used for piercing, slashing, chopping, blocking, parrying, stabbing, and other functions in battle. It has been used by most civilizations throughout history for close-quarters combat and in many cases, was the preferred weapon of war. The production of swords goes back to the Bronze Age. The first swords are dated 3300 B.C. and were found in modern-day Turkey. They were made of bronze and were actually just a longer variation of the dagger. The earliest found copper swords came from Harappa in modern-day Pakistan and date back to 2300 B.C. The earliest iron swords date back 1300 B.C. and were used by civilizations such as the Hittites and the Mycenaean Greeks.

The first swords in China were made of bronze and were produced during the Shang Dynasty (1766-1122 B.C.). The first steel blades were produced in 3rd century B.C. during the Qin dynasty and were the predecessors to the weapons used in modern-day kung fu training. In Asian countries, there's a distinct difference in nomenclature between single-edged and double-edged weapons. A single-edged blade is known as the *dao*, which is generally translated as saber or broadsword. The double-edged blade is known as the *jian*, which is called the sword. Thus, in Chinese martial arts it is not accurate to call all long-bladed weapons "swords", as the term is reserved only for two-edged blades.

The *jian* is one of the four principal weapons in Chinese martial arts--as well as one of the 18 traditional arms of *wushu*--bearing the nickname of "The Gentleman of Weapons." The first *jian* were produced around the 7th century B.C., during the Warring States period. *Jian* tend to be light and one-handed, although heavier variations that must be weld with both hands exist. The blade is straight, and there is a gradual taper to it, and occasionally the blade itself gets sharper near the tip. Some *jian* have a red tassel attached the pommel, which can be used for tangling the opponent's weapon or lashing across the opponent's face. As far as styles go, it is practiced a lot by students of Taijiquan (Tai chi quan), *wushu*, and other styles such as *choy li fut*.

As you can imagine, there is no shortage of the *jian* in Chinese cinema. However, since people often think of both the *jian* and the *dao* as both being "swords", one must be a little careful in distinguishing between the two whenever the word "sword" is mentioned. The *dao* and its variations are far more common in movies than the *jian* is. Nonetheless, most *wuxia pain*, or swordplay films, feature the *jian* in one form or another. A lot of movies that deal with *tai chi chuan* or wushu will have a character or two armed with the *jian* sword.

Some notable films featuring the *jian* would include the two Shaw Brothers classics, *The Master* (1980) and *My Young Auntie* (1981). In the former, Yuan Tak uses a tasseled sword against Johnny Wang Lung Wei in the finale. In the latter, Kara Hui Ying-Hung uses a sword while fighting against Yuen Tak. In *Kids from Shaolin*, several of the female protagonists use the sword throughout the film. In *Snake Deadly Act*, Angela Mao gets to show off some pretty good tai chi sword forms in an early fight, as does Linda Lin in the penultimate fight of *Dance of the Drunk Mantis* (1978). Most *wuxia* films made during the 1990s "New Wave" feature this weapon, as do the *wuxia* films made following the success of *Crouching Tiger, Hidden Dragon* in 2000.

While all of the films mentioned in the previous paragraph are period pieces, the *jian* occasionally finds its way into a more contemporary setting. In Tsui Hark's *The Master* (1992), Jet Li gets to show off his prowess with the *jian* in one of the later fight scenes. In *In the Line of Duty V: Middle Man* (1990), Cynthia Khan fights Kim Maree Penn with a *katana* blade, but uses techniques taken from *jian* forms. Something similar happens in *The Death Games* (1998), where Fan Siu-Wong and Kim Maree Penn duke it out with *rapiers*, but using traditional Chinese sword movements. That same year, *The Black Sheep Affair* (1998), Vincent Zhao Wen-Zhuo showed off some wushu-tinged swordplay with a *rapier* in his final duel with villain Andrew Lin. Skip ahead a few years, where Wu Jing, under Nicky Li Chung-Chi's tutelage, uses the *jian* in Triad melees and against Sammo Hung in *Fatal Move* (2008).

The Sword (1980)

In the late 1970s, Tony Ching Siu-Tung had entered the world of cinema as an actor and action director in a number of traditional "chopsockey" films, including fan favorites *The Master Strikes* (1980) and *Stroke of Death* (1979). Ching Siu-Tung showed off a certain knack for traditional choreography, and was just as physically talented and acrobatic as his contemporaries, including the Seven Fortunes and the Venom Mob. However, it was in 1980 that Ching Siu-Tung would find his special place in Hong Kong cinema: stylized *wuxia* swordplay. Beginning with *The Sword*, Ching Siu-Tung would go on to produce, direct, and choreograph countless films and TV series featuring over-the-top, wire-enhanced swordplay. Ching himself practically ushered in the 1990s "New Wave" with films like *The Chinese Ghost Story* franchise and the first *Swordsman* (1990) film. He has been one of the most-oft nominated action directors at the Hong Kong Film Awards and is commonly counted alongside Yuen Woo-Ping as the co-King of Wire-Fu.

It is in his first important *wuxia* film that Ching Siu-Tung gives us a good taste of what he'd be serving up for audiences for the next couple of decades. The final duel between Adam Cheng and Norman Tsui Siu-Keung is one of the better examples of his style of swordplay direction, as it's free of a lot of the qualities that purists tend to criticize in some of his work: overabundance of wires and FX-driven "esoteric" attacks, short duration, and a lack of actual martial arts content. The fight isn't very long compared to other films made during the same time; it's about three minutes long in total. However, there is more than enough energy in the sword fighting between Adam Cheng and Norman Tsui to make up for the short running time.

The style of the choreography is something of a transition between pure, technique-driven choreography involving the *jian* and Ching Siu-Tung's later, more balletic style of choreography. The fight goes on with little interruption and all of the moves are actual *jian* techniques, spiced up with wire-assisted somersaults. Ching Siu-Tung is a lot more restrained in both the usage of wires and quick cuts than he would be in the following decade, and that really contributes to a more compelling duel.

Adam Cheng plays here the role of the heroic swordsman, a role which he would play in quite a few films and TV series during his career, including the *Fong Sai Yuk* films of the 1990s and Tsui Hark's seminal fantasy *Zu: Warriors of Magic Mountain* (1983). This is certainly one of his best physical performances and he gets to do more here than in a lot of his other films. Norman Tsui, who plays the villain, also acquits himself well to the acrobatic swordplay that Ching Siu-Tung requires of him. Interestingly enough, Norman Tsui had only started performing kung fu in front of the camera three years earlier in *The Deadly Mantis* (1977) and before that he had never actually trained in the martial arts. Fortunately, he was very athletic and, like a number of other Hong Kong action stars, had the uncanny ability to do just about anything the choreographer wanted him to do.

If you're looking for some "flying swordplay" that strikes the perfect balance between the "flying" and the "swordplay", the final fight of *The Sword* is about as good as you can get. Ching Siu-Tung shows us that the *wuxia* genre practically belonged to him from the get-go and gives us one of the best examples of his style of action direction, which is in and of itself an art form.

Adam Cheng wields *The Sword* (1980).

Sword Stained with Royal Blood (1981)

It was at in 1981 that Chang Cheh and his Venom Mob troupe began to make period-piece films based on the *wuxia*, or swordplay, novels of acclaimed author Louis Cha (Jin Yong). As a result, the quality of the plots improved somewhat compared to a number of their earlier films. However, the quality of the action in their films really shot up in quality. Some of the finest *wuxia* action in the history of the genre was crafted in the four films they made based on Cha's books, including the finale to this film, which is one of the great fights featuring the sword.

At the climax of the film, Yuan (Philip Kwok) is in the Wen household and has discovered a number of dirty secrets about the family. After a failed attempt to poison him, the Wen men challenge Yuan to a "friendly" duel, in which he is to test out their "Five Element Formation." The duel is interrupted by the arrival of his martial brother, who is able to break their formation with the help of his abacus and metal paintbrush. Yuan gets in on the action and ends up challenging the entire family, first with the help of a jade hairpin, and finally with his special weapon, the Golden Snake Sword.

Standing in his way are the male members of the Wen Family. The Patriarch, played by Wong Lik, enters the fracas armed with a large metal staff. The Patriarch's sons are played by Chui Tai-Pang, Lu Feng, Chiang Sheng, and Chu Ko. Chui is armed with the double daggers. Lu Feng uses his favorite weapon: the *kwan do*, or long-handled broadsword. Chu Ko is armed with a pair of short spears. Finally, Chiang Sheng uses the tiger's head hooks. One could easily draw the parallels between this film and the finale of *Shaolin Rescuers*. All of them do stellar jobs with the fast and complex choreography put together by Philip Kwok, but the fight really belongs to Kwok himself.

Philip Kwok fights using a variation of the *jian* sword, the so-called "Golden Snake Sword", whose blade is undulated to appear similar to a slithering serpent. Kwok finds himself fighting four opponents simultaneously and thus as action director is saddled with the task of creating some of the fastest and most complex choreography of the genre. The blows come fast and hard, as Kwok must weave his way through the four Wens with all of his might, parrying, stabbing, swinging, and blocking all of them at breakneck speed.

There are a couple of moments where the camera lingers on the fighters for several seconds, allowing them to perform numerous moves per take. It has been said that the Venom Mob were capable of memorizing up to 200 movements without having to stop the take. Although the camera is a little bit dynamic here than in some of the previous fights in the movie, it is still quite impressive how many moves they can perform without having to stop. Today we see lots of complaints of martial arts movies that have been edited with hacksaws, presented in a way that the camera switches positions at every single punch thrown, making it difficult to discern what's going on. That is not the case here.

Philip Kwok had assumed the role as lead choreographer in the Venom Mob films after Robert Tai left the Shaw Brothers in 1979. From 1980 until 1984, Kwok took care of the choreography chores in the majority of the films that Chang Cheh did for the Shaw Brothers, especially the Venom Mob films. This fight represents the peak of his work. It is not as long and drawn out as several of the other climatic Venom Mob fights were; this fight only lasts about 5 minutes (12 minutes if you count the hairpin sequence, the abacus sequence, and all of the dialogue in-between). But he manages to cram in a lot of top-drawer swordplay and makes this a classic one-against-many set-piece.

As with all Venom Mob films, there is a bit of graphic violence in this particular fight scene, although not as much as most other Chang Cheh-directed movies. There's a severed arm and a face full of darts, but that's really about it. The other stabbings are considerably less bloody than in other *wuxia* films made in the same era.

The Venom Mob, especially Philip Kwok, Chiang Sheng, and Lu Feng were consistently the best in the business when it to portraying weapons of all sorts on film. This is yet another testament, one of their last, to their legacy and contributions to kung fu cinema. While not their last film, it was one of their last great movies. Kwok was the only Venom to have much of a career after the group broke up in the early 1980s, and his work as action director in numerous films afterward never reached the peak that he reached with this fight, a masterpiece of swordplay on film.

Martial Arts of Shaolin (1986)

One of the greatest swordsmen of martial arts cinema is Yu Chenghui. Yu was a Mainland Chinese *wushu* stylist, a master of the Drunken Sword technique and the Northern Mantis kung fu style. As a martial artist, Yu Chenghui's greatest contribution to the world of martial arts was his restoration of the two-handed straight sword, or *shuang shou jian,* which had been lost during the Tang Dynasty (618 – 907 A.D.). He spent fourteen years researching the weapon, which he restored and created several forms for, including one based on movements from the Northern Mantis style. In the 1980s, Yu Chenghui appeared in four Mainland Chinese kung fu epics, all of which are considered to be genre classics today. Three of those films are the *Shaolin Temple* trilogy that a young Jet Li starred in. The other one was *Yellow River Fighter* (1988). All of them showcase Yu Chenghui's prowess with the sword, although his best work is in *Martial Arts of Shaolin*, the third entry in the series.

The final fight of this movie is an epic battle between our three heroes (Jet Li, Wong Chau Yin, and Woo Gin-Keung) and Yu Chenghui, who plays the corrupt Qing official. There are a number of parallel fights going on this scene, including numerous scenes of Shaolin monks and Shaolin-trained laymen taking on Qing soldiers. There's also a nifty scene where Woo Gin-Keung does some excellent *hung gar*, taking on several soldiers with his "iron forearms" while standing in the fundamental posture. However, we'll turn our attention to the scenes in which Yu Chenghui is involved.

In the first part, Jet Li and Woo Gin-Keung take on Yu Chenghui inside of his personal boat. Jet Li is armed with a hook spear (*gou lian qiang*) and Woo Gin-Keung wields a saber (*dao*). As expected, Yu is fighting with his trusty two-handed straight sword and three go at with energy to spare. The fight between the two is made even more complex by the occasional interference by Yu's soldiers, making Li and Woo have to defend multiple blows and attacks while dishing out their own moves. The choreography becomes even more complex when Yu Chenghui starts attacking Wong Chau-Yin, who is tied up at the moment, leaving Jet Li to not only fend off the numerous soldiers, but to protect Wong from Yu's blows. There is so much going on this sequence that one must watch the scene in widescreen to really appreciate all of the movement and technique onscreen.

Wong Chau-Yin is freed and the fight moves up top where Yu Chenghui must contend with our three protagonists. Wong and Woo are armed with sabers while Jet Li is still wielding the hook spear. The choreography continues to be as complex as the previous scene, as Yu's guards occasionally step in to help their leader. The fight continues until the cavalry arrives in the form of the Northern Shaolin monks and the Southern Shaolin laymen. At this point, Yu Chenghui jumps off the boat and into the river in an attempt to flee.

Yu Chenghui doesn't make it very far before encountering Yu Hai, who plays a senior monk from the Northern Shaolin Temple. Yu Hai, who's armed with a pole, challenges Yu Chenghui to a duel. Their duel takes them into a large garden where a wooden lattice structure holds a number of vegetables growing on vines. After trading a number of blows with their weapons, Yu Hai is disarmed and uses the mantis style to disarm Chenghui. From this point on, Jet Li and Yu Hai are able to best Yu Chenghui in combat using their superior Northern Mantis and *pakua chang* skills.

The entire sequence is just incredible and the choreography is some of the best ever seen in a Mainland Chinese film. The action direction is provided by the Lau Clan, including Lau Kar-Leung. Mainland Chinese choreography is often a bit too "soft" and "flowery" when choreographed by Mainland *wushu* stylists, so Lau and his team help put a stronger edge on the choreography that it would have otherwise had. The movements look less like actors trying to perform *sets*, or forms, on each other and more like trained martial artists trying to hack each other to pieces. Yu Chenghui gets to show off his mantis and drunken sword techniques and looks absolutely stunning doing so. All of Yu Chenghui's films are excellent showcases for his swordsmanship; it is under Lau Kar-Leung's direction, however, that we can really see the way his techniques and forms were meant to be applied.

Crouching Tiger, Hidden Dragon (2000)

There are always films that are so popular that they set the trend for other filmmakers for years to come. Just look at Bruce Lee's movies and the number of "Brucesploitation" films made after. Or look at Jackie Chan's *The Drunken Master* (1978) and all of the kung fu comedies that followed the same formula. How about all of the ghost movies made in the wake of the success of *A Chinese Ghost Story* (1987)? That's to say nothing of all the "wire-fu" movies that flooded the theaters after the immense success of Tsui Hark's *Once Upon a Time in China* (1991). You can see where all of this is going: look at all of the big-budget historical kung fu fantasies that respected filmmakers started making with big name Asian stars after *Crouching Tiger, Hidden Dragon* was an international hit.

The cream of the crop of this film is the final weapons duel between Michelle Yeoh and Zhang Ziyi. By the time this film was made, Michelle was hot on her way to become the greatest female action star of her generation, with classic films like *Police Story III: Supercop*, *Wing Chun*, *Yes Madam!*, and a score of others. She had just got been a Bond girl three years earlier in *Tomorrow Never Dies*, in which she was considered to be the best Bond girl in a long time.

Zhang Ziyi was a relative newcomer when she appeared in this movie. Although not an actual martial artist, she was athletic enough that she could do anything almost everything that action director Yuen Woo-Ping asked her to do. She holds her own with the traditional sword, which she wields in most of the film's fights, including this one. We should note that after this film's success, Zhang was practically typecast in these historical epic fantasy films, something that she has tried to shake off recently.

In the final showdown between the two fighting women, Zhang Ziyi is armed with the Green Destiny, a powerful sword that once belonged to Li Mu-Bai (played by Chow Yun-Fat). Determined to take it back and return it to Li, escort Shu Lien (Michelle Yeoh) challenges Zhang to a duel and uses a number of traditional weapons to get the sword out of her possession.

The first weapons that Michelle Yeoh uses in this fight are the *shuangdao* and the spear. Michelle Yeoh's character had stated earlier in this movie that the former was her preferred weapon and she's awfully proficient with it. She does excellent work with all weapons, even though she gets disarmed each time. Nonetheless, it becomes very apparent that Michelle's character is the better fighter. Her techniques are indeed better and she gets in more powerful hits against her opponent than Zhang does. However, Zhang's sword is incredibly powerful is more resistant and has a greater capacity for slicing through other weapons, thus putting Michelle at a slight disadvantage.

Nonetheless, as powerful as Zhang thinks she is, she is really not more than the weapon she's armed with. Take the weapon away from her and Michelle would make mincemeat of her within the first minute of fighting.

Ang Lee should be praised for allowing Yuen Woo-Ping to use some weapons that weren't exactly common in martial arts movies. Michelle Yeoh's third weapon is the tiger's head hooks, a weapon that most mainstream audiences had only seen in the video game *Mortal Kombat III*, in which the character Kabal used it extensively. Michelle is quite slick with the weapon, especially when she uses one hook to swing the other, trying to hit Zhang Ziyi with the handle, which is shaped like a halberd's blade.

The other weapons Michelle Yeoh uses are heavy metal club and a two-handed broadsword. Both weapons are rarely used in Chinese kung fu movies. Both weapons overwhelm Zhang Ziyi, who is able to get the upper hand only because of the Green Destiny. According to the director's commentary on the DVD, Ang Lee had originally wanted Michelle Yeoh to use the rope dart against Zhang Ziyi, but Yuen Woo-Ping had advised that that weapon would be too complicated to choreograph, especially given the level of talent of the actresses involved.

This fight easily blows the other fights in movie out of the water. The teahouse fight had potential, as we were treated to a number of fighters armed with diverse weapons. However, Yuen Woo-Ping and Ang Lee opted to make Zhang Ziyi nearly invincible in that fight and thus we didn't get much opportunity to see those weapons in action. The bamboo forest fight wasn't so much a fight as it was a collection of wire stunts. This fight, however, used a minimum of wires and maximum of good old-fashioned kung fu weapon madness and, for all of the advances in CGI and digital wire removal, it is always the real deal that sticks in our minds longer. This fight is one of the best fights of the new millennium, no doubt about it.

Dagger

The dagger, like the axe, is one of the oldest weapons in existence and has its roots in prehistory. The first daggers were made of flint and bone and, as technology became more sophisticated, the materials used in making these small weapons became stronger and more durable as well. It is a weapon that has been produced in nearly all cultures and civilizations and is still standard issue for most military personnel and special forces operatives today.

The dagger is characterized as a short, two-edged blade, similar to a knife. While knifes are used primarily for cutting, a dagger's principal function is stabbing and thrusting, though most are designed to cut, too. In battle, daggers have generally been used as secondary or tertiary weapons because of their short range. While good for close range combat, taking on someone armed with a sword, a spear, or a bow and arrow would've been sheer foolishness!

According to Lau Kar Wing's *The Odd Couple*, the dagger is one of the eighteen principal weapons of kung fu. Like the axe, daggers are often seen in kung fu movies as being the preferred weapon of Triads and small-time robbers. Many of the first "chopsockeys" from the early 1970s featured large-scale melees involving multiple fighters armed with daggers. Throwing knives are also fairly common in traditional kung fu cinema as well.

While choreographing knife fights for large numbers of stuntmen isn't so difficult, there is a large amount of dexterity and coordination needed by performers and action directors to pull off good one-on-one fights involving daggers or knives. The two fights that shall be covered here are very good examples of both the dagger being used in a one-on-one situation and in a group fight.

Keep an eye out for well-choreographed dagger fights in *Daggers 18* (1980), *Vengeance!* (1970), *SPL* (2005), and the Japanese film *Versus* (2001). The advent of CGI in martial arts movies has resulted in exaggerated knife fare in films like *House of Flying Daggers, True Legend*, and the recent 3-D *wuxia* film *Flying Swords of Dragon Gate* (2011).

Sword of Swords (1968)

While Bruce Lee was of the earliest and easily the greatest of the "modern" martial arts heroes, the title of the "first modern martial arts hero" belongs to a man named Jimmy Wang Yu. It is with great irony then, that we point out that Mr. Wang Yu was not a martial artist. He was a professional swimmer and thus endowed with a certain athleticism that allowed him to adapt himself (up to a point) to the demands of the choreographers. Nonetheless, what really attracted filmmakers to him was that he was something of a brawler and was good enough in a street fight that film producers felt he was leading man material.

Throughout his career, Jimmy Wang Yu would have some certain difficulties in convincing audiences that he was a good fighter. If he had a weapon in his hands, he could pull it off quite nicely. However, remove the weapon from his hands and all you'd get was Wang swinging his arms wildly at his opponents. Apparently Wang was aware of his, as he would occasionally throw in a lot of bizarre elements into his movies to get past that. But that's another story. The point is that if you give Wang a sword or a spear, or a dagger in this case, Wang would become unstoppable.

The final fight from *Sword of Swords* can be seen as both an ode to Japanese *chambara* cinema and a continuation of Jimmy Wang Yu's personal theme that crippled people can be just as dangerous, if not more, than regular people. Wang Yu's character is blind by this point in this movie and has decided to arm himself with twin daggers. The blindness factor was obviously inspired by the Japanese *Zatoichi* films, which were wildly popular at the time. In this fight, the character's blindness helps his prowess become that much more entertaining and satisfying, but also leads up to the scenes most harrowing moments: the villains throwing Wang Yu's friends, who have been bound and gagged, at Wang, who unwittingly cuts them down with deadly efficiency.

Poster for *Sword of Swords* (Shaw Brothers, 1969).

Upon realizing what has happened, Wang is pushed over the top and is soon leveling a small army with his twin daggers. This fight can please on an emotional level, considering what has happened in the film up to this point, but also on a purely visceral level. Wang Yu's character has two disadvantages compared to his enemies, one being his blindness and the other being his weapons, which are small compared to the swords his enemies wield. Thus, watching Wang Yu go through them all like a reaper through a wheat field makes the entire sequence that much more entertaining.

We can also observe that the use of daggers in this fight would foresee the popularity of these weapons in a lot of films made at the beginning of the next decade. Dagger-wielding heroes and villains made up a large part of films made between 1970 and 1975. Actors like Bruce Lee, Ti Lung, and David Chiang would feature large-scale fights with knife-wielding thugs. The most famous of that era was *Vengeance!* (1970), starring David Chiang and directed by Chang Cheh.

The choreography for this scene was provided by Tong Gaai and Lau Kar-Leung, the Shaw Bros powerhouse choreographers. An early point in their careers, one can see the influence of Japanese *chambara* films in the fight direction: the movements are quicker and deadlier than the drawn-out, technique-based weapons choreography that both Tong and Lau would perfect in the second half of the following decade. Here, the movements are simple and this helps sell Wang Yu as a super-efficient killer, rather than a non-martial artist trying to do something that he wasn't even trained to do. The resulting battle is one that ranks with the best of the Japanese samurai movies being made during the same period.

Kwan Do – Assault Blade

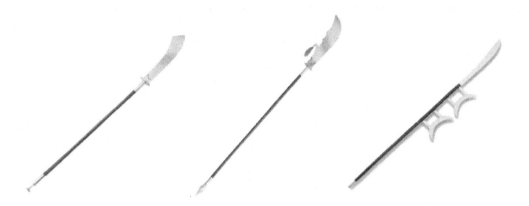

  A common weapon in Chinese martial arts is the long-handled broadsword, known in Chinese as the *pudao*. *Pudao* literally means "assault blade." It is a type of pole-arm, which consists of a long pole with a wide, curved metal blade at one end and a spear tip at the other for balance. A popular weapon with soldiers, the *pudao* was used for slicing the legs off of horses during battle. This has given the weapon the nickname of "horse knife." The weapon is commonly taught in most Wushu schools in China today, although the version they use a lot lighter than what soldiers used centuries before.

  There are a number of variations of the weapon. One variation is known as the "nine-ring blade", which gains its name from a number of metal rings found on the dull side of the blade, which are used for lessening the force of an enemy's attack when blocking. Another variation, *xiang bi da dao*, lacks a pointed blade and has a spiral design on the blade that gives it the nickname of "Elephant Nose Blade." A third variation, the *ying tou dao*, or eagle head blade, has a pronounced hook at the tip of the blade, used for pulling an enemy's weapon.

  The most famous variation, however, is the *kwan do*, or General Kwan's Broadsword. The legend is that General Kwan, who lived during the Three Kingdom Period (221 – 280 A.D.), was a big man and was able to master this weapon, which was both long and heavy. According to legend, his *kwan do* weighed in at about 107 lbs. The blade of the *kwan do* is very similar to that of any other *pudao*, but with a spike on the back of the blade and a slightly serrated back edge as well. The weapon was a simple of military rank, as it was wielded by higher-ranking officers instead of regular soldiers, who preferred to use the spear[63].

  The weapon appears fairly often in martial arts films, although not often in Hollywood films. The most notable appearance of the *kwan do* is in *Highlander: Endgame* (1999), in which there's a fight scene where Adrian Paul fights Donnie Yen, who's armed with the weapon. In Chinese cinema, the weapon is frequently (but not always) associated with villainy. This is true as many films feature corrupt officials, especially Qing dynasty ones, as villains and thus they wield the *kwan do* as their weapon of choice. In *The Kung Fu Instructor* (1979), villain Ku Feng wields a *kwan do* against Ti

---

[63] Some people often mistake the *pudao* and its variations for being a type of spear, which it isn't. In some kung fu movies, the weapon is often dubbed as "sword", which is also inaccurate.

Lung and Wang Yu in the film's finale. In the classic *Heroes of the Wild* (1978), Hwang Jang Lee fights Chen Sing with a medium-handled *pudao*, which has a ring on the handle to allow Hwang to twirl it. Hwang also uses a regular *kwan do* in the first half of the finale of *Tiger Over Wall*[64] (1980). Wang Lung Wei uses the weapon against Yuen Tak in *The Master* (1980). In the final battle of *Moon Warriors*, villain Kelvin Wong uses a medium-handled blade.

Nonetheless, there are a number of instances in which the hero of the piece uses this weapon. Chan Chung-Yung, who plays Tiger Lu in Jet Li's *Fong Sai Yuk* (1993), can be seen cutting down Manchu soldiers with a large *kwan do* at the film's climax. Jet Li himself uses the *kwan do* to dismember dozens of soldiers during a big battle scene in *The Warlords* (2007). Donnie Yen essentially recreates the aforementioned scene in an early fight in *Painted Skin* (2008). Yuen Biao uses a *kwan do* in wire-fu period piece *Sword Stained with Royal Blood* (1993). Another good example is the finale of *Shaolin Heroes*, where Ti Lung counters Michael Chan Wai Man's halberd with a *kwan do* in the film's final fight.

Fearless Hyena (1979)

The Fearless Hyena was the first movie Jackie Chan directed, coming hot on the heels of the hugely successful Seasonal Films, *Snake in the Eagle's Shadow* and *The Drunken Master*. Now that the kung fu comedy was the big thing, Lo Wei, with who Jackie Chan still had a contract, gave Jackie a lot more elbowroom when making movies. The result was *The Fearless Hyena*, a kung fu comedy that stood as a further example of how much Jackie wanted to revolutionize the genre by eschewing the confines of traditional kung fu for a more comic, acrobatic style of screen fighting.

The penultimate fight, which leads into the climatic duel between Jackie Chan and Yen Shi-Kwan, is the best and most creative fight in the film. In it, Jackie takes on three assassins who work for Yen. Three are armed with a pair of spear-tipped *pudao*, which have a joint in the middle of the pole, allowing them to be folded and stored. In order to save his teacher, Jackie must confront the three killers. He takes on one of them first, although soon the other two join the fight and Jackie must fight all three simultaneously.

The fight features some exceptional choreography, Jackie Chan himself being at the helm. The action direction is very complex, as Chan must use all manner of acrobatics to avoid being hacked to pieces with the *dao* end of the killers' weapons or skewered with the spearheads on the other end of their weapons. He puts on an excellent display of physical prowess as he contorts his body in numerous directions, lifting his leg, ducking his head, bending over backwards, etc. All the of the choreography is performed in awesome synchronicity, which, while being rather obvious, shows how difficult it was to perform Jackie's choreography and thus the fight gives us an idea of how talented both Jackie and the other three actors really were.

As was stated in the chapter introduction, the *pudao* was generally made to have a sharpened weight at the other end of the pole that served as a counterbalance to the (often) heavy blade that was the most important part of the so-called "assault blade." Here, the sharpened weight is pretty obviously a spearhead, and more so than in other

---

[64] See Chapter on Tae Kwon Do.

movies that feature the *pudao* and its variations, the spearhead is actually used quite a bit for piercing and jabbing techniques, much like a regular spear.

Jackie Chan fans will observe that this fight is something of a retread of a sequence in the climax of *Snake and Crane Arts of Shaolin* (1977), another Lo Wei-produced Jackie Chan film. In said scene, Jackie takes on a trio of spearmen who attack him simultaneously, leading Jackie to throw in some intricate moves in order to avoid getting impaled. That too is an awesome sequence, if a bit shorter and less acrobatic than this one; it was made before Jackie's success and thus any attempts at physical comedy had to be subtle.

This is one of our favorite Jackie Chan moments from his pre-*Project A* days. It's Jackie Chan at his prime and the *pudao*, which doesn't get often get so much attention, gets a rather creative showcase, something more than the swinging and chopping that it's usually relegated to onscreen.

Magnificent Ruffians (1979)

It would not be an exaggeration to say that Venom Mob team member Lu Feng was not only the best onscreen user of the *kwan do*, but the best actor to wield any pole-arm on film. He dazzled us with his spear displays in *Flag of Iron* (1980), *Kid with the Golden Arm* (1979), and *The Killer Army* (1980). He gave the three-pronged fork, or trident, the showcase it so richly needed in *Two Champions from Shaolin* (1980) and *The Masked Avengers* (1982). But most important, his ability with the *kwan do* has been unmatched throughout the past three decades. We mentioned it briefly when we talked about *The Shaolin Rescuers* (1979) and *Sword Stained with Royal Blood* (1981). However, it is in *The Magnificent Ruffians* that Lu Feng gave the best onscreen demonstration of the weapon in the history of the genre.

The final fight in this movie is between Lu Feng (playing the villain as always), Philip Kwok and Chiang Sheng, who are the two surviving protagonists. Lu Feng had previously framed Kwok for the murder of the owner of an escort company (Lo Meng) and then murdered Chiang Sheng's best friends to cover up the crime. With only Philip Kwok and Chiang Sheng alive, they train to take on Lu Feng and his powerful "Golden Sword" technique.

Poster for *The Magnificent Ruffians* (1979).

The final fight of this movie lasts about six minutes, but it is continuous martial arts weapons action from start to finish. By the time this film was made, Robert Tai had stopped working as head action director on the Venom Mob films and the choreography duties had fallen into the hands of Philip Kwok, Lu Feng, and Chiang Sheng. Thus, they show us from the outset that few action directors would have the same talent in choreographing weapons duels than they would, during this period or at any point in the history of the genre. In addition to the authentic weapons techniques, the Venoms throw in their typical acrobatics (simple flips and somersaults) to keep things going.

Lu Feng does wonders with the *kwan do* (dubbed "The Golden Sword") here. As he gets very ample time to show off the weapon, he gets to show off various techniques associated with it. Notice how the strikes and swings differ from technique to technique. For some closer-range attacks, he holds the weapon at both ends of the handle, giving him more control over the blade. However, for some of the long-range swings, he'd grip the weapon at the other end with both hands for maximum swinging power. In one sequence, Lu Feng lies on his back and starts swinging the weapon while twisting his body in an attempt to cut out his opponent's legs from under them. We also note that the way he twirls the weapon around his neck and over his back is quite impressive, considering the weight and awkwardness of the weapon—note that his weapon does not have a spearhead at the other end to act as a counterweight. The techniques that Lu Feng performs throughout the course of the fight are named after the movements of the sun, like "Sun Opens the Clouds" and "Sun Shines Everywhere."

Chiang Sheng and Philip Kwok provide excellent foils to Lu Feng's *kwan do*-wielding villain. The former enters the battle armed with the *shuangdao*, or double sabers, while the latter is armed with a pole. They perform at the same level as Lu during the fight. There are a number of gripping moments where the two perform flips and somersaults to narrowly avoid the powerful blows of Lu Feng's "Golden Sword." All of this creates a certain synergy that have led some people to label this fight as one of the greatest weapons duels ever filmed.

Three-Section Staff

The three-section staff (*san jie gun*) stands out as one of the more unique and complex weapons in Chinese martial arts. It consists of three small staves, made of wood (white oak or red maple) or metal, linked together by a chain or rope. The weapons unique construction gives it a variety of uses in combat. The chains that connect the individual staves make this a flexible weapon, giving it the capacity to trap an opponent's weapon or even strangle him at close range. Furthermore, the flexibility of the weapon makes it effective at long range, allowing the user to swing it around to build up momentum and then lashing it out at another fighter for maximum effect. When faced with an opponent who has a weapon with strong defensive capabilities, or a shield, the three-section staff is able to strike over or around it. Finally, a user may decide to hold the outer two staves at the ends closest to the middle, making the weapon behave similar to a pair of *arnis* sticks in *escrima*.

The origin of the weapon has been somewhat debated. Some have said that the weapon was created in the 18th century by the Shaolin monk San Te, who was famous for being the first monk to teach Shaolin kung fu to laymen. This event is dramatized in the Lau Kar-Leung's 1978 classic *The 36th Chamber of Shaolin*. However, it is also believed that the Chao Hong-Ying, the first emperor of the Song Dynasty (960 A.D.), created this weapon. Chao was a Shaolin-trained martial artist who worked as a bodyguard and escort previous to becoming emperor. The legend says that he usually fought with a pole in battle. In one particular scuffle, his pole broke. Chao then connected the two pieces of the pole with a chain, thus creating the "thrashing staff", or "sweeper". The pole eventually broke again and Chao connected that piece to the rest of the pole, thus creating the three-section staff.

The three-section staff does not get a whole lot of attention in film outside of China. The most notable example is in Jackie Chan's *Shanghai Noon* (2000), where Jackie uses the weapon against Yu Rong-Guang at the film's climax. In traditional kung fu cinema, the weapon gets a lot more attention and has done so for a long time. In "modern" kung fu cinema (i.e. movies made after 1970), one of the earliest examples of the three-section staff in action can be seen in *New One-Armed Swordsman* (1971), in which the weapon is villain Ku Feng's weapon of choice[65]. In 1973, David Chiang got to wield the three-section staff against Ti Lung in the Chang Cheh classic *The Blood Brothers*. Director-Choreographer Lau Kar-Leung has used the weapon in numerous films, including the aforementioned *The 36th Chamber of Shaolin*, *Legendary Weapons of China*, and in the superlative *Heroes of the East*, where Gordon Liu uses the weapon to counter Manabu Shirai's *nunchaku*.

The 1980 low-budget fantasy film *The Revenger,* starring Ti Lung, features a main villain who wields this weapon. That same year, Philip Kwok would put on a fairly memorable show with the weapon in the Venom Mob film *The Killer Army*. In the 1983

---

[65] One of the alternate English titles to this film is *Triple Irons*, as the exotic (to Westerners) weapon was marketing as the film's distinctive quality.

Mainland film *Kids from Shaolin*, there's a sequence in the big climatic fight where Jet Li uses the three-section staff against two bandits who are wielding the same weapon. In the 1989 action thriller *Burning Ambition*, the weapon appears in a big group fight set at a carnival.

The Victim (1980)

Sammo Hung is no stranger to the numerous styles and weapons portrayed onscreen in kung fu movies. At his prime, he was one of the most versatile and creative talents in the business, excelling as an onscreen performer, an action director, and a regular director as well. Sammo started directing in 1977, beginning a long directorial career with the adult-themed masterpiece *The Iron-Fisted Monk*. From there on out, almost every film he directed has been considered to be a genre classic. One of these many classics that he did was *The Victim*, a film that showcases the talents of not only Sammo Hung, but of Leung Kar-Leung, Chang Yi, and Wilson Tong. One of the great sequences in this film is a short fight between Sammo Hung and Huang Ha, in which Sammo gives an awesome display on the three-section staff.

The fight itself is simple: Sammo is challenging Huang Ha to a duel. Huang Ha is armed with a *kwan do*, or long-handled broadsword while Sammo chooses to fight with a three-section staff. The fight goes for about two minutes; Sammo wipes the floor with Huang with numerous well-executed staff techniques. For the greater part of the fight, Sammo attacks with the two end staves while using the middle staff to block Huang Ha's blows. Occasionally he swings the weapon for a good sweep or to score a good hit by letting the weapon wrap around Huang's *kwan do* and hit him in the side. He finally uses his weapon as a means of disarming Huang.

Like we said, the fight is short, but very sweet. The techniques are performed with a quite a bit of speed and agility, which is impressive considering Sammo's girth. Sammo makes his handling of the weapon look like a piece a cake, accentuated by his cocky demeanor throughout the fight. This is the third time Sammo wielded this weapon during the traditional "chopsockey" period. He had previous done so in *Traitorous* (1976), where he played a villain and took on Carter Wong; and in *Dirty Tiger, Crazy Frog* (1978), where he and co-star Lau Kar-Wing have a duel with three-section staves at the very end of the film. In the former, the choreography was a bit stilted—probably because of Carter Wong's stiffness as a fighter. In the latter film, the quality of the choreography is quite good, but hampered by Sammo's buffoonish handling of the weapon. Here he shows that the third time is a charm and does quite an excellent job in giving the *san jie gun* an excellent demonstration.

Fearless (2006)

Jet Li has often been called one of the greatest martial arts stars of all time, and to a certain degree, he is very deserving of such praise. Unfortunately, he has not always appeared in films that are deserving of his talent, nor have his action directors always brought out the very best in his talent. Although his first six movies are all *tour-de-forces* for his wushu and weapons skills, his movies made from 1991 onward have been a bit more spottier due to the growth in popularity of "wire-fu" and the filmmakers' inability to (for the most part) leave it alone in Jet's modern-day action thrillers. While few of his films have ever been less than entertaining and though the set pieces in most of these films are of a uniformly high standard; too many of these films either waste his skills (i.e. *High Risk* and *Swordsman II* are good examples) or have only a few great moments of authentic martial arts amidst the craziness (*Dr. Wai and the Scripture with No Words* and *Kung Fu Cult Master* fit in this column).

When Jet Li announced in 2005 that he was making his last kung fu film, it sent shockwaves throughout the martial arts cinema community. After all, he was still in his early forties at the time and Jackie Chan, in *his* early forties, had brought us some wonderful fight scenes in films like *Who Am I?* and *Gorgeous*, among others, so it sounded all too premature. There was some consolation, though, in that his last kung fu film was going to be a movie about Huo Yuanjia, the real life martial arts master who was the basis for Bruce Lee's *Fist of Fury* and Jet Li's masterpiece *Fist of Legend* (1994). Moreover, it was announced that Yuen Woo-Ping was going to assume the role as action director and, as Yuen had worked on *Fist of Legend*, expectations immediately shot through the roof. The result was like a wish granted to most of us: a movie with a good story, good characterizations, good production values, and numerous fight scenes of Jet Li displaying his prowess in numerous weapons (straight sword, saber, spear, etc.) and styles against a large variety of opponents. From a pure martial arts standpoint, *Fearless* was Jet Li's best film since *Fist of Legend* 12 years earlier.

Most people will say that the best fight in the film is the restaurant fight where Jet Li takes on newcomer Chen Zhihui with a large saber (*dao*). It is an excellent and a brutal fight to be sure. However, we were more impressed with the final fight, especially for the amazing agility and dexterity demonstrated by Jet, not to mention the character showed by Jet Li and opponent Shido Nakamura during their duel.

The setting of the fight is a tournament between Huo Yuanjia (Jet Li) and a number of foreign fighters. Having defeated three European fighters already, Huo is now ready to take on his final opponent: Anno Tanaka, a Japanese *bujutsu* expert. Tanaka enters the ring and has decided upon a weapon: the *katana*. Huo's weapon of choice is the *san jie gun*, or three-section staff. The two go at it wildly for some time. At one point, they disarm each other and end up with each other's weapon. Although Huo is quick to adapt the *katana* to Chinese martial arts techniques, Tanaka discovers that he doesn't quite have the coordination needed to wield the three-section staff. Huo stops the fight and hands the blade back to Tanaka, who in turn gives Huo the staff back. The two continue to go at it until a draw is reached.

Some say that Jet Li was already over the hill by his early 30s, due to a number of injuries he sustained while making movies. Nonetheless, you would not know that watching this film, especially this fight. Jet Li does it all with the three-section staff. He twirls it around his body with astonishing fluidity. He uses a numerous techniques in a short period of time. He swings it around for sweeping and wrapping attacks. He uses it for trapping. He uses the "Poison Snake Coils its Body" technique in which an end staff and the middle staff are gripped while the other end is swung at the opponent. The "Dragon Tiger Garb", where the middle staff is used for blocking and the outer staves for striking, are used as well. It's a wonderful showcase for the weapon, even it, like the fight in *The Victim*, only lasts for two minutes.

Shido Nakamura provides an excellent opponent for Jet Li and does an awesome job of wielding the *katana* blade in this particular fight. Yuen Woo-Ping furnishes some of his finest work in a long time with this particular fight—well, the same thing could be said for the movie on the whole. Jet Li looks magnificent and the three-section staff, which had seen very little screen time since the death of the traditional chopsockey in the mid-80s, is given one more chance to shine. And boy, does it shine brightly here.

Axe

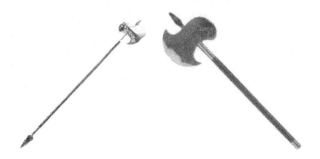

The axe is one of the oldest tools in existence, whose history dates back to the Neolithic period. It is considered to be a simple machine: a combination of a lever and wedge. Over the millennia the axe has served both a domestic purpose (i.e. chopping wood) and a martial one. A number of variations of the axe have been produced for specific purposes in practical and military use. In the latter case, axes have been made for armor piercing, throwing, and/or close combat. It is a universal weapon and has been used by practically all cultures in one form or another.

In film, there has been no shortage of the axe. Just watch any historical epic like *The Patriot* (2000) or the *Lord of the Rings* trilogy to see. The axe has also been a favorite weapon of psychopaths and serial killers in film. Jason of *Friday the 13th* fame has used one on many occasions. Some of Dario Argento's *giallo* movies feature axe-wielding killers. Let's not forget *The Shining* (1980), whose scene of Jack Nicholson chopping away at a door while saying, "Here's Johnny" has become an iconic moment in cinema history.

In Chinese cinema, the axe (and its sidekick, the hatchet) has been a traditional weapon of Triads and gangsters. From *The Boxer from Shangtung* (1973) to the more recent *Kung Fu Hustle* (2004), dozens of films have featured large gangs armed with hatchets for the hero(es) to take on. Both of these showdowns, along with a similar one in Jackie Chan's all-time classic *Drunken Master 2* (1994), have done down in the history books as some of the greatest mass fight scenes ever filmed. It's also used prominently in a major action sequence in Benny Chan's recent epic *Shaolin* (2010), although poor lighting spoils some of Corey Yuen and Yuen Tak's choreography.

However, while a lot of films have featured people armed with axes, few of them give attention to the axe as one of the traditional weapons of kung fu. While we've seen the axe as a normal chopping weapon, we rarely get to see it used with the grace and technique that other kung fu weapons have been afforded. With that in mind, let's take a look at two fight sequences that have given the axe their kung fu due.

Kid with the Golden Arm (1978)

One thing that makes the "Venom Mob" so popular among fans of kung fu cinema is they were always in favor of using lesser-known weapons in their movies. Oh sure, more commonplace weapons like swords, spears, and poles would frequently come up, but the Venom Mob never stopped there. Hooks, *kwan dos*, metal hoops, hammers, halberds, and a number of other weapons came in the numerous films they made from 1978 until 1984.

In this particular fight, we get to see Chiang Shang fight with the double axe. Granted, axes are nothing new in movies. Just watch any "slasher" movie and you'll probably get to see someone get knocked off with an axe. Or, a lot of Hong Kong movies have gangs whose members are armed with hatchets, which is a common HK action film cliché. But not many films allow us to see axes used from a kung fu standpoint.

The scene is simple. Chiang Shang, who plays "Short Axe", and Sun Shao-Pei, who plays "Long Axe", encounter a number of bandits led by Silver Spear, played by Venom Mob member Lu Feng. In the beginning both Short Axe and Long Axe fight off Silver Spear's minions, after which Short Axe and Silver Spear go at it one-on-one.

The fight starts off a bit awkward, mainly due to the awkward handling of Sun Shao-Pei's long-handled axe. However, once the focus of the fight shifts to Chiang Shang and Lu Feng, things pick up and we get to see two of the Venoms put their legendary weapons skills to the test. The rhythm and pace of the fight begins to intensify once the two start going at it, not to mention the complexity of the choreography and the inclusion of some solid acrobatics from both players. Chiang Shang's handling of the axe is as deft as any fighter who has fought with a sword or some other conventional weapon in any other movie. It is simply some great stuff.

Poster for *The Kid with the Golden Arm* (Shaw Brothers, 1978).

Fight director Robert Tai furnishes one of the best fights in the movie, which is probably only surpassed by the finale. While we feel that Robert Tai is somewhat overrated as an action director, we have to say that he was truly in his element when he worked alongside the Venoms. Probably the greatest part about the choreography is that we can see Chiang Sheng and Lu Feng performing up to twenty movements per cut. In a day and age where a fight scenes often come across as a collection of quick cuts, one can really appreciate the skills and dexterity of martial artists who could go through so many movements without stopping.

On a final note, the movie ends with one of the more memorable gore scenes in the movie: Chiang Shang gets impaled from behind by a spear, pulls the spear out through his stomach, and uses it to impale Lu Feng. There are some DVDs out that have this scene cut out, whereas others show the scene in its bloody entirety.

The Brave Archer III (1981)

When Robert Tai, who had essentially been the official action director of the Venom Mob films from 1978 to 1979, left the Shaw Brothers in 1980, the action directing duties were picked up in full by the three Venom Mob members who had Peking Opera experience: Kuo Chi, Lu Feng, and Chiang Sheng. They took care of the choreography of all of their movies until they disbanded around 1983. On the whole, the quality of the fight choreography of their films, especially in the weapons duels, really took off at that point and the movies they made from 1980 onward had some their best and most varied fight sequences. *The Brave Archer III*, a lesser-known film in which the Venom Mob appear in what are essentially extended cameos at the film's climax, has one their best weapons duels and is a fight that should be seen be each and every fan of martial arts cinema.

The fight sequence itself is a smorgasbord of martial arts skills, with a number of individual duels going on. Lo Meng gets to show off his Southern Mantis skills against genre favorite Alexander Fu Sheng, who does some solid Dragon style. Lu Feng, whose character is a fisherman, wields a double oar as if it were a *kwan do*. Sun Chien gets to do some weapon fighting with a fan in addition to his usual kicking. Wang Li, who plays a farmer, uses what is essentially a glorified garden ho[66] against his opponent, the techniques of which kind resemble those of a halberd.

In his scenes, Chiang Sheng, who plays a woodsman, fights two members of the Iron Palm Clan. The fighters from this fictitious clan are armed with weapons that are shaped like the palm of a man's hand, but are apparently sharpened around the edges. The first opponent Chiang Sheng takes on has one of these weapons with a long handle, which makes it comparable to a *kwan do*. After fighting to a stalemate, he and Lu Feng switch opponents and Chiang takes on another fighter with two short palm weapons, which might be considered analogous to the short axe.

In the last film we covered, *The Kid with the Golden Arm*, we praised Chiang Sheng's amazing dexterity with the short axe and noted his co-star's awkwardness in wielding a long-handled axe. In this fight we can see just how talented the late Chiang Sheng was as a martial artist. In this fight, he wields a long-handled axe with same speed and agility that he had done so two years earlier with the short axes. As usual, Chiang Sheng throws in his the usual acrobatics that his Peking Opera background had provided him. Moreover, as with the best of the Venom Mob films, each individual fight is made up of long takes full of complex moves and techniques.

We may have highlighted Chiang Sheng's axe-wielding skills for this fight, but the merits of this sequence are many and this film should be sought out if only for the last ten minutes, which is pure vintage Venom madness.

---

[66] We should point out here that in *The Magnificent Ruffians*, Wang Li's character fights with an axe.

Ring – Hoop

One of the more interesting weapons in Chinese martial arts is the ring (also known as the hoop). As it name implies, the weapon is simply a metal hoop that is generally smaller than a "hoola-hoop". The weapon's history can be traced back to Chinese literature and mythology to the Taoist deity Nezha. Nezha was originally a Hindu god that was adopted into the Taoist pantheon. In the book <u>Feng Shen Yan Yi</u>, Nezha is the son of Li Jing a commander of the evil Shang Dynasty king Zhou. Nezha becomes a rebel and fights against king Zhou and his demonic followers. One of Nezha's favored weapons was the ring, referred to in texts as a "fire wheel".

The ring is generally used for striking and trapping. It is not difficult for a practitioner to trap another fighter's weapon, such as a pole or sword, and twist it away from its user. Moreover, it can be thrown at one's opponent. Occasionally, a ring will be serrated and thus become useful for cutting and slashing, as well as trapping and disarming. It is studied in most *wushu* academies in Mainland China today.

The weapon comes up occasionally in Chinese kung fu movies, although not very often. The 1975 fantasy film *Na Cha the Great* features Alexander Fu Sheng playing Nezha and thus, using a ring in some of the fights. In *Last Hero in China* (1993), there's a Boxer in the first fight that calls on Nezha to possess him and fights Jet Li using a ring. Sammo Hung uses a ring against Leung Kar-Yan in the finale of *Enter the Fat Dragon* (1978). The weapon can also be seen briefly in *Avenging Warriors of Shaolin* (1979), *Demon Strike* (1979), and *Two Champions of Shaolin* (1980).

Shaolin Drunkard (1983)

In 1982, the Yuen Clan, led by famed action director Yuen Woo-Ping made a commercially successful Taoist magic film called *Miracle Fighters*. The movie mixed Taoist magic and kung fu to great effect, offering audiences something a bit different from your typical "chopsockey" films. The following year, the Yuen family got together once again to make a follow-up, which was *Shaolin Drunkard*. The movie follows the same formula of combining comedy, magic, and martial arts in a strange (to most Westerners) and yet compelling mixture and the result is a highly entertaining film that features kung fu frogs, bamboo tanks, acid-spitting snakes, a flaming hands kung fu style, spike walking, and more weird stuff than you can shake a *kwan do* at.

The crowning set-piece of this weird movie is the final duel between our hero, Yiao (Yuen Yat-Chor), the drunken Taoist priest (Yuen Cheung-Yan), and the vampiric Monster (Yuen Shun-Yi). In a nutshell, our hero has retired to his bedroom with his new bride, only to discover that it is Monster in disguise. The ensuing fight plays like a sex farce, as Yiao's grandmother (Brandy Yuen, in drag) watches the fight through the paper wall and thinks they're experimenting different positions. Luckily for Yiao, the drunken Taoist shows up and soon the two are up against Monster. It is when the grandmother enters the room and figures out what's going on that Monster pulls out the proverbial "big guns": a set of nine iron rings. Then things really get crazy.

What the Yuen Clan has done here is put together a madcap fight that is based on some combat principles of the ring and taken it to absurdity. Yuen Shun-Yi, who wields these weapons, does some traditional moves including your typical ring throws and trapping. Heck, he even breaks Yuen Yat-Chor's sword in the beginning. However, they the fight to whole new level when Shun-Yee starts using the multiple rings to trap and fit Cheung-Yan's and Yat-Chor's bodies into outrageous positions, like some sort of demented puzzle ring. It's quite ingenious to see how the Yuen think of ways to force the two protagonists into a horse/rider position and into a makeshift wheelchair position, and then execute the choreography in an imaginative, yet believable manner. While this is going on, Yiao's grandmother is experimenting with a set of real puzzle rings, trying to discover how to get the other two of their predicaments; it's a nice twist on the cliché of the master who watches the final fight while giving pointers to his student.

Here we have a fight with the five Yuen brothers doing what they do best: injecting your typical kung fu battle a high dosage of imagination and creativity. All five of them were involved in the choreography, while three of them: Cheung-Yan, Yat-Chor, and Shun-Yee, get up in the fighting. There isn't a whole lot of pure kung fu in the fight, although the Peking Opera influence -- seen in the use of acrobatics, back-breaking stunts, and an undefined mixture of styles--is present.

Yuen Cheung-Yan, best known by American audiences for his work in the *Charlie's Angels* movies, is more of a comic foil in this fight. He would play a nutty Taoist priest in later Yuen Clan movies, including *Drunken Tai Chi* (1984) and *Taoism Drunkard* (1983). Yuen Shun-Yee is once again playing the same role that he had played in movies like *Miracle Fighter*, *Dreadnaught*, and *Drunken Tai Chi*. Yuen Yat-Chor, the youngest of the Yuen clan, is basically playing the same role he played in *Miracle Fighters* and *Taoism Drunkard*.

The final fight of *Shaolin Drunkard* represents one of the pinnacles of creative choreography in kung fu cinema until the "New Wave" boom really caught big in the first half of the 1990s. It's the Yuen brothers at their most creative and Hong Kong cinema is richer for it.

Fan

The common fan has always been one of the more interesting weapons in Chinese martial arts, as it one of the most efficient concealed weapons out there. Efficient, we say, because a person could walk in public with one and nobody would expect said weapon to actually be an implement of death. Fans could be made with ribs made out of metal or wood, and thus could be used for trapping and parrying bladed weapons like daggers and swords. The edges were often sharpened so as to be useful for slashing. Moreover, darts and daggers were often hidden in the ribs, ready to be flung at an enemy or pierce him at close range.

Westerners will probably be most familiar with the martial uses of the fan through the *Mortal Kombat* video game franchise, in which the female character Kitana uses fans as her projectile weapon. In the movie *Mortal Kombat: Annihilation* (1997), Talisa Soto uses a pair of elaborate metal fans as a striking weapon, similar to *escrima* sticks.

Fans often appear in Chinese cinema as hidden weapons. In *Kung Fu Genius* (1979), villain Wilson Tong is armed with a fan with sharpened edges for scraping. In *The Snuff Bottle Connection* (1977), Hwang Jang Lee uses a fan against John Liu in the classic finale. Some people cite the fan duel between Jackie Chan and Fan Mei-Shang in *Young Master* (1980), as one of Jackie Chan's greatest moments; there's one move that Jackie performed that took more than 900 takes to get right! An iron fan was used as a weapon during Leon Lai's big fight in *Bodyguards and Assassins* (2009), which was interestingly enough a full-blown wire-fu fight, despite the relative realism of all the other action sequences.

It can be argued that our choice as a representative for the fan weapon isn't necessarily the best fight involving a fan, considering how many people enjoy *The Young Master*'s and *The Snuff Bottle Connection*'s offerings. Nonetheless, the fight we chose is not representative of the fan in action, but of a unique figure in Hong Kong cinema that we couldn't just pass up.

The Outlaw Brothers (1989)

One of the interesting anomalies of 1980s Hong Kong action cinema was Frankie Chan. Frankie Chan was a multi-talented man in the Hong Kong film industry, showing quite a bit of talent as a fight choreographer, actor, director, and even a music composer. What is interesting about the films he did that are set in the modern day is that he often would choreograph them as a traditional martial arts fight, sticking to traditional styles and weapons, despite the contemporary setting. Of course, he would make sure the fights were performed at a speed that would keep up with stuff Jackie Chan and Sammo Hung were producing during the era, but they often seemed rather anachronistic (who would enter a modern-day street fight with a 3-section staff hidden in their jacket?). Nonetheless, that is a special quality of Frankie Chan's films and most of his films are recommended at least on the basis of their fight scenes, if not the story.

The Outlaw Brothers is a Frankie Chan-directed film meant to be a showcase for both him and co-star Yukari Oshima. The main conflict of the film is between Frankie Chan's character, who is a car thief, and a gang of drug dealers led by Japanese actress Michiko Nishiwaki. In the final showdown, Yukari Oshima and Frankie Chan take on Nishiwaki's henchmen inside of a warehouse. After the obligatory gunplay and basic kickboxing, we get to the meat of the finale: Yukari Oshima vs. the *Six-String Samurai* himself, Jeffrey Falcon.

Wushu-trained Jeff Falcon enters the fray armed with a fan. His fan in particular has spikes at the tip of each rib. Squaring off against first Frankie and then Yukari, Falcon does some really agile *wushu* while swinging and striking with his unconventional weapon. There is some nice choreography as Yukari uses her more practical *karate* against Falcon. Oshima only really gets an advantage once she starts using a sash as a fair of *nunchaku*.

The fight was choreographed by Frankie Chan, who was assisted by Jackie Chan, Fung Hak-On, and Yuen Shun-Yi. They do a really good job of translating Jeff Falcon's *wushu* training into a fighting style that looks effective in a real fight. His fan work is more fluid that previous fights using the weapon, which isn't surprising, considering that Jackie Chan helped in the choreography. Yukari Oshima is about as solid as she ever was, getting ample opportunity to show off her flexibility, leg work, and *nunchaku* skills. There is a lot of style-based combat here, especially from Frankie Chan in his few moments with Falcon. There is also the improbability of modern-day drug dealers arming themselves with fans and broadswords. However, if you can suspend disbelief enough to get past that, this fight is one of the lesser-known treasures of 1980s Hong Kong cinema and to many, one of the classic *femme fatale* fighting moments.

Rope Dart

Two of the most powerful "soft" weapons in Chinese martial arts are the meteor hammer and the rope dart. The former consists of a cord, either a rope or a chain, with two spherical weights at each end. The cord is swung around the body, including around the neck and under the legs, in order to build up momentum, after which one end is flung towards the fighter's opponent, often with devastating results. For being something of a flexible weapon, the meteor hammer can wrap around a person's arm or weapon, either ensnaring it or hitting the person from behind. A user can strangle a person from a distance or up close, as well as hold the cord near both ends and strike with the weights in close-quarters combat.

The rope dart functions on the same principle—the user has to whirl the rope dart around his body in order to build up momentum. The difference is that instead of spherical weights, there's a pointed dart at the end. Thus, when the cord is thrown at the other person, the increased velocity of the cord allows the dart to pierce the other person. The weapon can be used in long distance combat or in close quarters fight, with the practitioner using the rope to bind and/or strangle his adversary.

The rope dart comes up occasionally in film, although there are only a few examples of the weapon being used outside of traditional kung fu films. Americans will recognize rope dart techniques in such films like *Shanghai Noon* (1999), *Romeo Must Die* (2000), and *Transporter 2* (2005). In *Shanghai Noon*, Jackie Chan has a memorable fight in which he attaches a horseshoe to a rope and uses it as a makeshift rope dart. In the other two films, both of which were choreographed by Corey Yuen, Jet Li and Jason Statham (respectively) use a fire hose as makeshift rope darts, to great effect.

In Chinese cinema, the rope dart is a little bit more common, although it's the type of weapon that generally doesn't get a whole lot of screen time. The weapon is most common in Mainland-produced films, where most *wushu* practitioners are trained in this weapon as part of the curriculum. All three of Jet Li's *Shaolin Temple* films feature brief fights with the rope dart. *South Shaolin Master* (1984) features an excellent, but very short, display of the rope dart right before the final one-on-one. In *Blade of Fury* (1993), which was Sammo Hung's "New Wave" film with several Mainland Chinese performers, one of the villains uses the meteor hammer in the climax. One of the earliest examples of this weapon in action is in Chang Cheh's *Five Shaolin Masters* (1974), where Choi Lang fights using a cord with an axe head at the end.

The Magnificent Warriors (1987)

Ironic how the movie we chose that features the best fight with the rope dart, one of the hardest weapons to use in kung fu, is the one whose user was not even a formally-trained martial artist. But there you have it: the best rope dart in a Chinese movie that we've seen in terms of technique, application, and choreography is performed by none other than Michelle Yeoh, the Queen of Action on the Jade Screen.

The fight scene is quite simple and rather brief, lasting just a little less than two minutes. Nonetheless, about three-fourths of that time is dedicated to showing Michelle

Yeoh use the rope dart in combat against a sword (or *jian*) wielding assailant and another one armed with an ax. Set during the Japanese occupation of China, a female Indiana Jones clone played by Michelle has just arrived home from her latest mission. Discovering that a couple of shady characters have entered her home and tied up her uncle, she sneaks into the house and drops in on the thugs, taking them by surprise. After a brief hand-to-hand scuffle, Michelle whips out the rope dart and proceeds to give a wonderful demonstration of the weapon to the two kidnappers, much to their displeasure.

Just about all of the techniques of the rope dart you can think of, Michelle Yeoh performs as if she were an old pro. She twirls and swings the weapon around her neck, under her legs, and all around her body as she fends off attacks from her two opponents. On a few occasions, she throws the rope out to wrap around and ensnare the two. She uses the weapon both at long range and in close quarters, blocking the one thug's sword strokes with the cord. Michelle's coordination is simply awesome in this sequence and you can see how much she deserves praise for being one of the great fighting females on film.

The choreography to this scene is brought to us courtesy of Stephen Tung Wei, one of the overlooked by very well-rounded action directors in Hong Kong. Westerners will recognize Mr. Tung for his cameo appearance in *Enter the Dragon* (1973) as the student Bruce Lee "teaches" at the very beginning. Tung Wei showed himself to be a very acrobatic fighter in a handful of classic chopsockey flicks like Sammo Hung's *The Incredible Kung Fu Master* (1978) and *The Golden Killah* (1979). Once he focused his career on directing and choreographing, he would find himself as one of the pioneers of the "bullet ballet" in John Woo's breakthrough film *A Better Tomorrow* (1986). His work on the action-comedy *Hot Hot and Pom Pom* (1992), is considered to be some of the best "gun-fu" ever filmed. He also worked on a number of wire-fu films including Tsui Hark's masterpiece *The Blade* (1995); horror films, including *Vampire vs. Vampire* (1990) and *Mr. Vampire 3* (1987); modern-day action, like Jet Li's *Hitman* (1998) and *Purple Storm* (1999); and historical epics, like *Warriors of Heaven and Earth* (2002).

Anyways, his work here is some of the best pure martial arts we've seen him direct, even in such a short sequence. He keeps it interesting, as we know that the moves that a person can do with this weapon are somewhat limited, especially in a one-on-one fight. Instead of having Michelle just swing the rope around in one of those demonstrations like Bruce Lee used to do with the *nunchaku*, he spices things up by having Michelle and her opponents use their surroundings, a few found objects, and a variety of moves involving ensnaring, trapping, and striking. He even throws in some painful stuntwork that was obligatory for a 1980s action movie in Hong Kong.

Michelle would "return" to the rope dart to one degree or another more than a decade later in *Silver Hawk* (2004), where her Silver Hawk character used a pair of cords with metal weights at the end as a "soft" weapon against Luke Goss' metallic arms. Nonetheless, it's this film that stands out the most with regards to this unusual, yet effective weapon.

Chain Whip

The term "whip" in the context of the action movie will bring to mind a lot of romantic images associated with characters like Indiana Jones and Zorro, both of whom used whips in their fantastic adventures. Video gamers will also associate the whip with the long-running *Castlevania* series, in which the protagonist always wielded a whip as his most basic weapon. However, the truth of the matter is, whips are not considered practical weapons in Western military history. Yes, they have been known for being torture devices—anyone who has seen *Passion of the Christ* will have a pretty good idea of how that works. But a whip is a time of tool that doesn't always lend itself out to personal combat, especially in smaller spaces.

Poster for *The Death Games* (1997).

More effective than the whip is the war flail. Most Westerners will recall seeing this weapon in a number of films, video games, cartoons; anything dealing with medieval knights will probably make mention of this weapon. It is simply a chain with a weight, usually a spiked ball (known as a "morning star") at one end and usually a handle at the other. It is a powerful weapon, capable of more damage in the hands of a skilled user than your typical melee weapon, like clubs, maces, and even some swords.

The weapon known as the chain whip in Chinese martial arts is a lot more like our Western war flail than your typical whip. The chain is made up of a number of long, slender metal links, ranging from three to nine. At the end of the whip is usually a flat, sharpened dart used for piercing and slashing. The whip is often swung around the arms, neck, and even under the legs to gain momentum. Like the Western flail, one of the advantages of the chain whip is its ability to wrap around a shield or block and still hit one's opponent. However, in a real fight, the user will often hold the whip by the two ends and use it to trap an opponent's weapon.

The chain whip is a very cinematic weapon due to the inherent beauty of it while being swung around its user's body. Nonetheless, the weapon requires a well-trained user to fully bring out the weapon's potential in front of the camera and an exceptional choreographer to set up a compelling fight with the weapon. The chain whip was used in modern kung fu movies as early as 1974 in *Five Shaolin Masters*, in which David Chiang uses a chain whip against three opponents in the big climax. Under Lau Kar-Leung's choreography, it was one of Chiang's better moments. He tried to do the same thing in that movie's prequel, *The Shaolin Temple* (1976), but the result was rather bland. In the obscure *The 36 Crazy Fists*, Jackie Chan choreographs a fight between the lead and perennial villain Fung Hak-On, who uses a chain whip. In more modern movies, Karen Shepherd uses a chain whip against Cynthia Rothrock in the classic *Righting Wrongs* (1986), which fight is considered one of the best femme fatale showdowns in the genre.

Under Yuen Woo-Ping's direction, Yu Rong-Gwong uses a chain whip against Hsiao Ho in the masterpiece *Iron Monkey* (1993). Slightly more recently, Kim Maree Penn, a beautiful Caucasian veteran of Hong Kong cinema, got to take on Riki-Oh himself, Fan Siu-Wong, with a chain whip in the obscure *The Death Games* (1998).

More recently, the weapon has popped up in the epic historical action drama *Bodyguards and Assassin* (2009), specifically in a scene where pop star Li Yuchun uses the weapon to keep the titular assassins at bay, at the cost of her own life. Mainland wushu stylist Jiang Luxia used the weapon the following year in Dennis Law's *Bad Blood*. With the exception of *The Shaolin Temple*, all of these fights are worth checking out.

Lion vs. Lion (1981)

The last time we had talked about Chin Yuet-Sang, it was in *Kung Fu vs. Yoga* (1979), in which he took a backseat to Dunpar Singh's amazing contortionist abilities. So once again we find ourselves analyzing the work of this great, but lesser-known actor and choreographer in a fight that online movie reviewer Mark Pollard refers to as "one of the most satisfying fights of all time." It is a great showcase for a weapon that doesn't always get attention, but it beautiful to see in use.

In this fight, Chin Yuet-Sang, playing a Qing spy, faces off against perennial Shaw Bros villain Johnny Wang Lung-Wei. They face off in Wang's house, starting with their fists and then going on to the main event, where Chin pulls out a chain whip and starts fighting Wang. As we mentioned, the first third of the fight is made up of hand-to-hand combat in that intricate, acrobatic style of choreography that dominated the genre after 1978. The fighting is fast and crisp and both actors hold their own quite well.

The fight really gets interesting once Chin Yuet-Sang produces the chain whip from his garments and starts swinging it with mad abandon. He uses a great variety of techniques in this scene, swinging it above his head, under his opponent's legs, around his neck, etc. In a number of scenes, he steps on the dart end of the whip with his foot while stretching the whip out and trying to trap Wang's hands.

What's interesting is how Johnny Wang, who's unarmed during the fight, tries to defend himself using chairs. Wang sets the chairs up in formations in order to keep the distance between the two. There is some neat choreography with the chairs, as Wang jumps onto and off of, walks over, and pushes the chairs around, trying to get the advantage against Chin. As you will see, chairs will play a pivotal role in the resolution of this fight.

Both actors do a very good job in this fight. Chin Yuet-Sang uses a mixture of Southern styles and acrobatics in the first part of the fight, including a two-finger strike labeled "the sword". His performance with the chain whip beats out similar displays from David Chiang and Chen Kuan-Tai in movies made in the same period. Johnny Wang Lung-Wei is not a single step behind in this fight, showing off some nice kicks and solid handwork as always—he's a very solid onscreen fighter.

As we stated in the beginning of this chapter, it's not enough to have talented actors, but good choreographers. Here we have the combined talents of director Hsu Hsia and from Chin Yuet-Sang himself. The former was a very talented choreographer, known for having worked alongside Yuen Woo-Ping frequently during the 1970s, in addition to a number of lesser-known, comedic kung fu films with the Shaw Brothers in the early 1980s. Chin himself had also worked on a number of fan favorites during the late 70s and early 80s, including a number of films starring kicking legend Hwang Jang Lee. While it's not quite their greatest work ever, it is indeed a fight that deserves more attention in a movie that should receive more attention.

Double Sticks – Tonfa – Escrima

In Chinese martial arts, there are two major short, blunt weapons. One is called the *tie jian*, or mace. The mace is not quite like the Western mace, which we generally imagine as a short stick with a spiked ball or oddly-shaped metal weight at the end. In Chinese martial arts, the mace is similar in appearance to the modern retractable steel baton. It consists of a metal shaft that has a diamond cross-section and a handle at one end. It is similar to a hard whip, but without any joints or tapering. The mace was created during the Jin Dynasty (265-420 A.D.), but became more widely used during the Tang Dynasty (616-907 A.D.), where it was often used by police constables. It is usually used in pairs, and is ideal for angled strokes, sweeping, and hitting pressure points.

Another, more popular weapon is the *guai*. It is generally translated as the "crutch" or "stick", and is known today as the nightstick. In Japanese and Okinawan martial arts, it's referred to as the *tonfa*. It is essentially a short, thick stick with a handle jutting out perpendicular to the stick itself. The weapon is very old, finding its origins in the Spring and Autumn States period (722 – 222 B.C.). In Okinawa, it is said that the weapon was adapted from a millstone handle after the weapons ban was placed on the country. The weapon is well-adapted for striking and sweeping, and the perpendicular handle allows the user to twirl at fast speeds, gaining momentum and thus strengthening the blow. If the user holds the weapon at the other end, the handle then can be used for trapping his opponent's weapon.

Although not Chinese, stick fighting of any sort will inevitably lead a person into a conversation about *escrima*, a name given to Filipino martial arts. The word *escrima* is derived from *esgrima*, which is Spanish for "fencing." Escrima refers to an entire class of martial arts, in which the emphasis is given on stick fighting, swordplay, and knife techniques. Escrima is often cross-trained with other styles, such *jeet kune do*, kempo karate, or *wing chun*, kung fu, often leading one to think that one style belongs to the other. Practitioners of *escrima* generally learn to fight with the double stick, although stick and knife combinations are common. Many *escrima* systems teach their users how to fight and defend at certain angles of attack, rather than specific blows and strikes. Thus, in theory, an *escrima* practitioner can hold his own in combat with any other fighter, as he or she can fend off blows from any angle.

It is usually rather tricky to discern in cinematic combat when a combatant fighting with double sticks of any type is using techniques taken from Chinese kung fu, *escrima*, or some combination of the two. Martial arts movie fighting, especially in modern-day action films, is generally a mish-mash of styles as it is. Thus, we made the decision to group all of these weapons techniques into one chapter, so as to avoid too much confusion on the subject.

Stick fighting is not altogether uncommon in movies. In American cinema, the most famous example of *escrima* is in the cavern sequence of *Enter the Dragon* (1973), where Bruce Lee unleashes some excellent stick skills against a horde of attackers. Kempo stylist Jeff Speakman does some nice *escrima* in a few sequences of his breakout film, *The Perfect Weapon* (1991). There is some stick fighting in the German martial arts film *Kampfansage* (2005). Japanese *tonfa* skills also get a brief showcase in the 1983 "classic" *Revenge of the Ninja*, as do they by genre veteran Yasuaki Kurata in the French martial arts fantasy *Samourais* (2002). Let's not forget the first *Lethal Weapon* (1987), where Mel Gibson uses a nightstick in the climatic brawl with Gary Busey.

In Chinese cinema, stick fighting, especially with the *tonfa*, is a little bit more common. In Jackie Chan's old school film *Dragon Fist* (1978), one of the main villains uses a stick with sharpened ends, which Jackie counters with a man's crutch. In *Invincible Iron Armor* (1977), hero Tino Wong uses the *tonfa* in several of the fight scenes. Jet Li gets to show off some awesome prowess with the double *tonfa* in the first part of the climax of *My Father is a Hero* (1995), giving the weapons a wushu twist. A Japanese weapons expert in *Heroes of the East* (1978) wields a *tonfa* and a nunchaku, only to be countered by Gordon Liu's three-section staff. There's a fight midway through *Crystal Hunt* (1991), where Donnie Yen uses some *escrima* against Caucasian fighter John Salvitti. In *Five Shaolin Masters* (1974), villain Kong Do is constantly accompanied by two baton-wielding assassins, who take on David Chiang in the finale. Finally, Stephen Tung's *Extreme Challenge* (2001), one of the characters fights with *tonfa*.

Spiritual Kung Fu (1978)

Many fans of Jackie Chan and of Hong Kong cinema in general automatically dismiss all of the movies Jackie made with Lo Wei during the four-year period of 1976 to 1979. They're dismissed for a number of reasons, which include cookie-cutter plots, the miscasting of Jackie in serious roles, mediocre choreography, and low production values. To Jackie's credit, he did make one great movie (*Snake and Crane Arts of Shaolin*) and a few rather enjoyable films, which include *The Fearless Hyena* and this one. *Spiritual Kung Fu* is often dismissed on the grounds of its low-budget special FX and bizarre costumes for the film's so-called "ghosts", but there are a number of good set pieces in this movie, including the fight we will address here.

One of Jackie Chan's greatest talents as an action director has been his ability to create believable and exciting fights involving him and multiple opponents. Too many one-on-many fights in Hong Kong cinema have the protagonist surrounded by multiple guys who circle him and then run at him one-by-one only to get beat up. While such a fight can still be entertaining, it does require a certain suspension of disbelief that most fans are willing to show, although your average filmgoer will simply laugh it off the screen. Chan, however, is able to keep things relatively realistic and his "jazz" style approach to choreography makes it easier for him to fend off multiple thugs simultaneously, giving the fight an extra sense of "Umph". The "night stick/*tonfa* fight" in *Spiritual Kung Fu* is one of the earliest examples of this particular talent of Jackie's.

Near the end of the movie, Jackie Chan decides to leave the Shaolin Temple to help the monks discover the whereabouts of a missing kung fu manual and the man responsible for the death of a Wu Tang master who had been visiting the temple. Having trained in the "Five Fists Style" under the tutelage of five Shaolin ghosts, Chan must face a formation of pole-wielding monks in combat in order to leave the temple. Armed with a pair of *tonfa*, he faces all of the monks and comes out victorious.

Poster for *Spiritual Kung Fu* (1978).

One of the more interesting aspects of this fight is the idea of the monks fighting in formations. At several intervals during the fight, the monks take on a number of different formations, allowing anywhere from four to six monks to attack Jackie from different angles at one time. There are a lot of movies that use the cliché of formations, especially with Shaolin monks. In *Shaolin Intruders* (1983) and *The Tai Chi Master* (1993), the Shaolin formations also involve monks armed with staves. In *Young Hero from Shaolin* (1984), they fight empty-handed. A number of people will point out that there is no realistic advantage to a formation in a real fight, which is probably true. Nonetheless, the formation does act as a springboard for Jackie Chan's excellent one-on-many fight choreography

Despite the fact that this is a 1978-produced classic kung fu film, Jackie Chan displays an early knack for fast-paced choreography and intricate exchanges of blows. Unlike *Dragon Fist*, whose *tonfa* fight was drawn-out and rather tedious, Chan keeps things moving at a nice pace and Chan's underdog position in the fight makes it a lot more compelling. Chan also puts on an excellent display of the *tonfa*, doing all of the twirling, striking, sweeping hits, locking, and disarming that you'd expect in a fight like this. He certainly looks better with the *tonfa* here than he did in *City Hunter*, made 14 years after this movie. The stuntmen playing the monks also put in some very solid work with the pole and compliment Chan nicely. It should be mentioned that although he's playing the underdog here, Jackie does a better job of selling his victory, if only for the fact that the last monk formation is a straight line where he must disarm or take down each monk individually.

As with many classic kung fu films, the camera sticks the actors for a lot longer than action films today. Thus, a take may last for ten movements or more, which is impressive considering the number of people involved and the level of complexity to the choreography Chan as crafted. Furthermore, Chan makes full use of everything on screen, making it essential that a viewer watch this movie in letterbox format. This is common for Jackie Chan movies: watching his movies in pan-and-scan format tends to take away from all of the movement—and there is A LOT going on here—happening onscreen. Thus, if viewed in widescreen format, this fight becomes an excellent showcase for the *tonfa*, proof to doubters of Chan's real-life martial arts mastery, and proof that Chan had been a genius in terms of action direction from an early age.

Chinese Stuntman (1981)

It's not very often that one can see pure Filipino *escrima* in action in a Chinese film. After all, as we mentioned earlier, styles tend to be mixed together in movies, not to mention the fact that are probably several places where Filipino *escrima* and Chinese weapons forms experience a sort of "convergent evolution" and thus it becomes more difficult to say where one stops and the other begins. Given the fact that most action directors in Hong Kong have more extensive training in Chinese martial arts than those from other countries, it's almost a given that there will be a Chinese "twist" to *escrima* whenever it is portrayed onscreen.

However, there is one name that we can almost certainly trust to give us a closest-possible-approximation to pure Filipino martial arts on film: Dan Inosanto. Inosanto is a Filipino *escrima* master who is best known for having taught Bruce Lee how to fight with the *nunchaku*. In *Game of Death* (1978), he plays the first person that Bruce Lee fights inside the pagoda/building, fighting first with a pair of sticks and then with the *nunchaku*. He was also a student of Bruce Lee, and today is considered one of the leading exponents of *jeet kune do*. Although *jeet kune do* is a style that preaches non-classicism and the incorporation of different styles, we can trust that in *The Chinese Stuntman*, the stick fighting performed by Inosanto is about as authentic as it gets.

When the fight begins, Dan Inosanto walks into an apartment where he finds John Ladalski. After a brief argument where Inosanto orders Ladalski to get out of town, the two start fighting with sticks. For the first two minutes, Inosanto simply wipes the floor with Ladalski, first with two sticks, then with one. Then, Ho Chung Tao (aka Bruce Li) enters the apartment and those two begin to fight. At first, Ho fights Inosanto unarmed, using mainly hand techniques. After getting beaten down, Ho picks up a pole, a weapon commonly used in *wing chun*, which was Ho's main style—starts to have more success in countering Inosanto's fast stick techniques.

We mentioned briefly back in the chapter about *wing chun* that one of the attacks commonly leveled at Brucesploitation films is that the choreography is often embarrassing and does little to show off the real talents of its actors. However, Ho Chung Tao eventually reached a point where he got tired of being known as "Bruce Li" and tried to make a few films that broke out of the Brucesploitation mold. One of them was *The Gold Connection* (1979), a praised action thriller with some brutal action. *The Chinese Stuntman* was another example, and it's often considered to be one of the great Ho Chung Tao films because the fights *are* high quality. Here, the action direction is provided by Liu Hok-Ming, who choreographed some mediocre Taiwanese films like *Blind Fist of Bruce* and *Killer of Snakes, Fox of Shaolin*, and Peng Kong, a very talented action director who worked on such classics as *The Leg Fighters; Woman Avenger;* and *Shaolin vs. Lama.*

Although not quite as fast and high octane as Dan Inosanto's fight in *Game of Death*, Inosanto gets a far-better workout here and gets to dominate the screen the greater part of the fight. He gets to show off ample techniques with the *kali* sticks, both single and double. He does a lot of neat twirling with the sticks when he isn't bashing his opponents into oblivion, although his actual stance work is calm and composed, as opposed to the elegant excesses of *wushu*. Inosanto throws a few kicks, but they never call attention to themselves or look too flowery. After all, Inosanto was a *jeet kune do* stylist, and thus believed in practicality as much as Bruce Lee himself did. It's a great moment for Filipino martial arts.

The Death Games (1997)

The Death Games is one of the lesser-known, but very special movies that more people should know about. It's a low-budget kung fu film made in Taiwan[67] starring Riki-Oh himself, Louis (or Terry) Fan Siu-Wong. The type of movie that every martial arts actor should have on his/her résumé, this movie shows Fan's skills with a variety of styles (*taijiquan*, wushu, *tae kwon do*) and weapons (*tonfa*, *jian*, and *spear*). The action direction is provided by Lam Maan-Cheung, a Taiwanese choreographer who is not only heavily underrated, but has shown himself able to reach the levels of kickboxing choreography that Sammo Hung reached at his apex in the 1980s. With a strong supporting cast of martial arts veterans like Kim Maree Penn, Billy Chow, and Collin Chou, *The Death Games* is an unsung classic of the genre.

The movie begins the way most kung fu movies should begin: a series of fights that have nothing to do with the plot, but exist only to show us how good a fighter the hero is. The very first of the film is a short stick duel between Fan Siu-Wong and another fighter. Fan Siu-Wong is armed with a pair of short, metal poles and his opponent wields a pair of *tonfa*. The two go at it, trading numerous blows with lightning-fast quickness. Fan Siu-Wong and his opponent keep things varied by incorporating some twirling and elegant wushu-inspired moves to their fighting. Furthermore, the two fighters compliment their weapon mastery with a number of twirls, cartwheels, and kicks (both wushu and tae kwon do-influenced). Although it's a short fight—the fight goes on for about a minute and a half—it shows off some excellent *escrima* and *tonfa* techniques.

Some people may feel that a short, seemingly inconsequential fight like this would be better suited to be mentioned in the chapter introduction. However, we must remember that at the time *The Death Games* was made, great martial arts movies were on the decline, a lot of talented actors were either going to Hollywood or just being forgotten by audiences, and Hong Kong cinema was dumbing down its action direction in order to make their films more marketable for foreign consumption. Thus, we must applaud and bring attention to the work of Fan Siu-Wong and action director Lam Maan-Cheung for having made this film, which hearkens back to the pure martial arts action that Hong Kong and Taiwan made during the 1970s and 1980s.

---

[67] - Is there any other type?

Miscellaneous Weapons

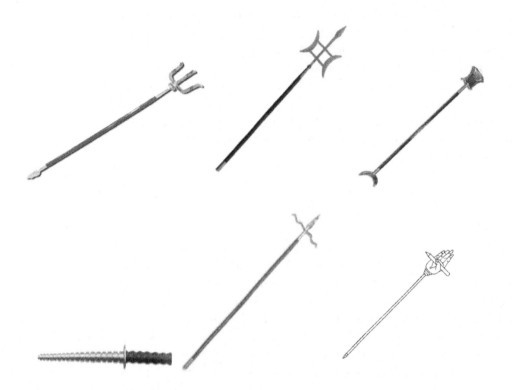

In Chinese martial arts, there are eighteen traditional weapons. Other weapons may be variations of one of these weapons, or may be a rare or secondary weapon. The most widely-accepted list of Chinese weapons goes as follows: the saber/knife (*dao*), sword (*jian*), spear (*qiang*), halberd (*ji*), axe (*fu*), rings (*yue*), hooks (*gou*), hunting fork (*cha*), steel whip (bian), club (*jian*), hammer (*chui*), the pen (*zhua*), trident-halberd (*tang*), 3-section staff (*gun*), the hook spear, pole (*bang*), stick/crutch (*guai*), and the meteor hammer (*liu xing*).

Nonetheless, this list is disputed and there are other variations of the list in existence. For example, in the opening scene of *The Odd Couple* (1979), Lau Kar-Wing and Sammo Hung's masterpiece, there is another list given for the eighteen traditional weapons of kung fu. This list in particular divides the weapons into long and short weapons. The long weapons are: the spear, pole, halberd, hunting fork, trident-halberd, rake, the hook spear, the pen/claw and the wolf's teeth club. The short weapons are the saber, sword, stick/crutch, axe, steel whip, short cudgel, hammer, claw, and the hook.

Now, it goes without saying that there a numerous weapons not included on this list that have gotten ample coverage in kung fu movies, like the rope dart, chain whip, fan, bench, and others. It's also a given that a lot of the traditional weapons, like the sword, saber, spear, and pole, are very common in these movies. On the other hand, there are a large number of weapons that get very little, if any, attention in martial arts films. Some of these weapons are even classified among the traditional weapons and even so, don't get a whole lot of, if any, attention. Here we will take a look at some of these weapons and give them the attention their deserve.

Among those forgotten weapons are:

The Hammer – The hammer in Chinese kung fu often resembles a large metal pumpkin or melon at the end of a pole. Naturally, it functions as a club and can be devastating if wielded by a strong fighter. Mainstream moviegoers will have seen a glimpse of it in the teahouse fight in *Crouching Tiger, Hidden Dragon*. Lu Feng gets to wield the double hammers in the *Ninja Death* series and we see it in the penultimate fight of Lau Kar-Leung's *Legendary Weapons of China*. More recently, Mainland actor Zhao Wen-Zhuo and Taiwanese singer Jay Chou go at it with melon hammers in the Yuen Woo-Ping epic *True Legend* (2010).

The Halberd – The halberd looks like a spear with a crescent-shaped blade sticking out of end. It is a versatile weapon, good for cutting, slashing, striking, piercing, and trapping. It gets ample attention in kung fu cinema, appearing in movies like *All Men are Brothers* (1975), *The Deadly Breaking Sword* (1978), *The Heroes* (1980), and a few others.

The *Hook* – The hooks are often referred to by some as hook swords, and they indeed resemble a sword that happens to curve at the end. They are almost always used in pairs, and together they become an optimal tool for trapping and disarming opponents. The Tiger's Head Hook is notable for a crescent blade coming out of the handle, giving both ends of the weapon deadly potential. It can be seen in movies like *Invincible Iron Armour* (1977), *Seven Grandmasters* (1978), and a few others, too. Westerns will remember it as the weapon used by Kabal in *Mortal Kombat III*.

The *Rake* – As the name implies, it is a simple garden rake adapted for combat. It can be briefly seen in the obscure Mainland film *Betrayal and Revenge* (1985).

The *Steel Whip* – Not a flexible whip, but a baton-like weapon with a shaft shaped into a spiral. It's reminiscent of the Japanese sai in that it was often used by policemen and was suited for attacking pressure points. Chiang Sheng fights with this weapon at the end of *Two Champions of Shaolin* (1980) and it can also be briefly seen in the Mainland film *Warriors of Liang Shan Po*.

The *Hook Spear* – Basically a spear with a hook-like blade coming out of the base of the spearhead. It was used in battle for disabling horses. Jet Li uses it briefly in the climax of *Martial Arts of Shaolin*.

The *Trident Halberd* – This weapon resembles a trident (or hunting fork), but the two outer prongs stick out perpendicular to the middle prong. The weapon is given a small cameo in Jet Li's *The Warlords* (2007) and is used briefly in *Seven Swords* (2005).

The *Pen* – This weapon appears to be a pole with a metal weight at one end that is forged to look like a hand holding a steel pen. It was used in combat between cavalry. We have not seen this weapon used in a movie yet, although it's mentioned in *The Odd Couple*.

The *Emei Piercers* – A pair of rods with sharpened ends fastened to a ring that fits on a finger, allowing the user to spin and manipulate them. They are Hwang Jang Lee's weapon in *The Secret Rivals 2* and *Canton Viper*, and show up in the Dorian Tan Tao-Liang films *Dynasty* (1976) and *The Knife of Devil's Roaring and Souls Missing* (1976).

Shaolin Rescuers (1979)

One of the most appealing characteristics of the Venom Mob, that quintet of five (sometimes six) great martial arts actors, were that their films tended to feature diverse styles and weapons in the set-pieces. As a result, few fights ever felt like "more of the same", but always had something new to them. One of the reasons for that was that three of the Venoms—Kuo Chi, Lu Feng, and Chiang Sheng—were Peking Opera trained and thus had knowledge of different styles and weapons. Not only that, their principal choreographer, Robert Tai, at his best, had an imagination that rivaled that of Ching Siu-Tung and Yuen Woo-Ping. One of the most diverse films they did in terms of weapons was *Shaolin Rescuers*.

In the final blowout, which lasts 17 minutes, the five heroes—played by Kuo Chi, Lo Meng, Chiang Sheng, Sun Chien, and Jason Pai Piao—take on a team of five hitmen in the employ of Pai Mei, the infamous traitor of Shaolin. The killers are led by Lu Feng. Jason Pai Piao stars here as Chinese folk hero Hong Xiguan (Hung Hei-Kwun in Cantonese), the first layman to study at Shaolin and the founder of the *hung gar* style. Each of the killers has a specific style or weapon and our heroes must use their skills and some hidden weapons of their own to beat the villains and get Hong Xiguan to safety.

Because of the number of people involved in the fight and considering that the players are always jumping back and forth between opponents, we'll look at each player individually.

First, we have Kuo Chi (also known as Philip Kwok). Kuo Chi's character has been trained in *Black Tiger* kung fu, although he ends coming off as a *faux* Jackie Chan more than anything else. During the first half of the fight, Kuo fights using a variety of found objects, including a sawhorse (i.e. a bench—considered a traditional weapon in *choy li fut* kung fu) and a stool. Particularly amusing is when he fights with a bowl and chopstick against Lau Shih Kwong, who's armed with ring. When Kuo confronts Lu Feng in the final melee, he arms himself with a pair of tiger's head hooks and does some great work with them.

Next, we have Chiang Shang, the most acrobatic member of the Venom Mob. In the first part of the finale, Chiang doesn't use any particular style, but uses a typical Peking Opera combination of Southern Chinese styles and somersaults. He also gets to fight Lu Feng with the aforementioned tiger's head hooks, although after being disarmed, he opts for the halberd. The halberd doesn't get a whole lot of attention in movies, so it's refreshing to see someone so talented use it.

Third, there's Sun Chien, the *tae kwon do*-trained kicker of the Venom Mob. Sun Chien didn't have much weapon's training, so he rarely used weapons in any of the movies he appeared in. Honestly, this fight in particular is not the best demonstration of his kicking skills[68], but he does impress us with his balance when he takes on Lau Shih-Kwong on top of a set of poles.

Fourth on the list is Lo Meng, the "muscle man" of the Venom Mob. Lo Meng was trained in the Southern Praying Mantis style, and gets ample opportunity to show it off while fighting multiple opponents in the first half of the fight. Lo Meng didn't use weapons very often in the Venom Mob films, but here he gets to wield the trident (also known as the three-pronged hunting fork) and holds his own when the heroes gang up on Lu Feng in the grand finale.

Finally, there's Jason Pai Piao, who was not a Venom Mob team member. Jason Pai Piao had been appearing in "chopsockey" films since the early 1970s, notably in some *tae kwon do* films filmed in Korea. Pai Piao fights using some handwork-based Southern styles—which is only appropriate, since he's portraying Hong Xiguan. According to legend, Hong's specialty was the staff. So, sticking (relatively) close to legend, Pai Piao gets an iron pole to wield in the showdown with Lu Feng. We should note here that the way he kills Tam Jun Tao with the pole is rather novel.

Lobby card for *Shaolin Rescuers* (Shaw Brothers, 1979).

As stated earlier, the bad guys are led by Lu Feng. Like the others, he fights with his hands in the first half of the fight. However, he really gets on fire in the second half, when he gets his hands on a *kwan do*. The *kwan do* was always Lu Feng's specialty and he does some awesome work in this film. Better yet, when he takes on the four surviving heroes in a big weapons duel, he looks absolutely stunning and easily convinces us that he could take on four armed men and hold his own. Lu Feng also has some secret weapons, including a few knives hidden in his queue and a pair of fork-shaped daggers.

The other actors playing the hired killers put in a good showing, too. Tam Jun Tao, who's dressed in a tiger loincloth vest, puts on a show with empty hands and his feet, doing some respectable spin kicks during the fight. Lau Shih Kwong fights with an iron ring and does some good work with it. He would fight with the ring in *Two Champions of Shaolin* (1980), another Venom Mob film. Yu Tai Ping fights with a saber and *rattan* shield, a typical combination. Finally, Yang Hsiung uses one of the rarest

---

[68] We think that the finale to *Five Deadly Venoms* (1978) and *Invincible Shaolin* (1978) had better showcases.

weapons in kung fu: the melon hammer. The melon hammer is a large hammer in which the metal weight at the end looks something a large pumpkin or melon. As you could imagine, even one hit with this weapon could mean certain death.

Robert Tai, Chiang Sheng, and Lu Feng, who collaborated on the choreography, understood that such a long fight would quickly become tiresome if there wasn't variation. Thus, the three action directors make a concentrated effort to include a large number of weapons, objects, and creative use the fighters' surroundings to shake things up. It works to an incredible degree. Admittedly, they would all later choreograph fights that had faster or more intricate moves on display, but the sheer diversity of the weapons makes this fight an event not to be missed.

Legendary Weapons of China (1982)

We wholly recognize the merits of Robert Tai's action direction. At his best, the man had both an accentuated sense of creativity and a keen eye for keeping things varied. Nonetheless, even at his best, Robert Tai could not match the best work of his contemporaries Lau Kar-Leung and Sammo Hung. In the former's case, *Legendary Weapons of China* was one of Lau Kar-Leung's final masterpieces. Filmed in 1982, one of the last great years for the traditional kung fu film, this movie would attempt to give a respectable showcase to as many kung fu weapons as humanly possible. Lau Kar-Leung and company succeeded.

In the final battle, Lau Kar-Leung and his brother, Lau Kar-Wing confront each other in front of temple with all of the traditional weapons of kung fu on hand for use according to their pleasure. The result: a ten minute fight in which we get to see more than *ten* weapons in all their Lau-choreographed glory. What might that mean, you ask? Well, the weapons techniques are not only done correctly (Lau Kar-Leung was generally a stickler for authenticity), but also we are treated to their applications and how one weapon could be used to counter or exploit the weaknesses of another weapon.

In the first part of the fight, we have Lau Kar-Leung armed with the *kwan do* and Lau Kar-Wing armed with the *shuangdao*, or the double saber. Pay attention to how Kar-Wing uses the sabers in comparison to the sword, which Kar-Leung uses after being disarmed the first time. The saber techniques are performed with more somersaults and swinging attacks than the sword. The sword techniques are more about piercing and appear to be simpler, yet more elegant looking. Kar-Leung attacks with the *kwan do*, using not only the blade, but the pole as well, generally to push his opponent back.

Kar-Wing switches over to the tassel spear and they continue fighting until both are disarmed. The weapons that the two fighters use next are rather interesting. Lau Kar-Wing arms himself with twin daggers, which in and of itself would increase the difficulty of the choreography dramatically. However, Lau Kar-Leung isn't content with taking upon himself the complications of choreographing a knife fight: he arms himself with the chain whip, which makes the choreography even more difficult than before. Watch how Lau Kar-Leung uses the chain whip not only long-distance attacks, but close up as well.

Lau Kar-Wing's next weapon is the double *tonfa*, popularly known as the "night stick". The *tonfa*, which functions both as an offensive and defensive weapon, allows Kar-Wing effective defense against Kar-Leung's whip lashes while allowing him to trap the whip and disarm his brother.

Soon, Lau Kar-Wing is armed with your basic pole while Lau Kar-Leung is ready for battle with the Monk's Spade. The latter is another rare weapon that consists of a pole with a shovel-like blade on one end and a crescent-shaped blade on the other. Instead holding the weapon at one end, Lau Kar-Leung holds the monk's spade in the middle, using the middle of the weapon to defend and the extremes to attack and, in the case of the crescent, to trap. Lau Kar-Leung switches over to the trident and does some solid work with it, showing us that it's not just for piercing and stabbing, but for trapping and disarming, too. And you know what? There are still some more surprises on the way.

Most people who watch this fight will be left in awe. Say what you will about the rest of the movie, which is often criticized for being needless convoluted, this fight is the real deal. It is one of the greatest weapons duels ever mounted. However, much like the finales to *The Martial Club* (1980) and *Heroes of the East* (1978), the fight ends without anyone dying. It shows how serious Lau Kar-Leung took his kung fu; he obviously wanted to show that a kung fu master could prove he was the better without killing his opponent, and that killing is not the goal of kung fu.

Part 6: Japanese Weapons

Kenjutsu – Kendo

The martial art most often associated with the Japanese *samurai* is *kenjutsu*. The word *kenjutsu* comes from the words *ken*, meaning "sword"; and *jutsu*, meaning "art". Japanese swords, which are known for being single-edged and curved, were first created in the Heian Period (794-1185 A.D.). Training in *kenjutsu* includes sparring; *kata*, or forms; and basic techniques, known as *kihon*. *Kenjutsu* can typically be distinguished from Chinese sword techniques not only by the type of sword involved, but by the fact that Japanese sword techniques tend to be more direct and less elegant. There exists an advanced branch of *kenjutsu* known as *nitojutsu*, in which practitioners learn to fight with two swords, generally a *katana* and a *wakizashi*.

Today, *kenjutsu* is the foundation of the competitive martial art known as *kendo*. *Kendo* practitioners practice *katas*, basic techniques, and often spar wearing armor and using bamboo swords called *shinai*. In competition, strikes and thrusts are directed toward certain specific (and protected) parts of the body, including the head and wrists. *Kendo* practitioners are known for performing *kiai*, or shouts, with every strike they perform.

There are a number of swords that *samurai* have used throughout history. The most well-known sword is the *katana*. The name refers to any curved, single edged sword that is anywhere between 27 and 35 inches in length. There is a lot of mysticism associated with the *katana*, especially the belief that it contained part of the *samurai*'s soul. It was created during the Muromachi Period (1392-1573) and became the preferred weapon of combat during the Tokugawa Shogunate. It is probably the most frequently-used Asian weapon in world cinema.

Samurai often carried another, shorter sword to accompany the *katana* in combat. This sword is known as the *wakazashi*. Like its larger cousin, the *wakizashi* had a curved, single edge blade and was anywhere between 18 and 24 inches long. A well-trained *samurai* could wield both swords simultaneously if necessary. The *wakizashi* was a preferred weapon to decapitate fallen warriors on the battlefield because of its smaller size. They were carried by *samurai* at all times, even in places where they were required to place their *katana* on racks.

There are number of other swords that have been used throughout Japanese history. There is the *nagamaki*, or "horse blade", which consisted of a long, curved blade and a long handle. Naturally, it was used for cutting down horses during combat. The *nodachi* was a long, two-handed sword that was used in open combat. The *uchigatana* is the predecessor to the modern *katana* and it was with this weapon that the act of unsheathing the sword and cutting down the opponent became a swift, lightning-fast movement. The *tsurugi* is a straight, two-edged sword that was brought over from China and Korea. The *bokken* are wooden practice swords that are used in *kendo* and *aikido* today.

Japanese swords have appeared in numerous films from various countries over the decades. It is arguably the most commonly-used Asian weapon in cinema. Any movie that claims to be about *samurai* or *ninja* will feature some sort of Japanese sword at one point or another. Films like *The Hunted* (1995), *The American Samurai* (1993), *The Last Samurai* (2003), and *Kill Bill vol. 1* (2003) all feature Japanese swords in action. The *katana* gained a certain degree of popularity among the younger generations through the *Teenage Mutant Ninja Turtle* films and cartoons during the late 1980s and early 1990s.

It goes without saying that Japanese cinema has cornered the market on these weapons. Some of the better Japanese films to showcase the speed and power of Japanese swordsmanship include the *Lone Wolf and Cub* series of the early 1970s and the more recent *The Princess Blade* (2002), which was choreographed by Donnie Yen. However, that does not discount the wealth of high-quality *samurai* films made by Akira Kurosawa, Kenji Fukusaku, and other later directors, each of these director's films having its own merits in terms of story and action.

Japanese swords have appeared in Chinese cinema ever since the early 1970s, when film producers discovered that heroic Chinese actors taking on sleazy Japanese martial artists was an audience draw. Thus, as early as 1972 we can see people like Bruce Lee and Angela Mao taking on those "dastardly" Japanese, what with their *katana* and whatnot. Japanese *kendo* probably wouldn't get any real respect until 1978, when Lau Kar-Leung casted Harada Riki as a *kendo* master in *Heroes of the East*. Japanese swords would pop up in dozens of *ninja* movies produced in Hong Kong and Taiwan during the 1980s, some of them classy, others not. One of the more interesting moments involving a *shinai* was in *Royal Warriors* (1980), where Michelle Yeoh fends off a team of *yakuza* thugs with this bamboo sword. In *In the Line of Duty V* (1990), Cynthia Khan and Kim Maree Penn duke it out with *katana* swords, although Cynthia does so with an obvious *kung fu* twist. Basically, where there are Japanese characters in a Chinese martial arts film, there's a good probability that you'll find someone wielding a Japanese sword of some sort.

Fong Sai Yuk II (1993)

Finding representative fights of Japanese swordplay in Chinese cinema is not really an easy task. It is not for a lack of examples, but because the measuring sticks for judging the fight scenes involving Japanese swords is quite different in Japan and China. First of all, if we compare typical Japanese *chambara* choreography with Chinese swordplay choreography, you'll notice that they are two almost entirely different creatures. Duels in Japanese films will end within the first few strokes, if not in the first stroke, whereas their Chinese counterparts can last up to several minutes. Moreover, we have to take into account the lack of respect given to Japanese martial arts in a good portion of Chinese cinema, not to mention that a lot of films simply casted Chinese actors in the roles of Japanese characters. All of these things must be taken into consideration when we judge the quality of Japanese swordplay on the Jade Screen.

The first movie we're going to talk about is *Fong Sai Yuk II*, which may call attention to some of you, as the fight we're talking about doesn't even involve any Japanese actors, let alone Japanese characters. Sure, there are Japanese *samurai* who appear in an earlier fight in this film, but they are nowhere to be seen in the climax. The *katana* used in this memorable fight are wielded by Mainland wushu master Jet Li, who, as far as we know, doesn't actually have any training in Japanese martial arts. However, that's nothing to really worry about, considering that the action direction duties are handled by genre stalwarts Corey Yuen and Yuen Tak, who have both worked as action directors on enough movies with enough different styles that they can easily adapt Jet's skills to the situation at hand.

In the set-piece leading up to the climax, Fong Sai Yuk (played by Li) enters a long alleyway filled with men wielding swords and spears. They are his brothers from the anti-Qing Red Flower Society and they have been given orders to kill Fong at any cost. Obviously, even a master of the "Invincible Magic Fist"[69] can't take on what appears to be a small army with his bare hands. Thus, he whips out a dozen Japanese *katana* swords and straps them to both sides of his waist. Not wanting to see the slaughter of his own brothers, he blindfolds himself and gets to work. Mass slaughter ensues.

This set-piece probably marks one of the first times since the early days of modern *wuxia* in the late 1960s that Chinese cinema was able to capture the feel of Japanese *chambara* films. In older movies like *Have Sword, Will Travel* (1969) and *Trail of the Broken Blade* (1968), actors like David Chiang and Jimmy Wang Yu could plow through a small army of men in a few sword strokes, occasionally exchanging a few blows or parrying a few attacks. Japanese *samurai* films of the same era functioned on the same principle. It was only later that *wuxia* films started featuring more drawn-out swordplay and traditional sword (*jian*) and saber (*dao*) techniques.

Scene from *Fong Sai Yuk 2* (1993).

Here we get to see Jet Li cutting down dozens of fighters in a series of fast and simple moves. At no point does he engage in the sort of drawn-out exchange of blows with one or several opponents that characterizes Chinese sword choreography. It is all done with the same direct, to-the-point attitude that so many Japanese movies have had over the decades. In this sequence, the failure to hit or draw your weapon, or getting your weapon parried results in almost immediate death. The choreography of the two Yuens can easily be seen as homage to Japanese cinema.

Jet Li shows us how versatile a fighter he is in this sequence. In movies like *Martial Arts of Shaolin* (1985) and *The Master* (1989), Jet Li gets to wield a sword and performs a number of elegant and beautiful movements that are part of *wushu* sword forms. He does none of that in this fight. A master of adapting his style to the whims of the action directors, he does the *katana* justice as he keeps all of his attacks fast, simple, direct, and practical. One of the more interesting aspects of the fight is how Jet Li fights blindfolded. This is an obviously not only a plot device, but a tribute to films like *Sword*

[69] - In the original international dub of *Fong Sai Yuk* (1993), Fong Sai Yuk describes his style as "The Invincible Magic Fist." In reality, Fong Sai-Yuk had studied southern Shaolin kung fu and was known as a *hung gar* stylist.

of Swords (1967) and the Japanese *Zatoichi* series, thus driving the Japanese influence of the sequence even further than before.

The penultimate set piece in *Fong Sai Yuk II* is a great moment in the 1990s "New Wave" of kung fu film. There are absolutely no wires used in this sequence. Jet Li adapts himself flawlessly to a weapon that not only outside of his formal training, but comes from an entirely different country. A classic moment in all respects.

So Close (2002)

Corey Yuen has always been considered to be one of the great action directors in regards to "Girls n' Guns" or "Girl-Fu" films. He has directed a number of classics including *Yes, Madam!* (1985), *She Shoots Straight* (1990), and *Enter the Eagles* (1998). Although he didn't make a whole lot of movies in the fighting female genre, almost all of the movies he did do (barring the recent flop *DOA: Dead or* Alive) are considered modern action classics. He has also shown quite a bit of talent for filming memorable fights around performers that had limited, if any, martial arts skills. Both of those skills of his came into play in the femme fatale action thriller *So Close*.

In this movie, Corey Yuen directs three non-martial artist women: Shu Qi, Vicki Zhao Wei, and Karen Mok Man-Wai. Although there are the occasional doubles and use of wires, this film is a breath of fresh air from the watered-down CGI fu that Corey Yuen was doing in films like *The One* (2001) and *Avenging Fist* (2001). In the final fight, Vicki Zhao and Karen Mok are challenged to a swordfight by the main villain's bodyguard, played by the legendary Yasuaki Kurata.

The fight begins with Vicki Zhao and Yasuaki Kurata fighting alone, as Karen Mok is in another part of the building fighting against Ben Lam. Vicki Zhao tries to shoot down Kurata, who simply sends sharpened pieces of bamboo in her direction with his *katana*. When Zhao finally picks up a sword for herself, Kurata doesn't even give her time to unsheathe it before unleashing a barrage of strikes at her. This leads to a beautiful moment where the two of them stop, eye each other down, and then suddenly the scabbard that held Zhao's sword falls into pieces by itself. As the two go at it again, Vicki Zhao is helped by some wire-assisted kicks and acrobatics, but is still no match for Kurata's superior sword handling. She receives a good deal more damage before Karen Mok comes to her rescue.

In the next part of the fight, we see Karen Mok and Kurata take each other on. Mok's character is decidedly a better swordswoman than Vicki Zhao is. The two trade blows and swings. In another beautiful moment, the two stop fighting in order to choose their next strategy. The camera then focuses on Kurata's suit jacket, which has been cut. Suddenly Mok's hair, which had been pulled into a ponytail, comes free and flows into her face. A brief look of surprise shows on her face as she realizes what a close call she had just experienced.

Soon, Mok and Zhao are attacking Kurata at the same time. Zhao is armed with a long bamboo pole this time. Kurata demonstrates some excellent dexterity as he defends himself against multiple blows holding his *katana* in the under-handed position. In one moment, Kurata uses a small *tanto* dagger that he has hidden in his suit to sneak in a surprise attack. The stakes steadily rise as the three sustain more and more wounds in the fight.

If the previously-discussed fight in *Fong Sai Yuk II* represents the best rendition of *kenjutsu* and traditional *chambara* choreography through the eyes of Chinese actors and action directors, this fight represents the ultimate translation of real *kenjutsu* into the Chinese mold of movie fighting. Yasuaki Kurata is, after all, a Japanese martial artist with ample knowledge of different arts, including *kendo/kenjutsu*. Thus, what we see him performing is real Japanese swordplay processed into typical Chinese movie fighting, with wire-fu flourishes and exaggerated moves. It's as if Corey Yuen had said of *Fong Sai Yuk II*, "Let's make Jet Li's wushu as Japanese as possible in this scene," and then said here, "Let's present Yasuaki Kurata's *kendo* in the most Chinese way possible."

Yasuaki Kurata was 56 when this film was made. He's obviously still in excellent shape and handles Corey Yuen's choreography with great aplomb. It's with little effort that he convinces us that he's not only the equal to the two female protagonists, but that he's probably their superior. In one of the fight's best moments, Kurata performs a spinning jump kick on Vicki Zhao that looks amazing, especially considering his age. With his knowledge of *aikido* and *kendo*, Kurata performs some of the best Japanese swordplay we've yet seen in a Hong Kong film.

Karen Mok and Vicki Zhao, as stated earlier, are not martial artists. Thus, it is safe to bet that not only were they assisted by camera tricks and wires, but were doubled in certain scenes as well. Nonetheless, they do hold their own in the scenes where their face is toward the camera. Karen Mok shows herself to be the more physically talented of the two, having been a singer and thus having something of a background in dance. She is ultimately more convincing in the fight than Zhao[70] and uses fewer wires in this particular sequence than her colleague does. Nonetheless, these observations aside, both girls are fairly impressive and fans and kung fu fighting femme fatales should find a lot to like here.

This movie was nominated for the Best Action Design Award at the Hong Kong Film Awards in 2003, but ended up losing to *Hero*, which featured stylized swordplay courtesy of Ching Siu-Tung and company. Nonetheless, after being totally ignored for his superlative work in Shannon Lee's *Enter the Eagles*, it's glad to know that an old fashioned girls n' guns film get critical recognition for its fight scenes, if nothing else. And this particular fight is stylized Japanese swordplay at its best.

---

[70] Vicki Zhao has since gone on to be the go-to girl for period-piece martial arts epics, starring in films like *Mulan; Painted Skin; 14 Blades;* and the *Red Cliff* films.

Sai

One the more popular weapons in Japanese martial arts is the *sai*. Like many weapons associated with Japanese *karate*, the sai was originally not a weapon, but a farming implement. The original function of the *sai* was to be dragged across the ground and create furrows for farmers to place seeds in. It was developed into a weapon after Okinawans were prohibited by the Tokugawa Shogunate from using weapons.

Despite the fact that is often referred to as a "short sword", the *sai* is a weapon that is more akin to a police baton than to a sword. The *sai* consists of a metal shaft and a wrapped handle. The shaft is generally either rounded or octagonal in shape. Depending on the weapon, it can either be sharpened at the tip or blunt. What really sets the *sai* apart is the presence of two—although there are occasionally only one—prongs that curve outward from the shaft. The prongs' function is to trap bladed weapons, especially the sword of a samurai. The shaft of the *sai* is not sharpened, and thus is used for striking and not cutting or slashing. *Sai* with blunt ends have been used in the past for striking pressure points.

In popular culture, the *sai* became somewhat popular after it became the preferred weapon of Raphael, one of the *Teenage Mutant Ninja Turtles*. Thus, mainstream American audiences can see this weapon in action in any movie or cartoon involving the *Ninja Turtles*. Also, this Japanese weapon put in an interesting anachronistic appearance in *The Mummy Returns* (2001), in which two Egyptian women—one a priestess; the other a princess— duked it with this weapon. Obviously, Japanese martial arts movies also feature this weapon from time to time as well.

Yasuaki Kurata wields a mean sai in *Twinkle, Twinkle Lucky Stars* (Golden Harvest, 1985).

The *sai* has been used a number of times in Chinese cinema. Perennial movie villain Chen Sing often used this weapon; movies like *Heroes of the Wild* (1978) and *New Fist of Fury* (1976) feature demonstrations by him with the *sai*. Japanese actor Yasuaki Kurata gave an excellent performance with them against Jackie Chan in *Twinkle, Twinkle, Lucky Stars* (1985). The example we'll talk about here comes to us courtesy of a martial arts actor who is neither Japanese nor Chinese: Richard Norton.

The Magic Crystal (1986)

One of the unsung heroes of Hong Kong action direction is a fellow named Tony Leung Siu-Hung[71]. His brother is Bruce Leung Siu-Lung, one of the great old school kickers and a solid fight choreographer in his own right. Interestingly enough, although the great majority of Tony Leung's credits are Hong Kong movies, his most important contributions to the genre have been in American films. Working with Seasonal Films in movies like *King of the Kickboxers*; *No Retreat, No Surrender 3*; and *Bloodmoon*, Leung has filmed some of the greatest fights in American martial arts cinema. While his Hong Kong credits have never quite reached the level of those films, *The Magic Crystal*, a screwball multi-genre film from trash director Wong Jing, has some of his best Hong Kong work.

There are three classic fights in this movie. The first one has Cynthia Rothrock taking on Tony Leung himself with traditional wushu weapons. The next one is a fight between Richard Norton, Cynthia Rothrock, and Wong Wang-Si in a cramped apartment. It features some good wushu from Wong and some saber forms as well. It features the climax, which we will look at here, is by far the best. By the end of the chapter, you will understand that what Tony Leung has done here is put together some of the greatest traditional fight choreography onscreen, in spite of the film's modern-day setting.

The last fight is a showdown between Interpol agents, played by Cynthia Rothrock and Andy Lau, and the KGB, led by Aussie actor Richard Norton. Andy Lau spends the first part of the fight fighting off Norton's lackeys while Richard Norton and Cynthia Rothrock go at it. There is something about those two that makes them so appealing to watch together. They've done quite a few movies together, including the *China O'Brien* and *Rage and Honor* series. They just really click together, whether they are fighting against each other or on the same side.

In the first part of their showdown, Cynthia gets to show off some of her traditional Chinese styles, most notably the Eagle's Claw technique and the Praying Mantis style. It's done very well with the appropriate amounts of speed and intricacy. This is indeed a rare sight, considering that all of Rothrock's films have been set in the modern day and thus normally translate her skills into a more modern kickboxing style. She looks as good as any Mainland performer has looked performing them in other movies, but with the benefit of Leung's assured action direction.

Richard Norton uses a style that almost looks like some sort of "soft" kung fu style. That is interesting, considering that his principal training was in *Goju-Ryu* karate and judo. Nonetheless, he's talented enough that he does everything that Leung asks him to do and make it look convincing. It's a nice start and a good lead-in to the main event.

It is when Andy Lau and Cynthia Rothrock team up to take on Norton together that Norton produces a pair of *sai* and the fun really begins. He begins to wield those *sai* with a prowess that leaves movies like the Ninja Turtles franchise and *The Mummy Returns* in the dust. The choreography is very complex, as Lau and Rothrock are attacking him simultaneously and yet Norton is blocking their attacks and striking them in such a calm manner that sometimes it doesn't look like he's even breaking a sweat. Every now and then he takes break in the middle of the fight to start twirling the *sai* in a way very similar to the way Bruce Lee would show off his *nunchaku* skills in his movies.

---

[71] We refer to him as Tony Leung #3, numbers one and two being Tony Leung Chiu-Wai (*Hero* and *Tokyo Raiders*) and Tony Leung Kar-Fei (*A Better Tomorrow III* and *New Dragon Inn*).

This fight is an excellent example of how a *sai* would be used in real combat, albeit a bit stylized. As we mentioned at the beginning of the chapter, the *sai* typically resembled a police baton more than a sword in its application. Here we can see Richard striking Andy Lau and Cynthia Rothrock in the face and torso with the weapon, but he also uses strikes to counter Lau's and Rothrock's strikes. Also interesting is that the butt of the handle is used a number of times during the fight. If you watch a *kata*, or form, of the *sai*, you'll notice that the practitioner will often turn the shaft and punch with handle pointing outward. Here you can see that being applied to great effect. Furthermore, in one move, Norton uses the prongs on his weapons to catch Andy Lau's arms, parry them, and open him up for a knee smash.

For fans and students of Japanese martial arts, this fight is highly recommended. It's an excellent demonstration for a weapon that gets sporadic coverage in martial arts movies and even then, mainly in the watered-down fights of the *Teenage Mutant Ninja Turtles* franchise. But Tony Leung doesn't sell this fight with just Norton's skills; he also throws in some excellent traditional choreography and that classical styles demonstration from Cynthia Rothrock. Heck, even Andy Lau looks good in this fight, which is impressive, considering that his martial arts training was pretty basic. Traditional choreography might've been all but an anachronism in this type of film, but Tony Leung Siu-Hung shows us that if it's done right, than suspension of disbelief comes easy. As for Norton, this is easily one of the best moments in his career.

Kama – Kusari-Kama - Shoge

The *kama* is one of the rarer weapons in Japanese martial arts, although in the hands of a master, it can be one of the deadliest. The *kama* is simply a sickle and is often used in pairs. The weapon, like many weapons used in Japanese and Okinawan martial arts, was originally used as a farming implement, in this case as a tool to harvest rice and cut grass. It was adapted into a weapon when Okinawa was annexed by the Tokugawa Shogunate about 350 years ago. The *kama* used for cutting and slashing, and can also be used for trapping an opponent's weapon and removing it from his grip.

One variation of the *kama* is the *kusari-kama*, or the sickle and chain. The *kusari-kama* was a weapon generally used by ninja. While it could be used for attacking and slashing an opponent from afar, it often was used to tie up an opponent, leaving him open for a deadly blow. A similar weapon to the *kusari-kama* is the *shoge*, which is a long chain with a blade that looks like the harpoon at the end. Both of these weapons could be used for attacking at a long distance, disarming an opponent, and even as makeshift grappling hooks.

Due to the rarity of these weapons, they aren't seen very often in movies. At the end of *The Octagon* (1980), Chuck Norris takes on a *kama*-wielding ninja, played by Tadashi Yamashita. They also make a brief appearance during the Chateau fight scene in *The Matrix: Reloaded* (2003). The *kusari-kama* and *shoge* weapons are just as rare. They can be seen briefly in movies involving ninjas like *Ninja Hunter* (1980) and *Dr. Wai and the Scripture with No Words* (1996). Action director Ching Siu-Tung gave us a Chinese variation of the *kusari-kama* in Zhang Yimou's epic *Curse of the Golden Flower* (2005) and more briefly in the first *Royal Tramp* (1992) film. Most recently, the *kusari-kama* was the weapon of choice of Korean pop star Rain in the Hollywood film *Ninja Assassin* (2009). Nonetheless, it was those masters of traditional weapons choreography, the Venom Mob, that gave one of these rare weapons the attention and showcase that it so rightly deserves.

Ninja in the Deadly Trap (1984)[72]

Ninja in the Deadly Trap is a low-budget Taiwanese film that stands out as being the only film that Venom Mob member Philip Kwok directed. The movie itself is a variation on the Shaw Brothers film *Five Element Ninja* (1980), one of the most over-the-top and violent ninja movies ever made[73]. In addition to the directorial chores, Philip Kwok handled the action sequences, though he was likely helped just as much by his co-stars, Venom Mob members Chiang Sheng and Lu Feng. Kwok handles the action with about as much grace as he did in a lot of the later Venoms films produced by the Shaw Brothers. Although he would never direct again, Kwok would become a solid action director not only in Hong Kong, but abroad as well later on.

---

[72] Depending on the source, the year of release of this movie varies from as early as 1981 or as late as 1985.

[73] It once led the author to muse that we need more movies in which the decisive moment of a fight is when one of the combatants trips on his own intestines.

The last 15 minutes of this film is a series of fights between our three heroes (Philip Kwok, Chiang Sheng, and Lu Feng) and different groups of ninjas. The first group of ninjas is dressed in shiny gold uniforms with mirrors on their chests to reflect the sun's light into their enemies' faces and distract them. The second group of ninjas is dressed in green—to blend in with the trees—and are armed with *shoge*. The third group is dressed in brown, burrow underground, and is armed with *rattan* shields and sabers. Let's take a look at the second group.

The ninja, hiding in the trees, surprise the three heroes and throwing their *shoge* at them. After acrobatically getting away from their attacks, our heroes are confronted by four ninja. Lu Feng and Chiang Feng each take on one ninja while Philip Kwok takes on two. The ninja use their weapon in almost every way possible. They swing it and throw it as you would a medieval flail. They hold the blade and fight up close as you would with a regular *kama*. Besides trying to pierce their enemies, the ninja use the *shoge* to trap their opponents' weapons and try to disarm them.

Our heroes fight back with some interesting weapons of their own. Philip Kwok is armed with what is essentially an umbrella with a sharpened point at the tip. Chiang Sheng uses a pair of butterfly swords. Lu Feng uses a short spear that can be wielded with one hand. Their movements are perfect in this scene and they use their weapons with excellent coordination. The Venom Mob was always great at weapon choreography, especially these three. They could mix acrobatics, highly-intricate choreography, and occasionally intense violence to create fights that are favorites among fans. Here they don't fail us, in spite of the fact that his portion of the fight lasts only two minutes.

One of the testaments to the skills of Kwok is his ability to make an interesting fight out of a weapon like the *shoge*. It is normally difficult to choreograph a fight utilizing a long-distance, flexible weapon like a *shoge,* a chain whip, or a rope dart, especially when the other fighters are using melee weapons like swords and knives. However, Kwok makes things interesting by arming our heroes with exotic weapons and diversifying the attacks of the ninja. It adds up to a neat little battle and another small, but important testament to the talent of the Venom Mob.

Yari – Naginata

For hundreds of years, two of the principal weapons in *samurai* combat were the *yari* and the *naginata*. They were both types of spears, the former having a straight blade and the latter having a curved blade. As a result, the former was better adapted to piercing while the latter was well adapted to piercing and slicing. While the *yari* was often considered to be the "straight spear", there were actually several variations of the weapon, each one having slightly different blade designs. In battle, infantry used both the yari and the naginata during the first half of the second millennium A.D. However, their use declined during the Tokugawa Shogunate (1603 – 1868) in favor of the sword, which was more effective in close quarters combat. Nonetheless, the *naginata* was the preferred weapon of *samurai* wives, who were expected to be able to defend their household while their husbands were away at war. The *naginata* was also a favorite of warrior monks.

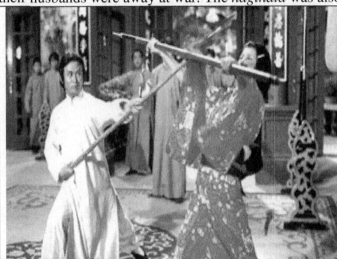

Yuko Mizuno (right) wields the yari in *Heroes of the East* (Shaw Brothers, 1978).

These weapons have gotten some coverage in movies all over the globe, although not quite as much as the Japanese swords, like the *katana* and the *wakazashi* have. In the Japanese *Lone Wolf and Cub* series, the protagonist Ogami occasionally uses the *naginata* while taking on hundreds of *samurai* simultaneously. In Chinese movies, these weapons occasionally appear in films dealing with *ninja*, like *Heroes of the East* (1978) and *Chinese Super Ninjas* (1982). In the latter, it is the main villain, played by Michael Chan Wai-Man, who is armed with the *naginata* in the bloody finale.

Shaolin vs. Ninja (1983)

Robert Tai basically became to the go-to guy for ninja movies during the first half of the 1980s. His first movie was the aforementioned *Chinese Super Ninjas*, which was directed by Chang Cheh. According to an interview, Chang Cheh had handed Tai a book about *ninja* and asked him to read it and use it as inspiration for the film's action design. The result was multi-colored *ninja* with a whole lot of secret weapons and special tactics, including disguises and ingenious hiding places to launch their bloody attacks. Robert Tai eventually left the Shaw Brothers in order to make movies in Taiwan, where he was offered more money. In Taiwan, he would go on to direct and choreograph films like *Mafia vs. Ninja* (1985), *Ninja vs. the Shaolin Guards* (1984), and his epic *Ninja: The*

Final Duel (1986). Crazy wirework, over-the-top *ninja* antics, and some pretty good fighting from star Alexander Lo Rei has given all of these films a pretty good cult following. The first of these movies he made in Taiwan, *Shaolin vs. Ninja*, features some of his best choreography.

It is of our opinion that Robert Tai is a very uneven choreographer. We recognize some of the advances he made in wire stunts and his talent for keeping the fights in his movies diverse and varied for the most part. However, far too often he allows the intricacy of his choreography to slow things down considerably, and often throws in too much unnecessary acrobatics into his choreography. Moreover, the low budgets he had to work with in Taiwan often reflected in the quality of his wire stunts, which were often awkward. Nevertheless, when he's good, he's pretty darn good.

Shaolin vs. Ninja is a pretty good example of how uneven Tai was, with the movie featuring some rather bland fights near the beginning and some pretty great fights near the end. A large portion of the last act is taken up by a tournament sequence pitting a number of Japanese warrior monks against some Shaolin monks. In each round, two fighters will duel on top of a red carpet; whoever steps off the carpet is the loser.

In the third fight of the tournament, a Japanese fighter armed with a *yari* takes on a monk armed with a *rattan* shield and a saber. The variation of the *yari* that the Japanese fighter uses is called a *kata kama yari*. It is different from a traditional *yari* in that the spearhead is straight, but there is a hooked blade coming out of the base of the spear, used for trapping and disarming. The fight goes on for about two-and-a-half minutes, until the Japanese fighter is able to disarm the Shaolin monk and win. Right here we can draw a comparison between the fights in this tournament and those in *Heroes of the East*. In the latter, Gordon Liu won all of his matches against the different Japanese fighters. Here, we actually get to see the Japanese fighters win a few of the matches, which kind of makes up for the racist portrayal of the Japanese villains in the film.

In the next fight, a Japanese fighter armed with a *naginata* takes on a senior Shaolin monk armed with a pole. The quirky part about this fight is that the monk tries to act playful (or drunk), but ends up coming off effeminate due to the bad dubbing. Like the last fight, there is some great, intricate choreography here with some great moves from both and some solid acrobatics from the Shaolin monk. However, it is easy to tell that Robert Tai was mixing the *naginata* techniques with Chinese kung fu, as there are a number of moments where the Japanese fighter throws his spear into the air so he can flip and catch it and other such indulgences. Japanese martial arts tend to be a bit less ornate and pretty much "to the point" (no pun intended) in their execution.

So, aside from some excesses on the part of Robert Tai, this portion of the tournament sequence in *Shaolin vs. Ninja* is quite solid and is as good as some of the showdowns in *Heroes of the East*, one of the pinnacles of Japanese martial arts on film. The fights aren't violent[74], so there's a bit of appeal to younger audiences. This is some of Robert Tai's best work here, especially outside of his Venom Mob films. Highly recommended.

---

[74] We're referring to the fights in the tournament sequence; there are some bloody moments in the film itself, although nothing compared to the gore on display in *Chinese Super Ninjas*.

Nunchaku

One of the most popular and well-known weapons in all of martial arts is the *nunchaku* or "nunchucks", as some people pronounce it. The weapon is generally associated with Japanese martial arts, mainly because of the legend regarding its development as a weapon. The legend states that the *nunchaku* was a sort of flail used by Okinawan farmers to beat grain. However, when the infamous weapons ban was placed on the Okinawan people, they started adapting farming implements to use as weapons. Thus, the *nunchaku* became a weapon. Nonetheless, there are martial arts scholars that suggest that the weapon was originally not as popular as it is today, citing that there is no official *kata*, or form, for the *nunchaku* in Okinawan karate. Nonetheless, today it is taught in a number of non-Japanese/Okinawan martial arts, including *tae kwon do*, *hapkido*, and some Chinese styles.

The person who was responsible for bringing the *nunchaku* into the mainstream consciousness was none other than Bruce Lee. His *chaku* skills were practically second to none and we owe most of the weapon's popularity onscreen to Lee's memorable fights with it. The mainstream popularity of the weapon has further been cemented, at least in the West, by the popularity of the Teenage Mutant Ninja Turtles, as it was the specialty of Michelangelo. The weapon has made numerous appearances in films, many of the being martial arts films, but occasionally they show up as being weapons wielded by some street gangs.

The weapon is often regarded as being somewhat limited because of its short range. Its main limitation, however, has been the difficulty in doing something really innovative with the weapon onscreen. A lot of fights involving the *nunchaku* are very similar, as it involves the user whipping the weapon around his body, and then simply cracking a bunch of people in the head when they try to come at him. Thus, we decided to take a different route with this chapter and provide a short commentary on a number of fights involving the *nunchaku* in Chinese cinema.

Fist of Fury (1972) - In one of Bruce Lee's most famous fight scenes, he enters a Japanese dojo and starts wiping the floor with all of the students present, first with his feet and then with his *nunchaku*. One of the most iconic fights involving this weapon.

Way of the Dragon (1973) - In the second fight behind the restaurant, Bruce Lee takes on a bunch of Italian thugs with his superior skills, including some pole work and the *nunchaku*.

Call Me Dragon (1974) - Bruce Leung Siu-Lung uses the *nunchaku* to counter Yasuaki Kurata's *tonfa*. One of the better fights involving this weapon.

Kidnap in Rome (1974) - Another Bruce Leung Siu-Lung film that features some *chaku* fighting from a young Meng Hoi. Ironic, considering that Bruce Leung was the Bruce Lee imitator and yet it's not him that uses Bruce Lee's signature weapon.

Secret Rivals (1976) - In one of the later fights, Don Wong Tao takes on a couple of thugs with the weapon in question. Don Wong had previously tried to become the "successor" to Bruce Lee in *Slaughter in San Francisco* (1973), thus making his use of the *nunchaku* seem like another attempt for him to do the same thing.

New Fist of Fury (1976) – In his final fight against villain Chen Sing, Jackie Chan uses a three-section staff to counter Chen's *sai* swords. One of the sticks if broken off, transforming Jackie's weapon in a *nunchaku*. His handling of the weapon, however, is nothing compared to that of Bruce Lee's handling of it in the original *Fist of Fury*.

Along Comes a Tiger (1977) - More *chaku* goodness courtesy of Don Wong Tao.

Game of Death (1978) - Bruce Lee and escrima master Dan Inosanto whip out the *nunchaku* in the first part of one of the greatest fight scenes ever filmed.

Enter the Fat Dragon (1978) - In Sammo Hung's supreme tribute to Bruce Lee, Hung does some excellent *nunchaku* work against a bunch of thugs (including Meng Hoi and Yuen Biao) at his uncle's restaurant.

Heroes of the East (1978) - In another of the most creative fights using this weapon, a Japanese fighter wields the *nunchaku* and the *tonfa* simultaneously while Gordon Liu counters with the three-section staff. This is an excellent fight to compare Japanese and Chinese weapons techniques.

Half of a Loaf of Kung Fu (1978) – This was Jackie Chan's parody of kung fu movies. In the final fight Jackie Chan pulls off villain Kam Kong's hairpiece and uses it like a pair *nunchaku*, swinging the improvised weapon by the queue.

Shaolin Daredevils (1979) - Midway through the film, Lo Meng gets a brief fight scene in which takes on Wang Li. During the fight, Lo Meng gets to briefly use his *nunchaku* against Wang Li's *sai* variation.

Flag of Iron (1980) - In this Shaw Brothers film featuring the Venom Mob, there's assassin who wields an abacus that breaks apart into two pairs of *nunchaku*. He is quickly killed, however, by Philip Kwok's character.

Shaolin vs. Ninja (1982) - In the opening fight scene, Alexander Lo Rei takes on a couple of Japanese baddies with two-fisted *nunchaku* in one of the film's better fight sequences. Before that, he does some nice double *nunchaku* form work as well.

Martial Monks of Shaolin Temple (1984) - Korean Bruce Lee imitator Dragon Lee uses the *nunchaku* briefly in the climatic duel against Hwang Jang Lee. He fails, however, to beat Hwang with this weapon, not mention fails to convince the audience that he could actually make it out of the fight alive.

Ninjas and Dragons (1984) - In the climax of this Mainland Chinese-Japanese co-production, the Chinese protagonist uses two pairs of *nunchaku* against the Japanese villain at the end of the climax.

Angel III (1988) - In the film's best fight scene, Moon Lee takes on a mansion full of blade-wielding killers with a pair of *nunchaku*. The choreography here is provided by Stanley Tong, who'd go on to do several Jackie Chan films, including *Police Story III: Supercop* (1993) and *Rumble in the Bronx* (1995).

Skinny Tiger, Fatty Dragon (1990) - This is Sammo Hung's other tribute to Bruce Lee. At the film's climax, Sammo does some more excellent *nunchaku* work against a gang of thugs led by Lau Kar-Wing.

Dragon from Russia (1990) - In one of the film's training sequences, Sam Hui fights Yuen Tak using this weapon. In a creative bit, Yuen Tak dips the end of the sticks in paint and then tries to leave marks on Hui's face. Sam Hui also does some *nunchaku* training while performing sit-ups. Yuen Tak's choreography is slightly wire-enhanced in this particular scene.

God of Gamblers 2 (1990) - Stephen Chow homages Bruce Lee (something that would become recurring theme in his films) using a pair of plungers as *nunchaku*.

King of Beggars (1992) - Another homage to Bruce Lee by way of the *nunchaku*.

The Inspector Wears Skirts IV (1992) - In a running gag at the film's climax, Kara Hui Ying-Hung keeps pulling numerous weapons, including a *nunchaku* and a *kwan do* out of a rather small sports bag.

Fist of Legend 2: Iron Bodyguards (1996) - Jet Li-imitator Jet Le uses the *nunchaku* in a well-choreographed fight by Robert Tai.

House of Fury (2005) - In am homage to Bruce Lee, Anthony Wong uses the arm bones of a plastic skeleton as a pair of *nunchaku*. Choreography by Yuen Woo-Ping.

Dragon Tiger Gate (2006) - Based on a popular comic book, the hero Turbo Shek, played by Shawn Yue, is a *nunchaku* expert and gets to show off his prowess in a number of fights scenes, including the finale. Choreography by Donnie Yen.

Legend of the Fist: Return of Chen Zhen (2010) – A sequel-cum-remake of Bruce Lee's *Fist of Fury*, the finale includes a recreation of the original's famous dojo fight scene. Unfortunately, Donnie Yen fails to do anything new with the material and the scene ends up looking like a rehash of both Bruce Lee's classic fight and Donnie's previous recreation of said scene from his 1995 TV series *Fist of Fury*.

Bibliography

Allison, Keith. "Bastard Swordsman." *Teleport City*. 06 January 2007. 17 June 2010
< http://teleport-city.com/wordpress/?p=795>.

Allison, Keith. "Enter the Ninja." *Teleport City*. 20 December 2002. 11 December 2008
< http://teleport-city.com/wordpress/?p=624>.

Allison, Keith. "Kung Fu vs. Yoga" *Teleport City*. May 2000. 17 June 2010
<http://web.archive.org/web/20000523100428/www.teleport-city.com/movies/reviews/kungfu/kfvyoga.html>.

Allison, Keith. "Shiri". *Teleport City*. 30 August 2001. 17 June 2010
< http://teleport-city.com/wordpress/?p=576>.

"Ba Gua Zhang". *Shen Wu*. 7 November 2008 < http://www.shenwu.com/bagua.htm >.

"Bingqi." *AraChina*. 2010. 17 June 2010 <http://www.arachina.com/culture/bujyutu/bingqi.htm>.

Brian. "The Hong Kong Actors Index". *Hong Kong Cinema: View from the Brooklyn Bridge*. 17 June 2010. < http://brns.com/hkactors/pages/intro.html>.

Burr, Martha. "Eagle vs. Eagle." *Kung Fu Magazine*. 2001. 14 April 2009.
< http://ezine.kungfumagazine.com/magazine/article.php?article=137 >.

Chinavoc. November 2008 < http://www.chinavoc.com/kungfu/index.asp>.

Drake, Brian. "Nin-Gu." *Ancient Japanese Weapons*. 17 June 2010
< http://cs.bluecc.edu/StuProj/CS121w02/Drake/page%204/page%204.htm>.

"Eagle Claw History". Lily Lau Eagle Claw. *Lily Lau Eagle Claw Kung Fu Federation, International*. 2001. 14 April 2009. < http://www.lilylaueagleclaw.com/eaghist.html >.

"Five Animals." Wikipedia. 19 March 2009. 5 May 2009
<http://en.wikipedia.org/wiki/Five_Animals >.

Funk, Jon. "History of Praying Mantis Kung Fu." *Mantis Kung Fu*. 23 April 2009
< http://www.mantiskungfu.com/HistoryofPrayingMantisKungfu.htm >.

Garafolo, Michael P. "Zhang San-Feng, Taoist Master, Circa 1300 C.E." *Green Way Research*. 1 August 2007. 23 November 2008.
< http://www.egreenway.com/taichichuan/chang1.htm#Main >.

Gentry III, Clyde. Jackie Chan: Inside the Dragon. Dallas, TX: Taylor Trade Publishing, 1997.

"History of Choy Li Fut – Page One." *White Lions of Shaolin*.
17 June 2010. < http://www.whitelionsofshaolin.com/HistoryofChoyLiFut.htm>.

Hong Kong Movie Database. 18 June 2010. < http://www.hkmdb.com >.

"Japanese Sword". *Wikipedia*. 11 January 2009. 20 January 2009
< http://en.wikipedia.org/wiki/Japanese_sword >.

"Katana." *Wikipedia*. 14 January 2009. 20 January 2009 <http://en.wikipedia.org/wiki/Katana >.

Lanuque, Arnaud. "Interview Bruce Leung: Crazy Kung Fu Fighter". *Hong Kong Cinemagic.* 16 March 2006. 24 November 2007 <http://www.hkcinemagic.com/en/page.asp?aid=208&page=1 >.

"Nezha." *China History Forum.* 09 July 2004. 17 June 2010 <http://www.chinahistoryforum.com/index.php?showtopic=12996>.

Pollard, Mark. "Dirty Tiger, Crazy Frog." *Kung Fu Cinema.* 2 March 2009 <http://www.kungfucinema.com/dirty-tiger-crazy-frog-1978-234>.

Pollard, Mark. "Lion vs. Lion." *Kung Fu Cinema.* 19 November 2007. 19 December   2008 <http://www.kungfucinema.com/lion-vs-lion-1981-494>.

Richards, John. "100 Greatest Fight Scenes – 90-81." *Wasted Life.* 21 October 2007 < http://homepage.ntlworld.com/john.richards250/100fightscenes2.htm >.

Rovin, Jeff and Kathy Tracy. The Essential Jackie Chan Sourcebook. New York: Pocket, 1997.

Shaolin Gung Fu Institute. 18 April 2008 < http://www.shaolin.com/>.

"Southern Praying Mantis (Martial Art)." *Wikipedia.* 13 April 2009. 23 April 2009 < http://en.wikipedia.org/wiki/Southern_Praying_Mantis_(martial_art) >.

"Staff and Nunchaku Info". *West Coast Juggling.* 18 March 2009. 17 June 2010 <http://westcoastjuggling.net/?page_id=200>.

"Three-Section Staff." *Flying Eagle Academy.* 16 February 2009 <http://flyingeagleacademy.com/samjitgwun.html>.

"Tonfa Martial Arts Weapon." *MartialArm.* 2008. 3 December 2008 < http://www.martialarm.com/weapons/weapons-tonfa.html >.

Valentin, Albert. "The Art of Kicking Part 1: The Kickers of Classic Kung Fu." *Kung Fu Cinema.* 31 October 2008. 03 November 2008 <http://www.kungfucinema.com/?p=3346>.

"Weapons History." *Warrior Wonders.* 08 December 2008 < http://www.alaska.net/~rlw/warriorhome.htm >.

Western Australia Chin Woo - Perth. 5 December 2008 < http://www.chinwoo.com.au/joomla/index.php >.

"Wing Chun". *Martial Arts Database.* 03 Jan 2009 < http://www.mardb.com/wing-chun/>.

"Wu Tang Death Squad." *Martial Artist's Guide to Hong Kong Films.* 15 January 2006. 8 March 2008 < http://www.magthkf.ronlim.com/martial6.html#anchor487693>.

"Xing Yi Quan." *Shen Wu.* 7 November 2008 < http://www.shenwu.com/hsingi.htm >.

"Yoga Schools of Purna Yoga, Raja Yoga, Hatha Yoga, and Others." *Life Positive.* 2010. 10 December 2008 <http://www.lifepositive.com/Body/yoga/yoga-schools.asp>.

Made in the USA
Monee, IL
30 November 2020